THE HERB & SPICE COMPANION

Marcus A. Webb

Richard Craze

Eagle Editions

AN OCEANA BOOK

Published by Eagle Editions Ltd
11 Heathfield
Royston
Hertfordshire SG8 5BW

This edition printed 2000

ISBN 1-86160-395-9

QUMH&SC

This book is produced by
Quantum Publishing
6 Blundell Street
London N7 9BH

CONTENTS

THE HERBAL COMPANION

THE SPICE COMPANION

I dedicate this book to my wife, Mhairi. I seem to take on major projects just as new additions to our family are due. When our first baby, Cameron, was born I was in the middle of finishing an academic thesis, and just as our second baby was due, I decided to undertake the writing of this book. Mhairi, without your support and understanding neither of these projects would have been possible.

Acknowledgments

I owe special thanks to: Sue Wallander of Enzymatic Therapy (USA), Melanie Cook of Enzymatic Therapy (UK), Jen and Janyn Tan of Bioforce (UK), Pamela Cranston, Jan de Vries and Kathy Steer of Quintet Publishing.

A special thanks goes to Terry Griffiths for his introduction to Quintet Publishing and to my wife, Mhairi, for reading through the final copy so carefully and correcting my dreadful spelling!

THE HERBAL COMPANION

The Essential Guide to Using Herbs for Your Health and Well-Being

MARCUS A. WEBB

HERBS CAN DO far more for you than just garnish a finished dish: they can actually promote and protect your health. The use of traditional herbal remedies is a growth area in health care that is reflected in the 1994 sales figures for the United States of $1.6 billion. This enormous consumption of herbs is proof that something positive is gained by their use.

In 1995 the World Health Organization published figures that showed that more than 80 percent of the world's population used herbal medicines as their primary source of medication. This figure comes as no surprise when you consider that this form of medicine can be considered as original medicine, not alternative medicine.

The interest in herbal extracts has increased in the "developed" world as people look for safer ways to treat everyday illness and improve general health, while scientific interest is growing as the search for new therapeutic agents broadens. The potential discovery of, for example, a new anticancer drug extracted from a plant is a tempting and highly profitable reality. But as we purify the natural agents, we lose the very concept of herbal medicine that incorporates the whole plant, utilizing active agents and other essential factors that are naturally present in the herb. The whole plant extract will still be effective, but its action will be buffered by the cofactors present. Remove these and a pure "drug" is born with its undesirable side effects.

The aim of this book is to guide the interested reader through all aspects of herbs, from their growth through their medicinal uses. The discussions will, by the confines of this book, be brief but concise and easy to use. All the herbs in the directory are listed in Latin order. For quick reference there is a list of herbs with their common names on pages 46 and 47.

CAUTIONARY NOTE:
At all times it is recommended that you consult a health-care professional before embarking on a program of self-treatment. Herbal medicines are effective and safe when used in the correct circumstances. This book has been written to educate, and every effort has been made to make the book as accurate and as informative as possible, but the advice contained within is no replacement for professional guidance.

TRADITIONS AND HISTORY

In the Beginning

The use of herbs for the promotion of health can be dated back to the days of Hippocrates, who compiled a *materia medica* (a book containing information on herbs and their prescription) of more than 400 medicinal herbs during his lifetime (c. 460–370 B.C.). The works he left behind were soon built upon. The Greek philosopher Aristotle (c. 372–287 B.C.) wrote his monumental 10-volume compendium called *The History of Plants*, making him one of the most important contributors to our knowledge of botanical science.

Throughout history, herbs and their powers have played a very important part in our lives, so much so that the Egyptians immortalized their uses in stone tablets and tomb paintings.

Herb gardens first appeared during the eighth century.

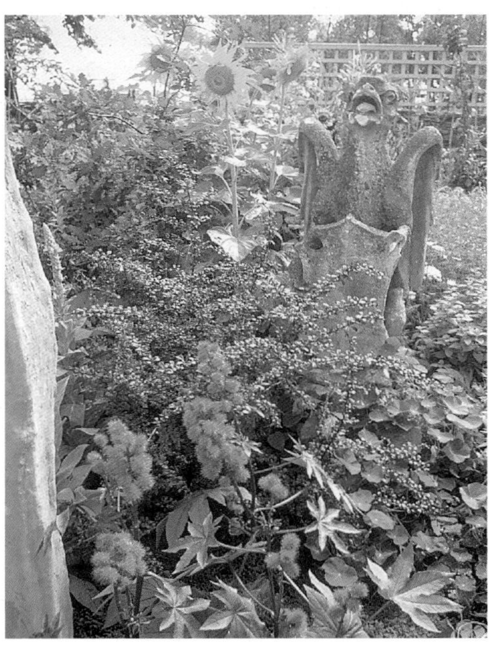

An apothecary's garden displaying different therapeutic herbs and flowers.

Monks grew medicinal herbs for treating of illness and for healing of wounds. The medieval opinion was that illness resulted from an imbalance in the four humors (phlegm, black and yellow bile, and blood) contained within the body. A popular treatment of the day was bloodletting. It was believed that this procedure allowed an excess of one of the humors to be drained away, and a preventive, quarterly bloodletting was performed on all monks living in the monasteries in an attempt to prevent an outbreak of disease. Herbs were frequently given to assist in the removal of excessive humors. Lavender was said to aid "pains in the head," violets were taken for diseases of the lung, and pennyroyal aided those with toothache. There were no physicians in the monasteries; the monks would train each other in treatment procedures and herbal applications. The information passed down from generation to generation firmly supported the effectiveness of herbal remedies and dictated the necessity for a well-stocked herb garden.

The first illustrated book on herbal preparations was written by the English herbalist and surgeon John Gerard. *The Herball, or Generall Historie of Plantes* was published in 1597 and gave comprehensive details of each plant including its origin, history, uses, methods of planting and the type of soil needed for each different species.

Unfortunately, one of herbal medicine's best-known advocates, Nicholas Culpeper, actually brought the practice of herbal cures into serious disrepute. Culpeper, who was an astrologer as well as a physician, classified the herbs according to astrological influences. The medical profession of Culpeper's day shunned him, since his teachings mixed magic and mystery with the old and accepted art of healing with herbs. Despite this, medicine came to acknowledge the power of plants in healing, and stronger extracts were purified to a point where only a few milligrams could exert a dramatic effect on the body.

The stage that conventional medicine has reached today is a long way from Hippocrates' original writings, even though the profession has taken his teachings and swears an oath in his name.

Important Influences on Herbal Medicine

It was not until the first century A.D. that the Roman physician Galen started to form a classification for the prescribing of herbal medicines based on the teachings of Hippocrates and formed his own classification for prescribing herbs. This was the first attempt to form a system of medicine that could be taught and followed by others, and it created a definite division between the physician and the traditional healers.

Inasmuch as this system of medicine helped to elevate herbal medicine, it did nothing to forward free thinking, and for approximately 1,500 years, the teachings of Galen were not challenged in Europe. It has been said that Galen did more to paralyze herbal medicine than anyone else, allowing the Galen-minded physicians to take over by prescribing herbs according to his teachings without actually considering the patient. In the days of the traditional herbalist, however, this would have been unthinkable because each patient was considered as an individual. Galen's teachings were, in fact, a direct contradiction to the faith the herbalists had in *vis medicatrix naturae*, the healing powers of nature.

During the sixteenth century Paracelsus challenged the teachings of Galen with his theory of the *Doctrine of Signatures*. This suggested that the physical characteristics of an herb indicated the area of the body that it was intended to treat. Paracelsus described illness as an external event (at this time syphilis and plague were widespread) for which the internal use of herbs was indicated.

*Goldenseal (*Hydrastis canadensis*) originally grew in North America and became a popular remedy for relieving constipation.*

By 1785 herbs were being used for the treatment of many problems, one of which pushed forward the science of pharmacology dramatically. An English physician, William Withering, discovered that dropsy (heart failure) could be successfully treated with an extract of foxglove (*Digitalis*). This extract is still used to the present day in the form of the drug Digoxin.

The use of herbal medicine now appears to be turning full circle as scientists calculate that at least 328 new drugs could be developed from the plants of the tropical rain forests. Fresh interest is being generated in the healing powers of plants, an ancient wisdom that has stood the test of time.

The American Influence

The Americas offer many different climates and growing habitats for plants. Nearly all of the most important North American medicinal preparations originate from spices that grow native to the region.

As settlers adopted these remedies and discovered how effective they were for many different complaints, commercial growing was required to meet the demand. In 1838 the use of American herbal- and spice-based remedies spread to Europe, where their popularity soon grew. Remedies such as passionflower, goldenseal, witch hazel, sassafras, slippery elm and many other familiar preparations originally grew in North America.

From Central and South America the rain forest yielded, and is still yielding, a fascinating collection of plants with medicinal actions. As far back as the fourteenth century, a Florentine navigator, Amerigo Vespucci, discovered Colombian tribes chewing coca leaves, a practice stemming back to 2100 B.C. The alkaloid extracted from these leaves, cocaine, has become a valuable topical anesthetic as well as a lethal and addictive substance. Other commonly used plants from Central and South America include the chili pepper, Mexican yam, pawpaw, strychnine, boldo, allspice, Jamaican dogwood, vanilla and maize.

Conservation of this vital resource is essential, especially when cultivation for coca alone has accounted for the loss of more than 2 million acres (809,372 hectares) of rain forest in Peru since the early twentieth century.

GROWING HERBS

Careful planning can create wonderful visual effects in any garden or patch of land.

HERBS ARE NOT DIFFICULT to grow, and great satisfaction can be gotten from cultivating an herb garden or even growing just a pot of herbs.

Plant herbs outside when you can avoid having them damaged by excessive heat or cold. Most herbs enjoy a sunny location, but chives, feverfew, horseradish, lemon balm, mint, comfrey, ginger, violet, angelica, chervil, sweet woodruff, parsley and cicely are best planted in a shady place.

Selecting special herbs to plant in your herb garden will protect your crop from pests. If you plant rosemary and/or sage with your other herbs, you will prevent garden pests from destroying crops without needing to resort to chemical agents. This is important, especially if you are going to consume your produce.

Selecting the correct patch of land is important. Most herbs like at least six hours of light per day. Check the consistency of the soil: A sticky, muddy soil may need a little sand worked into it, but a stiff clay-based soil would benefit from some peat.

For your herbs to obtain optimal nutrition from the soil, make sure that the pH is slightly acidic to neutral (pH 6.5–7.9).

Herbs That Like Clay Soil

Angelica	Fennel
Chives	Lemon balm
Comfrey	Peppermint

Most garden centers will stock a pH testing kit. If your soil is too acidic, add some lime powder and if it is too alkaline, add some sulfur.

When choosing the most suitable herbs to grow, it will be necessary to select the best aspect, or exposure, of the ground. A southern exposure is considered the best, but the patch should be screened to the north and west by high-growing shrubs, conifers or a wall. Keeping the south and east aspects of the herb garden exposed is essential.

Water is a vital resource. Herbs should not be planted too far away from a hose or sprinkler. Herbs do respond well to rainwater, so storage is desirable for collecting this precious resource.

The best soils are generally loam-based, tending toward a sandy texture rather than a clay texture. A soil that has the characteristics of strength and lightness is perfect; this will make the best medium in which to grow any herbs irrespective of their species.

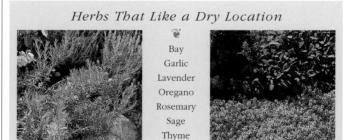

Herbs That Like a Dry Location

Bay
Garlic
Lavender
Oregano
Rosemary
Sage
Thyme

Herbs in the Garden

Growing herbs in a large garden will take some planning, and a visit to an established public herb garden will give you valuable ideas to bring home. An herb border is a good method of growing herbs for a kitchen garden. After seeing the plants growing in an established garden, you will get an accurate idea of how much certain species branch out and to what height they grow. For example, rosemary plants need to be spaced at least 3 feet (90 cm) apart, while fennel and marjoram need about 1 foot (30 cm) between each plant.

Herb borders make a very attractive addition to any garden as well as provide a great source of fresh herbs, but care must

Herbs can look impressive in different shaped beds.

Shade-loving Herbs

Angelica	Horseradish
Chervil	Lemon balm
Chives	Parsley
Cicely	Peppermint
Comfrey	Sweet woodruff
Feverfew	Violet
Ginger	

be taken not to overplant the area. In a smaller garden the available space for planting is the important restricting factor, but with imagination there can be an infinite number of ways to create an impressive herbal display. Whether the beds are spread out in squares or circles depends on the location and number of herbs required.

Keep in mind that a kitchen garden needs to be close to the back door for ease of access. In this case it is likely that some of the area will be in shade for some of the day. Luckily there are some very useful herbs that thrive in the shade.

Herbs in Containers

Planting herbs in pots and containers is a very popular method, but they do need to be watered regularly and kept as near to the sunshine as possible. Container growing is also ideal if space is very tight. The pots may be piled up pyramid fashion if necessary. The number of herbs kept in a container

An unusual and attractive way of growing herbs is in a cascade.

depends, of course, on the size of the pot or container being used and its location. Don't forget that herbs spread out and some grow very fast, so allow plenty of room at the time of planting.

Window boxes are ideal placed on the kitchen window.

Window boxes planted with herbs are colorful and decorative. These can liven up any dull wall, and they do not have to be confined to a window ledge. The choice of pots and containers is wide, but a classic wooden design is probably the best. If herbs are planted in a hanging wrought-iron container, the wind will have a dramatic drying effect on the soil. Some new designs of hanging baskets now have a built-in reservoir at the base of the container that can provide up to a week's water supply to the plants. This is a very good idea, especially in the hot summer months. Freestanding terra-cotta or glazed, decorative pottery containers look beautiful when planted, but they must be protected from frost, which may crack them. Some are frost protected, making them the pots of choice where possible.

Herbs can be planted in any container such as a pair of old kitchen scales.

Herbs Suited to Containers

Basil	Oregano
Bay	Parsley
Chives	Peppermint
Feverfew	Rosemary
Hyssop	Sage
Lavender	Tarragon
Lemon balm	Thyme

A great way to start growing herbs is in a strawberry pot. This pot stands about 3 feet (90 cm) high, and it contains pockets around its circumference in which small plants can be planted. This method makes the most economical use of space and can be used in restricted areas such as a balcony, roof garden or outside the back door within reach of the kitchen.

When planting in a container, it is advisable to place some broken pots in the base of the pot to allow for drainage, then fill over with good-quality soil mixed with compost. Plant the herbs about 2 inches (5 cm) deep and press the soil down firmly. If planting seeds, scatter the seeds over the top of the soil, then cover with a little soil. Water well after planting.

Even in containers, some herbs such as fennel grow tall, whereas tarragon is naturally kept small by the restricted root space. Pruning will keep your container crop in check.

Essential Herbs to Grow

The planning of your herb garden is most important. Do you need herbs for cooking or are you looking to make medicinal remedies from your crop?

The commonly used culinary herbs are worth considering,

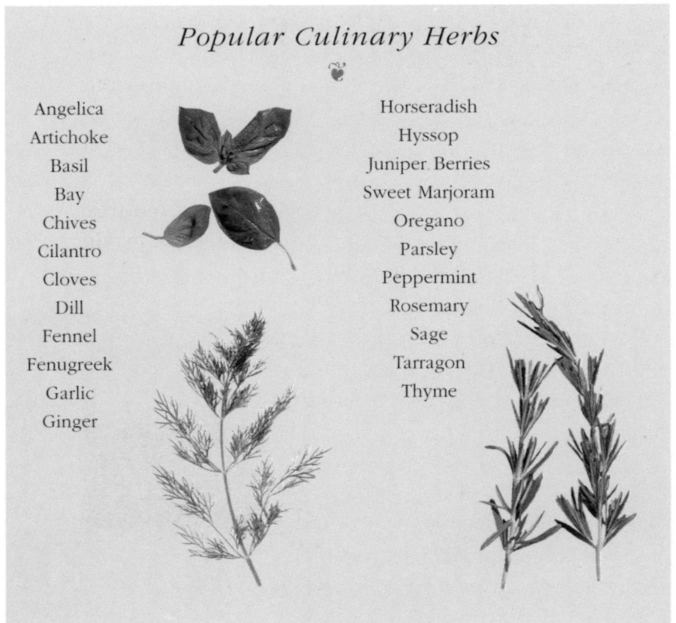

Popular Culinary Herbs
Angelica
Artichoke
Basil
Bay
Chives
Cilantro
Cloves
Dill
Fennel
Fenugreek
Garlic
Ginger
Horseradish
Hyssop
Juniper Berries
Sweet Marjoram
Oregano
Parsley
Peppermint
Rosemary
Sage
Tarragon
Thyme

Popular Medicinal Herbs

Caraway	Hyssop
Chamomile	Lavender
Cloves	Lemon balm
Comfrey	Peppermint
Echinacea	Rosemary
Feverfew	Sage
Garlic	Thyme

Toxic Herbs

Cowslip
Foxglove
Glory lilies
Lily-of-the-valley
Madagascar periwinkle
Meadow saffron
Opium poppies
Poke root

but grow only the ones that you use on a regular basis. Check which herbs are running low in the kitchen and plan to grow those first, as at least you know that they will be used. As you learn more about herbs and become more adventurous, you will be able to add new plants to your collection.

When choosing an herb crop to grow at home, don't forget that some are quite toxic and should be avoided whenever possible or at least positioned with great care, especially if you have young children or pets who may nibble the plants.

When and What to Plant

Garlic (*Allium sativum*) The bulbous root of the garlic is made up of 12–15 smaller cloves. The plant is grown by detaching the cloves and planting them. The soil should be light, dry and finely broken up. The cloves are planted 2½ inches (6 cm) apart and 1½ inches (4 cm) deep. They are best planted in early spring, and by the summer it is recommended that the leaves are tied in knots to prevent the stronger garlic plants from turning to flower.

The crop is harvested toward the end of summer. The roots are tied in bunches and hung in a dry room for later use.

Chives (*Allium schoenoprasum*) Chives are readily grown by dividing the roots, either in the fall or spring, and will grow in any soil or situation. They should be repeatedly cut during the summer, which will cause successive leaves to grow through.

A small bed or border is easily managed and will continue to supply a productive crop for three to four years, after which a new planting should be cultivated.

Angelica (*Angelica archangelica*) Angelica is easily raised from seed that should be sown soon after it is gathered. It grows best in a moist soil and thrives exceedingly well by the side of a ditch. Though a biennial plant, it may be made to continue for several years by cutting down the flower stem before it goes to seed.

Celery (*Apium graveolens*) There are two varieties of celery: one with a hollow stalk and one with a solid stalk. The solid stalk is generally the preferred form to grow.

Celery must be sown at several different times in order to ensure a succession of plants throughout the year. The first sowing is made at the beginning of spring, in a sheltered border. The next planting can start at the end of spring in a moist border. By the middle of spring the plants of the first sowing will be ready for transplanting to nursery beds of rich earth, in which they can be planted 2 inches (5 cm) apart. Water is given, and the plants are shaded from direct sunlight for a few days. Toward the end of spring, the most mature plants can be transplanted into trenches for blanching. The normal method for transplanting and blanching follows:

Dig trenches 3–4 feet (90–120 cm) apart, 1 foot (30 cm) deep and 1 foot (30 cm) wide. Make sure that the soil at the base is fine and of good quality. The soil for celery needs to be moist, deep and rich, but still light. The earth dug from the trench is laid on either side ready to be drawn back in as wanted. The tops are cut off of the long leaves and any side roots, then the plants are placed in the base of the trench 2 inches (5 cm) apart. As they grow, the earth is drawn in toward them every 10 days. Care should be taken to do this in dry weather and not to cover the center of the plant with soil. When the plants rise above the ground level, the earth from around the edges of the trench will have become used up, so another trench needs to be dug between the rows for a supply of soil to continue the earthing up until the leaf stalks of the celery become blanched for 3 inches (8 cm). The last sowing can withstand a mild winter, and the soil into which the plants are transplanted should be dry. In severe winters, loose straw is thrown over the beds.

Horseradish (*Armoracia rusticana*) The soil for horseradish should be rich and deep. It is grown from cuttings of the knotty parts of the root that have one or two eyes present. They are planted in early spring, in rows, leaving 1 foot (30 cm) between each row. The cuttings are placed at a depth of at least 1 foot (30 cm). The roots are not used until the second year, when they are dug up as needed. The bed should last for four to five years.

Caraway (*Carum carvi*) The caraway is a biennial plant and should be sown soon after the seed is ripe in the fall. Thin out the plants during the next spring to within 4¾ inches (12 cm) apart. A moist soil suits the caraway plant best.

Artichoke (*Cynara scolymus*) Artichokes are grown by means of rooted slips or suckers taken off the main plant during spring. They like a light loam soil—cool, rich and deep but dry. In preparing for the crop, the soil should be dug in 3-foot (90 cm)-deep trenches and left to mature for a few days before planting. The plants should be placed 4 feet (120 cm) apart, and by the end of the season, a small crop of artichokes can be cut. In the second year the crop will be plentiful, and at the time the heads are gathered, by the fall, the whole stalks will be broken down close to the ground.

Hyssop (*Hyssopus officinalis*) a poor, dry soil is most suitable for hyssop. It may be grown in the spring months from seed, rooted slips or from cuttings.

Lavender (*Lavandula officinalis*) Lavender is grown from cuttings or young slips any time in the spring months. It should be planted in a dry, gravelly or poor soil.

Peppermint (*Mentha piperita*) Peppermint likes most soils and is readily grown from slips in the spring, by means of cuttings in the summer and by dividing the roots in the fall. Because peppermint plants are sometimes destroyed in a severe frost, it is advisable to cover them lightly with straw.

Sweet Marjoram (*Origanum majorana*) This herb is best grown from seed. Pot marjoram is propagated by cuttings and is hardy to withstand the winter. Winter sweet marjoram requires a sheltered border and a dry soil. It is a perennial plant and is propagated by dividing the roots in the fall.

Parsley (*Petroselinum crispum*) Parsley may be raised in shallow furrows on the edge of a border. The seeds may be sown in early spring.

Rosemary (*Rosmarinus officinalis*) Rosemary is easily grown from slips or cuttings in the spring. It should be planted in a dry soil in a shaded location.

Sage (*Salvia officinalis*) The lighter and poorer the soil, the better the sage will thrive. It is grown in the spring from slips and in the summer from cuttings. The cuttings should be up to 4¾ inches (12 cm) long, stripped of all the lower leaves and plunged nearly to the top in the earth. They must be well watered. The plants should be replaced every three to four years.

Thyme (*Thymus vulgaris*) Thyme grows best in a light, dry soil that has not been recently manured or fertilized. It is grown by parting the roots and planting the slips or by sowing the seeds in spring.

HARVESTING HERBS

PICKING HERBS TENDS to encourage new growth and stimulates the healthy development of the plant.

When picking the flowers it is best to take the bud just before it opens up, as most herbs reach their optimal flavor just prior to flowering. Perennial herbs can yield two or three good crops during their growing seasons, but it is best to give them one year to get established before harvesting. When collecting from perennials, it is important not to cut into the woody growth. For annuals it is possible to cut the crop to 4 inches (10 cm) from the soil twice during the growing season with a final harvesting just before the first frost.

If you wish to collect the seeds, wait until the seed pods change color. To confirm if they are ready, just give the pods a tap; if seeds fall out, they are ready to be gathered.

It is important to harvest your crop from healthy plants in order to obtain the best extracts. The active agents and volatile oils will be plentiful. When collecting herbs, it is best to avoid contamination of aromas by placing each cutting in a separate collection bag; this will preserve the fragrance and oil content.

Harvesting Herb Parts

Leaves and Stems Select the young fresh leaves and stems before they undergo a tough and woody transformation.

Seeds Collect the seed heads or seed pods before they become overripe. Cut them and store them in a warm, dry place to ripen.

Flowers As the flower opens and reaches its peak, cut it from the stem just below the flower head.

Berries and Fruits These are best collected when ripe but before they become overripe or subjected to injury from the birds. Pick the fruits and use immediately or preserve.

Rhizomes, Roots and Tubers Once the above-ground stems and leaves have died and the plant goes into a dormant state, collect the underground structures.

Woods and Bark Many plants have bark or wood that can be used. Never cut bark away in a circular manner from the plant as this gives it no protection from infection. Collect the bark from harvested twigs or branches, making sure to seal any cut areas left after their removal.

DRYING HERBS

Air-drying is the most natural way for preserving herbs, and they look attractive hung upside down in bunches.

THE BEST HERBS to dry are thyme, tarragon, bay leaves and rosemary. These hold their aroma and taste for a good long time, but for most herbs there is no comparison to that of a freshly picked sprig. In general it is not wise to keep dried herbs for more than 12 months since the aroma and flavor will reduce dramatically after this period.

When drying the leaves, it is best to collect them just before the buds open to make sure that the leaves contain the highest concentrations of oils and essential agents. Herbs such as thyme and tarragon can be tied together and hung in bunches to dry. For the larger-leaf varieties of herbs, such as mint, basil and sage, pick only perfect leaves early in the day before the sun has a chance to dry out the essential oils. Once they have been picked, hang the bundles in a warm place (an airing cupboard is perfect) to dry out to a point where they are brittle enough to crumble and store in a bottle.

Once your herbs are dried, keep them in individual storage bottles that are clearly marked with the name of the herb and the date harvested. The bottles need to be clean, airtight and kept in a dry, dark place.

Air-Drying

This is the most widely used and easiest method of preserving the herbs. Simply spread them out on a dry surface or bunch them up and tie with a length of twine. The herbs should be dried within two days, otherwise the potency of aroma and effectiveness of the active agents will decline dramatically. If the leaves turn a dark brown-black and show signs of mold, then the process is too slow, and the herb has become unusable. Ideal drying conditions are 68°–73°F (20°–23°C) in a dry and fume-free environment. The traditional method of hanging the herbs in bunches will increase the efficiency of the drying method. Spread flowers and large leaves out on blotting paper and allow to dry on a wire cooling rack.

Seed heads should be hung upside down so that the seeds may fall out during the drying process and land on a piece of clean blotting paper placed underneath.

Oven-Drying

This method is not recommended for fragile leaves and flowers because heat will destroy all the active agents and oils. Oven-drying is most suitable for the larger structures, such as roots, rhizomes and tubers, which need intense drying at 122°–140°F (50°–60°C) for successful preservation. The drying process will take about three hours.

Storage Containers

Once your herbs have been dried, the containers in which they are stored will make all the difference to their shelf life. A clear glass container will allow the herbs to become bleached by light, which damages the valuable chemicals contained within the plants. Plastic containers may encourage a moist atmosphere that in turn can cause molds to grow and spoil the dried preparations. The best containers are dark glass or ceramic pots with airtight lids. These protect the contents from becoming damaged by light or air. Keeping these containers in a cool, dark place will increase the shelf life of the herbs.

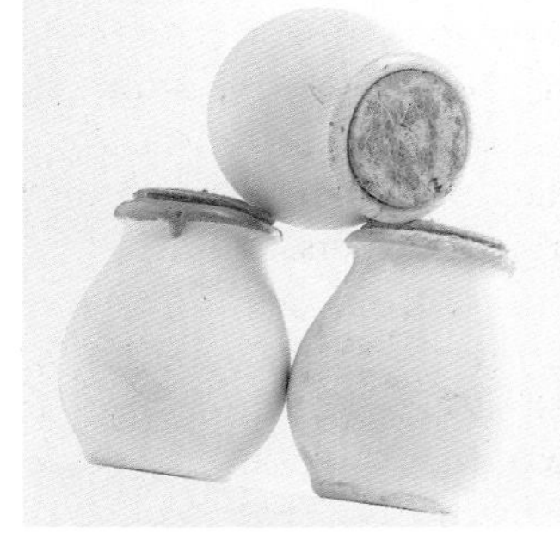

MAKING REMEDIES

A relaxing infusion of Chamomile (Anthemis nobilis)

Infusions and Decoctions

Infusions are made by adding boiling water to the delicate parts of the herb—the flowers, leaves and seeds. An infusion is normally made from a single herb, and it should never consist of more than three herbs.

To make an infusion, try mixing 1 oz (25 g) dried herb, or double this amount for a fresh herb, with 2½ cups (600 ml/ 1 pint) boiling water. Pour the boiling water over the herbs, cover and leave to steep for 15 minutes. Strain the mixture, squeeze out the herbs to obtain the maximum amount of juice, and drink a cupful twice daily. Good herbs to experiment with include sage, mint and chamomile.

For the hardy parts of a plant—the wood, bark and stems—a decoction is used to extract the active agents from this tough material. The same quantities are used as for an infusion, but the water and herbs are brought to a boil from cold, then simmered for 20 minutes before they are strained and drunk.

Infusion and decoction preparations are best taken the day they are made, but they can be kept in the refrigerator for about 24 hours.

Tinctures

The herbs (any part can be used) are steeped for just over two weeks in an alcohol-and-water mixture. The process extracts the active agents out of the plant matter, while the alcohol content of the mixture preserves the tincture for about two years from the date of manufacture. After about two weeks, press out the mixture to obtain the final tincture. Seal in an airtight container and use as needed. It is best to make tinctures of single herbs and only combine them with other tinctures when needed. Your local pharmacy can supply you with the alcohol needed for the extraction process. Commercial tinctures use ethyl alcohol but you can make tinctures at home using vodka (37.5%). Dilute 3¼ cups (750 ml) vodka with 2½ tablespoons (37.5 ml) water and use this mixture to steep the herbs in.

Oils

The extraction of oils from plant material is a complex process. The majority of oils are extracted by steam distillation. In this method water is heated to its boiling point, and the steam is directed to a large chamber containing the herbs. As the steam passes through the bed of herbal material, vaporized water and essential oils are released. These run through a condenser to be collected as oil and floral water. Oils such as lavender, myrrh, sandalwood and cinnamon are collected in this way.

The process isolates the volatile oil from the plant material. Other substances such as tannins and bitters are excluded from collection. A redistillation at different temperatures can separate different constituents of the essential oil such as camphor, which can be broken down by further distillation into white, yellow or brown camphor. Essential oils tend to evaporate when brought into contact with the air, so it is vitally important to keep the lids on bottles of essential oils firmly closed to preserve the aroma.

When mixing oils for use in massage, it is recommended that the combination be kept simple, and no more than four oils are used together in any one remedy. It is perfectly acceptable to use a single oil, and this may actually exert a more powerful effect than if it were combined with others.

Oils in Massage Oils for use in massage have been classified according to the part of the plant from which they have been extracted. Oils derived from the flowers are termed the top notes and carry the presenting aroma that is first noticed; those from the leaves are called the middle notes and have a more therapeutic action; oils from the wood and roots are known as the base notes as they provide a "fixing" characteristic to a blend since they have a more long-lasting aroma. A formula with a balanced blend of oils, therefore, carries all of these notes.

The oil into which the essential oils are mixed is referred to as the carrier, or base, oil and is commonly grapeseed or almond oil. Others, such as wheatgerm or avocado oil, can be used, but these are normally reserved for very dry skin types because of the nutritive nature of the oil.

Oils in the Bath The addition of a few drops (about five) of essential oil to a bath can be very relaxing and therapeutic. For those with very sensitive skin, this method of use may cause irritation, and the advice of a professional aromatherapist is best sought. Try a bath with chamomile or lavender to relieve stress or insomnia or rosemary oil to help aching muscles and stiff joints.

Oils in Vaporization Making use of the evaporative properties of essential oils can be a fun and delightful way to scent a room. Placing a few drops over a piece of tissue paper draped over a radiator can generate a marvelous aroma in the

Burning a few drops of essential oil in a burner is a great way to scent a room.

room, strong enough to clear the air of unwanted cigarette smoke if needed. When taken to the sick room, essential oils can help purify the air and ease the congested breathing of the bed-bound patient. The oils may even lift his or her mood. Try vaporizing essential oils of eucalyptus or peppermint in the sick room.

To lift the mood and induce relaxation, fill a room with the fragrance of cedarwood and frankincense. This can be achieved by using an oil burner or placing a few drops around the light bulb ring used to fasten a shade to the light fitting.

Oils in Steam Inhalation
There is no better way to clear the chest and sinuses than by the traditional method of steam inhalation. Add three to five drops of peppermint, eucalyptus or thyme to a bowl of hot water, cover your head with a towel and lean over the steam. Breathe in deeply and feel the passages clear.

CAUTIONARY NOTE:
In certain sensitive asthmatic people, the oils used and the steam itself may trigger attacks during the inhalation treatment. It is strongly advised that professional guidance is followed when using this method of treatment in an asthmatic person.

Oils Taken Internally The internal use of essential oils is not recommended unless you have been given specific instructions on what oil to use and how much to take. Many oils can be extremely irritating to the stomach and may cause serious adverse reactions when taken this way.

Poultices and Compresses

The best method of making a poultice is to use the fresh leaves, stems and roots. Chop and crush the material into a paste, adding water as needed to form a good consistency. A short whiz in a blender or food processor can speed up the process. The final processed herb can be either applied directly to the skin or placed between two thin layers of gauze and bound firmly to the area.

The poultice can be bearably hot or cold, but the best method of keeping it active is to place a hot water bottle over the gauze for about 30 minutes. This can be repeated every two to three hours as needed.

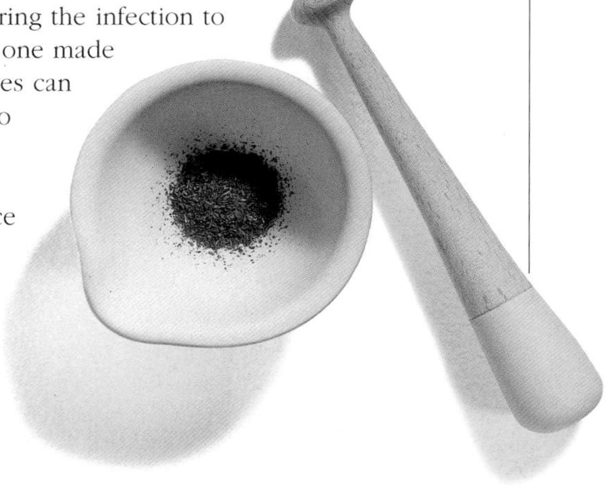

A poultice made from bread can help ripen a boil and bring the infection to the surface, while one made from cabbage leaves can bring great relief to arthritic joints.

For a compress, simply soak a piece of cotton fabric or clean dish towel in a fresh herbal infusion (hot or cold), a decoction or diluted herbal tincture. Apply it directly to the affected area. When using a hot infusion, allow the compress to cool before changing it. If a cold application is used, repeat when the compress dries out. A compress is best used when healing is needed, especially when there is damage to muscles and ligaments.

Ointments and Creams

Ointments are designed to sit on the skin, especially in areas of weakness or where extra moisture is needed. They are made of oils and fats (such as petroleum jelly or paraffin wax) and contain no water. Any herbs can be used but comfrey (*Symphytum officinale*), calendula (*Calendula officinalis*) and goldenseal (*Hydrastis canadensis*) are particularly beneficial.

Once you have melted down the oil or wax of your choice using a double boiler, slowly add your chosen herbs. Continue to heat for about two hours. Remove from the heat and filter the mixture into a bowl using a piece of cheesecloth, squeezing out the mixture thoroughly. Decant the liquid quickly into clean jars and leave to solidify. Use as required.

Creams are used when the herb needs to be absorbed into the skin. Obtain some emulsifying ointment from your local pharmacy. Melt this down and add a little water and the herbs, then slowly heat the mixture for about two-and-a-half hours. Filter the mixture through a cheesecloth and squeeze out firmly. Transfer the cream to clean jars and store in a cool place. Your cream may be kept in this way for two months.

MEDICINAL USES

IT IS IMPORTANT to keep in mind that plant extracts can be very toxic as well as beneficial to health. Just because they are natural does not mean they are safe; some of the most powerful poisons are obtained from plants.

In order to make the use of herbal medicine safe and effective, you need to know how much and how often to take an extract. Just as a medicine bottle from the pharmacy tells you how much aspirin is in each tablet, so a bottle of herbal medicine should tell you how much active agent is contained in it. This not only safeguards against overdosage, but it also reassures you that you are taking a good-quality extract. Consider the label taken from an over-the-counter remedy (see box).

> Korean ginseng root extract (3:1)
>
> (*Panax ginseng*) 100 mg
>
> Siberian ginseng root extract (5:1)
>
> (*Eleutherococcus senticosus*) 150 mg
>
> Standardized to contain 1% eleutheroside

What does this mean? The common name is given as well as the botanical name, thus allowing for a complete understanding of the extract contained in the preparation. The dosage, given in milligrams, gives the weight of root extract, but only when the extraction concentration is given (e.g. 3:1 or 5:1) do you know how strong the extract is. When the extract is expressed in the form 3:1, this means that each tablet or capsule has the same potency as three capsules of the powdered herb; 5:1 means that each capsule has the same potency as five capsules of the powdered herb. In other words, the extract has been concentrated.

When an extract has been standardized, its content is at a pharmaceutical grade and is consistent. The 1 percent eleutheroside in the example states that the dose of the active agent for that manufacturer's ginseng compound is one percent. A poor-quality ginseng will still weigh the same when powdered, but there is no law at present that requires the manufacturer to tell the customer if the extract actually contains any active agent, so it is well worth understanding how to read the labels.

With a liquid tincture, the descriptive terms change again. Tinctures are normally made at a dose of 1:5 or 1:10 concentration, meaning that one part herb is soaked in five or 10 parts liquid. In other words, they include five or 10 times the amount of solvent than herb. Tinctures are normally made by using a water-and-alcohol solvent. The herb is soaked in this solvent for hours to sometimes days before being squeezed out and bottled as a tincture.

Fluid extracts are made by soaking the herbs in solvents such as vinegar, glycol or glycerin, and then distilling off some of the liquid using vacuum distillation or countercurrent distillation, both of which achieve the final 1:1 concentration without using heat. This leaves one part herb to one part solvent. Fluid extracts are, therefore, five to 10 times stronger than tinctures.

Solid extracts are generally made by thin-layer evaporation methods, in which the solvent is completely removed, leaving behind the dry, solid plant material. This can be finely powdered and used to fill capsules. The powdered extract can be reconstituted by adding back the water or alcohol. Probably one of the greatest improvements that modern science has been able to offer herbal medicine is the ability to produce pure, safe and standardized methods of extraction. This has aided the effective use of herbal remedies as well as the research into the plant constituents. The ability to offer the herbal user a standardized extract allows a universal understanding of the dose taken regardless of the crop quality or method of extraction.

Standardized Extracts

Since the beginning of time, people have used herbs to promote health and well-being. To make the best possible use of herbal extracts, pure standardized extracts (PSE) have been developed to ensure the highest level of quality and consistency. To obtain a PSE, concentrate the herb by mixing the crude plant with an appropriate amount of alcohol and water. The alcohol and water is then either partially or completely removed to produce a liquid, soft or solid extract. Making an herbal extract is rather like refining pure gold from crude ore.

These modern laboratory methods preserve the beneficial botanical compounds. These extracts are normally available in capsules as a dry or powdered form because this offers the greatest stability to the final extract.

The PSE is not a method of isolating chemicals. All PSE formulas contain the same chemicals found in the crude plant including essential oils, flavonoids, alkaloids, glucosides and saponins. It is important not only to have these compounds present, but also to have them in the proper ratio.

Importance of Standardization

*Korean ginseng (*Panax ginseng*) is used to improve stamina.*

Herbs can vary tremendously in chemical composition and quality depending on where they are grown, soil factors and how and when they are harvested. A nonstandardized herbal remedy cannot, therefore, guarantee any consistency.

To consider an example, Korean ginseng (*Panax ginseng*) has been featured in a number of studies. Independent research and published studies have clearly shown a tremendous variation in the content of the active agent, called ginsenoside, in commercial preparations. Most contained only trace amounts of ginsenoside, while some contained none at all! To solve this problem, manufacturers of herbal preparations needed to guarantee the level of these compounds. The method of preparation and extraction needed to do this is the PSE process. This gives manufacturers the ability to state, for example, "*Panax ginseng* standardized to contain 17 percent ginsenosides." This method allows the user of herbal preparations to be aware of the exact strength of the preparation he is taking and to be reassured that it will be consistent.

The Phytosome® Method

This method is probably the most advanced way of preparing an herbal extract for human use. Phytosomes are created when herbal molecules are bound to phosphatidylcholine, a natural component of lecithin, which is found throughout the body in our cell membranes. The Phytosome method allows a water-soluble herbal extract to be surrounded by a coat that makes it readily absorbable across a cell membrane. The cells will actively take up this Phytosome complex from the circulation. Herbal extracts normally find their way into cells by a process of passive diffusion. This process intensifies the herbal compounds by improving their absorption and increasing their biological availability. Some herbal compounds are not very bioavailable, and very large doses are needed for an effect to be noticed. The Phytosome process has revolutionized the use of such herbs.

Medicine Cabinet Staples

There are a number of essential herbs that are best kept as tinctures or ready-made tablets or capsules so that they are always ready for instant use. Tinctures of echinacea (*Echinacea purpura*) and valerian (*Valeriana officinalis*) are always good to have in store, as well as preparations of licorice (*Glycyrrhiza glabra*), Korean ginseng (*Panax ginseng*) and cranberry (*Vaccinium macrocarpon*).

The choice and variations of herbs to keep in the medicine cabinet are almost limitless and are dependent on you and your family's needs.

Basic Medicinal Herbs

Aloe vera (*Alo barbadensis*)
Chamomile (*Anthemis nobilis*)
Cranberry (*Vaccinium macrocarpon*)
Echinacea (*Echinacea purpura*)
Feverfew (*Tanacetum parthenium*)
Garlic (*Allium sativum*)
Ginger (*Zingiber officinalis*)
Ginseng (*Panax ginseng*)
Licorice (*Glycyrrhiza glabra*)
Valerian (*Valeriana officinalis*)

*Echinacea (*Echinacea purpura*) stimulates the immune system.*

COSMETIC USES

Making your own cosmetic preparations is rewarding as only natural ingredients are used.

PLANT EXTRACTS HAVE been used in body painting since the time of the ancient Egyptians. Woad (a blue dye obtained from *Isatis tinctoria*) was used by the ancient Britons to paint their bodies much in a way similar Native Americans used plant dyes and oils.

Flower Water

Many plants can be used fresh or dried. Plants with aromatic leaves are most effective at the end of summer, but they are considered to be freshest at the start of summer. These plants can be dried and, when stored correctly, can be used throughout the year. For best results the plants need to be dried just after picking in order to preserve the aromatic oils.

After rinsing the plant in cold water and removing all the dead material, place in a clean pan that is big enough to hold two handfuls of plants. Add enough water to cover the material. Then cook the plants over low heat to release the aromatic oils. In general, cook the plants 15–20 minutes. After cooking, strain the mixture, decant into small storage jars and transfer to a cold place to keep the extracts fresh.

Cleansing Milk

1 cup (250 ml/8 fl oz) buttermilk
2 tablespoons chamomile flowers
2 tablespoons elder blossom
2 tablespoons lime blossom

*Chamomile (*Anthemis nobilis*)*

Place all the ingredients in a pan and simmer for 30 minutes; do not allow the mixture to boil. After simmering, leave the mixture to cool for just over two hours before straining and decanting into a storage bottle. Store in the refrigerator and use within a week of making. Use the cleansing milk before the herbal toning lotion.

Toning Lotion

Mix together equal parts of flower waters (rose, lavender, elderflower and orange), combine and mix well. Take 2 tablespoons of the mixture and add it to 2 tablespoons lemon juice and 2 tablespoons witch hazel. For a soothing effect, add a few drops of essential oil (lavender, geranium or rose), and mix the ingredients together well. Store the lotion in a cool place, and apply morning and evening to restore the skin's natural texture and cleanse the pores.

Astringent

Infuse a good handful of lime blossom or meadowsweet flowers, allow to cool, and then strain. Mix 1¼ cups (300 ml/ ½ pint) boiling water with 1 teaspoon witch hazel. Then combine the flower water with the witch hazel mixture.

Witch hazel has the ability to soothe and soften skin while acting as a deep cleansing agent. Use this formulation morning and evening.

HOME USES

HERBS AND AROMATIC plants have been used in the home for centuries. Potpourri and incense balls were widely used in medieval times for freshening the air. The ancient Egyptians were also known to use combinations of aromatic herbs in rooms for decorative and medicinal purposes.

*Lavender (*Lavandula officinalis*) is one of the few flowers to retain their aroma after drying and is ideal for potpourris.*

Potpourri

Making a potpourri can introduce a unique aromatic characteristic to your living room or bedroom. A potpourri comprises four component parts—flowers, leaves, spices and a fixative (called the base note in aromatherapy). The fixative is needed to keep the potpourri together. The aromatic substance chosen releases its scent slowly, giving a long-lasting aroma to the mixture.

The advantage of making your own potpourri, rather than buying it, is that you can choose the combination that will suit your taste exactly. Select the ingredients for your potpourri from the following suggestions.

FLOWERS
- *Elder*
- *Honeysuckle*
- *Lavender*
- *Lily-of-the-valley*
- *Lime blossom*
- *Narcissus*
- *Orange blossom*
- *Rose*
- *Sweet rocket*

AROMATIC LEAVES
- *Basil*
- *Bay*
- *Bergamot*
- *Lemon balm*
- *Lemon verbena*
- *Rosemary*
- *Sage*
- *Sweet marjoram*
- *Tarragon*
- *Thyme*
- *Woodruff*

SPICES
- *Allspice*
- *Aniseed*
- *Cardamom*
- *Cloves*
- *Coriander*
- *Dill seeds*
- *Ginger*
- *Nutmeg*
- *Star anise*
- *Vanilla beans*

BASE-NOTE FRAGRANCES
- *Frankincense*
- *Myrrh*
- *Sandalwood*
- *Sweet flag root*

Potpourri must be aged before using. Place in a sealed container and leave in a warm, dry place for four to six weeks.

Drying the Flowers The ideal drying temperature is about 75°F (24°C). The flowers need to be spread out evenly, without overlapping, on gauze or newspaper. They will need to be turned every day. For an effective drying process, the smaller petals need to be dried for up to seven days, while larger, thicker petals may take up to three weeks to be fully dried. Flowers such as lavender and chamomile can be dried on the stem and are best tied in bunches and hung upside down for drying.

Spicy Spring Potpourri

Flowers
3 cups rose petals
2 cups lavender
1 cup cloves

Leaves
¼ cup rosemary
½ cup bergamot
¼ cup bay leaves
½ cup southernwood

Colored Flowers
¼ cup calendula
½ cup forget-me-not

Spices
½ tablespoon ground cloves
1 tablespoon allspice

Base-note Fixative Oil
5 tablespoons sandalwood oil

CULINARY USES

Aromatic oils are useful for adding flavor to any salad dressing. All oils should be kept in a cool, dark place.

WHEN USED IN cooking, the tender aromatic plant tips tend to be classified as herbs, while the dried aromatic extracts of the plants' barks, flower buds, fruits, seeds and roots are known collectively as spices. The term "condiments" refers to spices that are added to the food at the table after cooking.

Many composite spices and herbs are also available. Apple spice is a mixture of cinnamon, nutmeg and sugar as well as other aromatic spices. Pumpkin spice is made by mixing cinnamon, ginger, nutmeg and cloves. For savory foods, a good meat tenderizer can be made from salt and papain (from the pawpaw fruit). On the barbecue, try using a mixture of Indian and Italian herbs to create a special flavor.

There is also an interesting variety of composite condiments available. These often contain sea salt and a mixture of up to 16 different herbs such as bell peppers, garlic, onion and many others. The herbal salt combination Herbamare (produced by Bioforce) is prepared from organically grown herbs that have been allowed to steep with sea salt for six to eight weeks before the moisture is removed using a special vacuum method at low temperature. This method of manufacture preserves the aroma and flavor of the herbal ingredients. Herbamare, therefore, contains nutrients and natural plant-based iodine. This salt combination is based in celery leaves, leeks, celery root, watercress, onions, chives, parsley, lovage, basil, marjoram, rosemary, thyme and kelp. A similar method of production is used in the manufacture of a more spicy version, Trocomare, which also contains horseradish and red bell pepper.

It is important to remember that the art of flavoring in cooking is to use just enough to enhance the dish, not to overpower the final result with the flavor of the herbs. As a rule, ground spices lose their flavor quickly and are not suitable for dishes that require long cooking times. For stews or soups, add them within the last 20 minutes before serving.

In most cases, use at least twice the amount of fresh herb to give the same intensity of flavor as its dried equivalent, but remember that the flavor quality of the fresh herb cannot be compared to the dried. Different herbs and spices have an affinity with different foods, which makes cooking an exciting and enjoyable activity.

Herbs can be added to preserves to enhance the flavor. A single or a mixture of herbs makes delicious combinations.

Herbs for Cooking

Garlic (*Allium sativum*) Garlic tends to be more pungent than onion. Do not use a wooden board for chopping or crushing it because the wood will become saturated with the aromatic oils. Use garlic in soups, fish dishes, roast lamb, meat stews, poultry dishes and pasta. Vegetables are especially good when prepared using garlic. Try it with tomatoes, green bell peppers, artichokes, eggplant and spinach. Vinaigrette dressing would not be the same without a good dash of garlic. Also try using garlic in marinades and mixed with butter for oven-baked garlic bread.

Chives (*Allium schoenoprasum*) Chives give a mild onion flavor that is best released by snipping the leaves and adding them to the dish immediately before the oils evaporate. Try adding chives to vegetables of all kinds, fish, salads, baked potatoes, omelets and egg dishes. As a garnish, chives are irreplaceable as a source of color. Chives mix well with chopped parsley. Use the flowers to garnish soups and savory dishes.

Dill (*Anethum graveolens*) Dill has a slight anise flavor. Use the chopped leaves in salads, vegetable dishes (they are especially good with large zucchini, tomatoes, beets and cabbage) and egg dishes. Use a sprig and the leaves as garnishes for fish. The seeds may be used in fish dishes, grilled lamb and pork, stews, sauerkraut and cabbage. Dill is also a good addition to cheese dishes.

Angelica (*Angelica archangelica*) Angelica has a penetrating flavor. Care is needed since some may find the taste overpowering. The stems are crystalized and used to decorate cakes and desserts. Try using the leaves and roots for stewing with fruit to give an alternative sweetness to sugar. Chopped angelica may be used in salads, hot wine and fruit drinks.

Horseradish (*Armoracia rusticana*) Horseradish gives off a hot, strong and pungent aroma rather like mustard. When shredded, the root can be used as a sauce, mixed with cream and vinegar. Add to shellfish and smoked fish dishes. As the classic accompaniment to roast beef, it is said to help digestion. Other foods that work well with horseradish include poultry, beets and tomatoes.

Caraway Seeds (*Carum carvi*) Caraway seeds have a licorice flavor that's stronger than anise. The whole seeds are used in dumplings for soups and stews, goulash and vegetable dishes, especially red and white cabbage, cauliflower, beets, turnips and potatoes. Try adding the seeds to a rye bread mix or just to a standard bread mix for a special flavor and aroma. Grind the seeds when adding caraway to stews and vegetables such as zucchini, beans, cabbage, tomatoes and potato salad.

Cilantro (*Coriandrum sativum*) Cilantro is a versatile herb and the leaves and green coriander seeds have a very pungent aroma. Use a small handful of young chopped leaves in soups, beef stews, poultry dishes, salads, vegetables and even desserts. Try adding the leaves and green seeds to curries.

Turmeric (*Curcuma longa*) Turmeric is unmistakable with its distinctive color and delicate aroma. It is used ground in fish and shellfish dishes, curries, stews and in rice and vegetable dishes. Try adding a little turmeric to homemade relish and chutneys.

Fennel (*Foeniculum vulgare*) Fennel has a more concentrated flavor than dill and has the similar anise taste. It goes very well with fish, particularly the oily types. Try grilling the fish over sprigs of dried fennel. Otherwise, use it in exactly the same way as dill. The seeds can be used in a fish bouillon or try adding them to bread mixes.

Hyssop (*Hyssopus officinalis*) Hyssop is slightly bitter with a hint of mint. The tender young leaves can be used in soups and with oily fish. Stews, salads, stuffing mixes and fruit cocktails also benefit from the addition of hyssop. Cranberries, peaches and apricots are delicious with hyssop.

Juniper Berries (*Juniperus communis*) Juniper berries are generally used dried. They can be lightly crushed to release their strong bittersweet flavor. Try adding a small handful of berries to rice dishes, sauces, marinades and relish, or use them with game meats, pork and as a delicious ingredient in stuffing mix.

Bay Leaves (*Laurus nobilis*) Bay leaves should be added at the start of cooking. They deliver a strong spicy flavor to soups and stews. Bay can be added to all meat dishes. For sweet dishes, try adding it to milk desserts and custards.

Bay leaves form an essential part of a bouquet garni. To make, take one bay leaf, three or four sprigs of parsley, including stalks, and a sprig of thyme, and wrap in a small piece of cheesecloth, and tie tightly. You can add other herbs to taste.

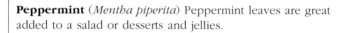

Peppermint (*Mentha piperita*) Peppermint leaves are great added to a salad or desserts and jellies.

Basil (*Ocimum basilicum*) Basil gives a peppery flavor to a dish. The leaves, torn not chopped, may be added to soups, fish, egg and game dishes. Try basil mixed with rice, vegetables or pasta during cooking. Finely grind and use as part of a vinaigrette dressing for salads.

Sweet Marjoram (*Origanum majorana*) Sweet marjoram has a sweet and spicy flavor and is very versatile in cooking. The leaves can be chopped and added to soups or meat dishes, poultry and vegetables. Potatoes, carrots, cabbage and celery are especially good mixed with a little marjoram. Try adding it to cheese, egg and fish dishes. Oregano (*Origanum vulgare*) belongs to the same family as sweet marjoram but has a stronger flavor. Use chopped leaves in salads and pasta dishes.

Parsley (*Petroselinum crispum*) Parsley can be considered one of the most versatile herbs with its own distinctive flavor. The stalks have a stronger flavor than the leaves, so in stews, stocks and marinades it is best to use the stalks. For a bouquet garni, try adding the whole sprig. For soups, fish dishes, meat and poultry, use the freshly chopped leaves. As a garnish, parsley adds color and texture to any dish.

Rosemary (*Rosmarinus officinalis*) Rosemary can overpower a dish because it is a very strong and aromatic herb. Use whole sprigs under roast lamb or placed inside a chicken. The chopped leaves are suitable for soups, fish dishes, bacon, ham and any meat or game stew. Rosemary combines well with large zucchini, peas, bell peppers, potatoes and bread mixes.

Sage (*Salvia officinalis*) Sage has a strong and distinctive flavor. It is slightly bitter and goes well with fatty foods probably because it stimulates the flow of bile that aids fat digestion. The chopped leaves go very well with pork, duck and sausages. With vegetables, sage combines well with tomatoes, bell peppers, dried beans, eggplant and onions. In a stuffing, sage is a vital ingredient.

Cloves (*Syzygium aromaticum*) Cloves have an unmistakable sharp and spicy flavor. The whole clove can be stuck into an onion and added to soups or stews to produce an aromatic flavor to the finished dish. Try studding a ham or beef with cloves before cooking. Use the ground spice in meat dishes and curries with vegetables. Cloves go very well with beets, sweet potatoes and Belgian endive. Baked fruit and fruit pie fillings lend themselves to spicing up with a few cloves. Use ground cloves in pumpkin pie. Mulled wine and ale should never be without cloves.

Thyme (*Thymus vulgaris*) Thyme has a distinctive, strong flavor. A sprig of thyme is a must in a bouquet garni, stocks and marinades. The chopped leaves may be added to soups, fish and shellfish dishes, meat and poultry. It is a very versatile herb, combining well with beets, mushrooms, pasta, rice, tomatoes, beans and bread mix.

Fenugreek (*Trigonella foenum-graecum*) Fenugreek has a background flavor of bitterness. Use it ground in vegetable and bean soups, curries, meat stews and homemade chutneys.

Ginger (*Zingiber officinale*) Ginger, when fresh, gives off a fabulous aroma. The hot, strong characteristics of this spice make it a good accompaniment to Chinese and Indian food. Use the whole dried root in relish and chutneys. When ground it can be scattered over melon or grapefruit and added to soups, vegetable dishes and cake mixes.

Culinary Cupboard Staples

If you like to experiment in the kitchen and you have advanced cooking skills, a wide range of herbs is essential. If, however, your culinary expertise is limited, then choose a basic range of herbs. It might be wise to start with just parsley, sage, bay, peppermint, garlic, cilantro, oregano, cloves and ginger; then, as your confidence increases, you could add to the selection you keep in stock.

Basic Culinary Herbs

Basil	Parsley
Bay	Peppermint
Cilantro	Rosemary
Fennel	Sage
Garlic	Sweet Marjoram
Ginger	Tarragon
Oregano	Thyme

THE HERB DIRECTORY

Cautionary note:

At all times it is recommended that you consult a health-care professional before embarking on a program of self-treatment. Herbal medicines are effective and safe when used in the correct circumstances. This book has been written to educate, and every effort has been made to make the book as accurate and as informative as possible, but the advice contained within is no replacement for professional guidance.

HERB LIST BY COMMON NAME

Common name	Botanical name	Page
Agrimony	*Agrimonia eupatoria*	51
Alfalfa	*Medicago sativa*	108
Aloe vera	*Alo barbadensis*	56
American cranesbill	*Geranium maculatum*	94
Angelica	*Angelica archangelica*	59
Arnica	*Arnica montana*	67
Artichoke	*Cynara scolymus*	84
Astragalus	*Astragalus membranaceus*	70
Basil	*Ocimum basilicum*	111
Bilberry	*Vaccinium myrtillus*	150
Black cohosh	*Cimicifuga racemosa*	79
Blackthorn	*Prunus spinosa*	124
Borage	*Borago officinalis*	72
Burdock	*Arctium lappa*	64
Butcher's broom	*Ruscus aculeatus*	128
Calendula	*Calendula officinalis*	73
Californian poppy	*Eschscholzia californica*	88
Caraway	*Carum carvi*	76
Cayenne	*Capsicum frutescens*	74
Celery	*Apium graveolens*	63
Centaury	*Centaurium erythraea*	77
Chives	*Allium schoenoprasum*	55
Cilantro	*Coriandrum sativum*	81
Clary	*Salvia sclarea*	132
Cloves	*Syzygium aromaticum*	139
Coltsfoot	*Tussilago farfara*	145
Comfrey	*Symphytum officinale*	137
Crampbark	*Viburnum opulus*	154
Cranberry	*Vaccinium macrocarpon*	148
Dandelion	*Taraxacum officinale*	142
Devil's claw	*Martynia annua*	107
Dill	*Anethum graveolens*	58
Echinacea	*Echinacea purpura*	85
Elder	*Sambucus nigra*	133
Eucalyptus	*Eucalyptus globulus*	89
Evening primrose	*Oenothera biennis*	112
Eyebright	*Euphrasis officinalis*	91
Fennel	*Foeniculum vulgare*	92
Fenugreek	*Trigonella foenum-graecum*	144
Feverfew	*Tanacetum parthenium*	140
Garlic	*Allium sativum*	53
Ginger	*Zingiber officinale*	156
Ginkgo	*Ginkgo biloba*	95
Ginseng	*Panax ginseng*	117
Ginseng (Siberian)	*Eleutherococcus senticosus*	86
Goldenseal	*Hydrastis canadensis*	98

YARROW

Achillea millefolium

THE LATIN NAME for this plant is believed to come from the Greek hero Achilles. It is said that he used it to heal his soldiers' wounds during the Trojan War.

Taken internally, this herb is used to stimulate the circulatory system and help reduce blood pressure. It has a diaphoretic action, so it is helpful in reducing fevers brought about by colds and flu. Yarrow has antiseptic and anti-inflammatory properties, so it is used to control excessive bleeding and helps reduce diarrhea and dysentery. This herb can be used to relieve indigestion, flatulence and dyspepsia.

Externally, yarrow is used to help heal minor wounds and for cleansing and toning the skin.

PARTS USED

- *Leaves and flowers*

DOSAGE

- *As a tea, add about 2 teaspoons (5–10 ml) of herbs to 2½ cups (600 ml/1 pint) of boiling water and infuse for 5 minutes.*
- *For external application, use as a poultice for minor cuts and scrapes.*

POTENTIAL BENEFITS

- *Stimulates the circulatory system*
- *Helps reduce blood pressure*
- *Helps to reduce fevers*
- *Has antiseptic properties*
- *Has anti-inflammatory properties*
- *Can reduce diarrhea*
- *Can relieve indigestion*

COSMETIC USES

- *Flowers can be used in creams and lotions to cleanse the skin. Yarrow can also be used in skin tonics as an astringent for oily skin.*

CULINARY USES

- *The fresh young leaves are used in salads.*

WARNING: Do not use yarrow for long periods as it may cause skin irritation. Avoid during pregnancy.

SWEET FLAG

Acorus calamus

THIS HERB HAS both medicinal and culinary uses. Candy made from this plant is produced by crystalizing tender slices of the roots (rhizomes). The roots contain volatile oils that have profound antibiotic actions. Taken internally, sweet flag can be very useful in the stimulation of digestion and as a remedy for bronchitis and sinus congestion. An external application can be used to relieve rheumatic joint and muscle pains. It is also a carminative agent and can reduce muscular spasms that are associated with nerve pains.

PARTS USED

- *Roots, rhizomes and oil extract*

DOSAGE

- *As a liquid tincture, take 20 drops twice daily before eating.*
- *For external application, use as a compress for joint and muscle pain.*

POTENTIAL BENEFITS

- *Helps bronchitis*
- *Reduces sinus congestion*
- *Stimulates digestion*
- *Eases joint and muscle pains*
- *May help in neuralgia*

CULINARY USES

- *Used to make candy*

HORSE CHESTNUT

Aesculus hippocastanum

THE LEAVES OF this tree leave a horseshoe-shaped scar behind on the twig as they fall off, but it is named horse chestnut because the fruits were used as fodder for cattle and horses.

Herbal medicine has found a number of applications for this herb. When taken internally, it has a mild diuretic activity and can exert an anti-inflammatory action. This herb can improve the flow and exchange of tissue fluids in the body and can reduce the swellings associated with poor circulation. Therefore, the congestion that occurs in cases of varicose veins can be relieved by regular use of an extract of horse chestnut. Its value in circulatory problems can be seen by the benefit reported by those who have suffered a stroke or suffer from erythema or other conditions associated with poor circulation—it promotes the flow of oxygenated blood to every area of the body.

PARTS USED

- *Bark and seeds*

DOSAGE

- *As a liquid tincture, take 15–20 drops twice daily.*
- *For external application, apply as a cream directly to varicose veins as needed.*

POTENTIAL BENEFITS

- *Acts as a mild diuretic*
- *Regulates circulation*
- *Reduces tissue inflammation*
- *Eases varicose vein symptoms*
- *Promotes flow of oxygenated blood to all areas of the body*

COSMETIC USES

- *May be used in a lotion to improve the skin's circulation.*

AGRIMONY

Agrimonia eupatoria

DURING ANGLO-SAXON times, agrimony was used externally as a wound-healing agent. This use was practiced by the French during the fifteenth century, when they applied the herb after gunshot injuries. The agents responsible for the medicinal actions have been identified as astringents. These substances have the ability to close wounds and control the flow of blood.

Other medicinal functions of this plant rely on the bitter principles present in the extracts. Bitters can cause the gallbladder to contract and release its stored bile as well as stimulate the flow of digestive juices. Agrimony can reduce the inflammation of the stomach lining that often results from food allergies. Used externally, this herb can also help relieve symptoms of eczema.

PARTS USED
- *Whole plant*

DOSAGE
- *As a liquid tincture, take 20 drops twice daily before eating.*
- *For external application, use as a compress for eczema.*

POTENTIAL BENEFITS
- *Controls bleeding wounds when applied as a compress*
- *Assists liver function and digestion*
- *Helps in some cases of food allergy*
- *Helps reduce skin irritations from eczema*

COSMETIC USES
- *The leaves can be used in a facial wash to improve the skin's complexion.*

LADY'S MANTLE

Alchemilla vulgaris

THE LEAVES OF Lady's mantle were considered to hold special magical powers once, so much so that the translation of its botanical name, *Alchemilla*, means "little magical one."

It has been used for many feminine problems and was thought to restore a lady's beauty. In the treatment of menopausal disorders, the astringent and anti-inflammatory properties help control irregular bleeding, an effect that prompted its use for menstrual problems in younger women. Taken internally, lady's mantle can help regulate excessive or irregular menstrual bleeding and can also be used as a treatment for diarrhea. Applied externally, its properties make it very useful for the treatment of vaginal discharge.

PARTS USED

- *Whole plant*

DOSAGE

- *As a liquid tincture, take 20 drops twice daily.*
- *As a douche, infuse 1 tablespoon (15 ml) dried powder, strain and apply in the morning and evening.*

POTENTIAL BENEFITS

- *Controls excessive bleeding*
- *Regulates menstrual bleeding*
- *Aids in vaginal infections*
- *Relieves diarrhea*

COSMETIC USES

- *The leaves can be used in a lotion as an astringent to help oily skin.*

GARLIC

Allium sativum

IT SEEMS THAT not a day passes without some new benefit of garlic being discovered. The ancient Egyptians actually worshipped the herb and fed it to their slaves to keep them fit and well.

Taken internally, garlic's volatile oils keep the lungs clear of infections. The treatment of pneumonia, bronchitis and asthma should be followed up by a preventive dose of garlic daily.

The risk of heart disease due to cholesterol deposits can be reduced by regular doses of garlic. It has been shown that the "bad" cholesterol (low-density lipoproteins [LDL]) is reduced, while the "good" cholesterol (high-density lipoprotein [HDL]) is increased after garlic is ingested. At the same time the stickiness of the bloods platelets (small fragments that cause a clot to form) is dramatically reduced.

Garlic has a powerful antimicrobial action and can be applied directly to infected areas. Fungal infections, often difficult to control, can be reduced by a garlic application.

New research is suggesting that garlic contains anticancer substances, but this is still a new area of study.

The aromatic oils contained in garlic give it many of its health-promoting actions. Whenever possible, deodorized garlic preparations should not be used.

Aioli is a classic French dish and originated in Provence where it is called "beurre de Provence."

PARTS USED

- *Bulb*

DOSAGE

- *Take 2 or 3 garlic capsules daily with a meal.*
- *As a liquid tincture, take 1 or 2 teaspoons (5–10 ml) daily.*
- *For external application, crush and apply a paste topically to the affected area.*

POTENTIAL BENEFITS

- *Protects against heart disease*
- *Lowers LDL cholesterol*
- *Can reduce blood pressure*
- *Exhibits antimicrobial activity*
- *Kills fungi*
- *Clears chest infections*
- *May have cancer-protective action*
- *Protects against blood clots*

CULINARY USES

- *Garlic enhances the flavors of most foods. Whole, roasted garlic bulbs are sweet and mild. The dressing Aioli is made out of puréed garlic using 6–12 garlic cloves and a pinch of salt.*

WARNING: When applying topically as a paste, do not tape in place because the oils can cause skin burns with chronic exposure. Eating more than five cloves at a sitting may cause a stomach upset.

CHIVES

Allium schoenoprasum

A MEMBER OF the lily family first discovered more than 5,000 years ago in China, this common herb can now be found in every food store.

Chives are high in vitamin C and iron. For this reason they are considered to be a highly nutritious food and excellent for building up the blood. Chives also have a mild stimulant effect on the appetite and can aid digestion.

PARTS USED

Leaves

DOSAGE

Eat a large sprig of the whole herb daily.

POTENTIAL BENEFITS

- *Restores blood iron levels and combats anemia*
- *Stimulates appetite and aids digestion*

CULINARY USES

Used in salads, soups and omelets, where onions would be too strong, and also as a garnish and in dressings. To make a chive and lemon vinaigrette, put one garlic clove and a pinch of salt in a bowl and crush together. Add the finely grated rind of one lemon, 4 tablespoons (60 ml) of lemon juice and 1½ teaspoons (7.5 ml) of mustard and stir until smooth. Slowly pour in 4 tablespoons (60 ml) of olive oil, whisking constantly until well emulsified. Add 2 teaspoons (10 ml) of chives and season with pepper. This is delicious over potatoes.

ALOE VERA

Alo barbadensis

ALOE VERA IS an ancient remedy. The body of Jesus was wrapped in linen impregnated with aloe vera and myrrh.

Contained within the leaf is a special gel that is used in cosmetics as a natural skin moisturizer. A topical application of the juice can help with minor skin burns, sunburn, insect bites and sometimes with eczema.

The juice is taken internally for digestive disorders and inflammation of the stomach. The juice can be either commercially prepared or extracted from the leaves by scraping it out with the blunt side of a knife. Other benefits have been attributed to aloe vera, such as its ability to act as a natural laxative as well as an appetite stimulant.

PARTS USED

- *Leaves that contain the sap*

DOSAGE

- *Take 1 tablespoon (15 ml) juice twice daily.*
- *For external application, use as a cream or lotion on the skin as required.*

POTENTIAL BENEFITS

- *Keeps skin supple*
- *Helps speed wound healing*
- *Reduces inflammation of stomach*
- *Acts as a laxative*
- *Heals sunburn*

COSMETIC USES

- *Can be made into lotions and creams for soothing irritated and inflamed skin.*

WARNING: Internal use not advised during pregnancy. Always seek medical attention for serious burns.

MARSHMALLOW

Althaea officinalis

USED BY THE ancient Greeks in the ninth century B.C., marshmallow has been a favorite herb for the treatment of colds and chest infections including sore throats and coughs. Its soothing action can be helpful to inflammations of the stomach and lower intestine, especially in conditions such as colitis. Ulcerations of the stomach are eased with the use of marshmallow, which can make a very effective antiulcer remedy when combined with licorice. Conditions of the respiratory tract, such as asthma and bronchitis, have been reported to respond well to this herb. The peeled and washed root can be given to children to chew on as a teething aid. Used externally, marshmallow can also help heal boils and abscesses.

PARTS USED

- *Leaves and roots*

DOSAGE

- *Take 2 or 3 tablets (100 mg) of dried extract after meals.*
- *For external application, use as a poultice for abscesses and boils.*

POTENTIAL BENEFITS

- *Soothes stomach inflammation*
- *Helps heal stomach and skin ulcers*
- *Soothes colitis*
- *Helps speed recovery from chest infections*
- *Helps relieve asthma and bronchitis symptoms*
- *Acts as a teething aid for children*

DILL

Anethum graveolens

DILL IS A popular culinary herb, and it has been used medicinally by doctors since ancient Egyptian and Roman times. The word "dill" comes from the Saxon word "dilla," which means to lull or soothe.

Taken internally, this herb can relieve an upset stomach and nausea. It has an antispasmodic action that helps to reduce flatulence, stimulate the appetite and aid digestion. In babies, dill can be taken to help reduce colic.

The seeds can act as a sedative, and chewing them can sweeten the breath. Dill can also stimulate the flow of breast milk in nursing mothers.

Used externally, dill is useful for soothing muscular tension. It can also be used to strengthen fingernails.

PARTS USED

- *Leaves and seeds*

DOSAGE

- *As dill water, put 2 pinches of dill seeds in 1 cup (250 ml/8 fl oz) of water and bring to a boil. As the water changes color, keep boiling for 1 minute. Strain and cool before drinking. Keep it in the refrigerator.*
- *As a tea, add 2 teaspoons (10 ml) of crushed seeds to 1 cup (250 ml/8 fl oz) of boiling water and let stand for 5 minutes. To reduce flatulence, drink 1 cup before eating.*
- *For external application, use as a compress, for muscular tension.*
- *For external application, use as an infusion of dill seeds to strengthen nails.*

POTENTIAL BENEFITS

- *Relieves nausea*
- *Aids digestion*
- *Helps reduce colic*
- *Stimulates the flow of breast milk in nursing mothers*
- *Soothes muscular tension*
- *Strengthens fingernails*

CULINARY USES

- *Popular in many dishes. Fresh leaves can be used in salads, poultry and fish dishes. Dill pickles are also popular.*

ANGELICA

Angelica archangelica

LEGEND SAYS THAT angelica was a cure for plague, which has secured it a place in traditional herbal medicine as a protector against evil.

Angelica appears to have a beneficial effect on the circulation of blood and body fluids. For the treatment of menstrual cramps and fluid retention, there can be no better herb to take than angelica. The medicinal effect that angelica exerts on the body has offered those suffering from rheumatism and arthritis a noticeable easing of symptoms. This effect may be a result of the removal of inflammatory chemicals accumulated in the tissues. Angelica is also useful in relieving symptoms of cystitis.

As a remedy for stomach upsets, gastric ulcers and migraines, angelica can be combined with chamomile (*Anthemis nobilis*). For an effective remedy against bronchitis and congestion of the lungs, angelica can be combined with yarrow (*Achillea millefolium*). An infusion can act as an expectorant in cases of colds and flu.

Candied angelica

PARTS USED

❦ *Leaves, seeds, stems and roots*

DOSAGE

❦ *As a liquid tincture, take 20 drops two or three times a day or 200 mg of dried herb daily.*

❦ *As an infusion add 1 tablespoon (15 ml) of dried herb to 2¼ cups (500 ml/ 18 fl oz) of boiling water.*

POTENTIAL BENEFITS

❦ *Eases symptoms of rheumatism and arthritis*

❦ *Soothes an upset stomach*

❦ *Acts as an antispasmodic to soothe menstrual cramps*

❦ *Relieves symptoms of cystitis*

❦ *Acts as an expectorant for chest infections*

CULINARY USES

❦ *Angelica leaves will give a salad a lively and aromatic flavor. The best-known application for angelica is its candied form used for cake decoration. This is not difficult to make at home. After collecting angelica stems, place them in boiling water until they are tender enough to remove the outer skins. Return the peeled stems to the pan and bring to a boil again. Cool the stems and add an equal weight of sugar to the stems, cover and leave for two days. Then place the stems and the syrup in a pan and bring to a boil again. Preheat an oven to 200°F (100°C) and place the stems (after sprinkling with confectioners' sugar) on a tray until they have completely dried out. Store in an airtight jar.*

WARNING: Avoid during pregnancy as large doses of angelica may disrupt blood pressure. This herb should also be avoided by people who suffer from high blood pressure. Some people suffer sunlight sensitivity due to a substance called furocoumarin, which may also cause skin irritation.

ROMAN CHAMOMILE

Anthemis nobilis

THE ANCIENT EGYPTIANS make reference to the use of chamomile in their writings, making it another herb with a long and trusted history.

Chamomile has been taken for centuries to calm the nerves and induce rest. When taken internally, the herb assists in soothing an upset stomach and menstrual cramps and dulling muscular aches and travel sickness, as chamomile has an excellent antispasmodic action.

Chamomile tea can be drunk to help reduce nasal congestion and lower temperatures associated with colds and flu. A tincture is especially useful for childhood teething problems, as chamomile has natural painkilling properties. It is also safe to use for children. Chamomile is an excellent antiseptic and can help to relieve urinary infections, including cystitis. The best method is to drink copious amounts of chamomile tea, sit in a chamomile bath and place hot compresses on the lower abdomen. Chamomile is also a mild diuretic which helps reduce fluid retention. This may be helpful in premenstrual syndrome as it may alleviate bloating. This herb is a good antidepressant and may relieve anxiety and tension. An aromatherapy application may be beneficial for helping depression.

An external application rapidly soothes sunburn, hemorrhoids, skin wounds, mastitis and skin ulcers. An immune-stimulating action has also been reported.

Chamomile (Anthemis nobilis)

PARTS USED

- *Flowers and essential oil*

DOSAGE

- *As a tincture, take 15–20 drops twice daily.*
- *As a tea, follow the manufacturer's instructions.*
- *As an aromatherapy application, use 6 drops essential oil mixed with 2 teaspoons (10 ml) of almond oil. Massage in the usual way.*
- *For external application, use as a cream or compress.*

POTENTIAL BENEFITS

- *Calms the nerves*
- *Reduces internal inflammation, especially of the stomach, and reduces flatulence*
- *Aids in teething pain*
- *Helps reduce nasal congestion*
- *Soothes irritated skin and skin wounds*
- *Eases menstrual cramps*

COSMETIC USES

- *Chamomile can be used in a cleansing milk for dry and chapped skin and in a shampoo for fair hair. It is also useful as a hand cream. A few drops of chamomile oil can be added for a relaxing bath.*

WARNING: Avoid using the essential oil during early pregnancy as it can stimulate menstruation.

CELERY

Apium graveolens

CELERY WAS PRESENT in the tomb of Tutankhamen (c. 1370–1352 B.C.) and has been used as a food and spice for as long as records have been kept.

Celery can reduce blood pressure probably as a result of its diuretic action. Inflammation of the bladder, gout and arthritis all show improvements when treated with celery extracts. An external application helps in cases of fungal infections, and drinking celery juice has been reported to stimulate menstruation. For this reason its use is not advised during pregnancy.

PARTS USED

- *Whole plant*

DOSAGE

- *Drink a small tumbler or ⅔ cup (150 ml/¼ pint) of fresh juice daily (best diluted 50:50 with water).*
- *Add 5 drops of oil extract to a tumbler or ⅔ cup (150 ml/ ¼ pint) of water daily.*
- *For external application, add 6 drops of essential oil to 2 teaspoons (10 ml) almond oil and massage into the area twice a day to eradicate fungal infections.*

POTENTIAL BENEFITS

- *Acts as a diuretic*
- *Has anti-inflammatory properties*
- *Promotes menstruation*
- *Reduces arthritis symptoms*

CULINARY USES

- *Celery can be washed, and eaten raw.*

WARNING: Avoid concentrated extracts or tinctures during pregnancy.

BURDOCK

Arctium lappa

BURDOCK HAS SWEET roots and bitter leaves. The roots contain a mucilaginous substance that has a calming and anti-inflammatory action on the stomach.

In herbal medicine burdock has traditionally been used internally for the treatment of psoriasis, eczema, rheumatism and gout. In Chinese medicine, burdock was said to be of benefit in treating pneumonia and throat infections. Burdock also acts as a mild diuretic and detoxifying agent in chronic diseases such as arthritis.

Externally burdock can be very soothing when applied to eczema or other inflammatory skin conditions.

PARTS USED

- *Roots, stems and seeds*

DOSAGE

- *As a liquid tincture, take 15 drops twice daily.*
- *For external application, apply as a cream, compress or poultice as required.*

POTENTIAL BENEFITS

- *Acts as a mild diuretic*
- *Has a detoxifying action*
- *Soothes skin irritations*
- *Reduces muscular stiffness associated with rheumatism*
- *Controls blood sugar levels*
- *Stimulates the immune system*

CULINARY USES

- *Burdock root can be cooked like carrots, or the stalks of the young leaves can be scraped and eaten like celery.*

UVA-URSI (BEARBERRY OR UPLAND CRANBERRY)

Arctostaphylos uva-ursi

THE BACTERIUM *E. coli* is very susceptible to the chemicals found in uva-ursi. The antibacterial agent arbutin has given this herb a special place in the treatment of urinary tract infections, especially cystitis. In addition to its antibiotic activity, the herb has a beneficial diuretic action that helps in the elimination of the infective agent. In addition, uva-ursi has high astringent actions that can help relieve minor vaginal infections.

PARTS USED

- *Leaves*

DOSAGE

- *Take 2 tablets (100 mg) of dried herb daily until symptoms are relieved.*
- *As a douche, infuse 1 tablespoon (15 ml) of dried herb, strain and apply.*

POTENTIAL BENEFITS

- *Soothes symptoms of bladder and mild kidney infections*
- *Acts as a diuretic*
- *Relieves minor vaginal infections*
- *Reduces symptoms of cystitis*

HORSERADISH

Armoracia rusticana

THIS VERY AROMATIC herb contains oils that can control microbial infections and even lower fever by increasing perspiration as the volatile oils are eliminated.

It is an excellent remedy for lung infections. During the elimination of the oils from the lung, the antibacterial activity permeates through the entire lung, cleansing as it goes. As a diuretic, horseradish is quite effective, but its stimulating action on digestion is greater. A horseradish poultice has been traditionally used over areas of infection, especially over the chest for the treatment of pleurisy. The drawing properties of horseradish are said to clear the infection.

PARTS USED

- *Leaves and roots*

DOSAGE

- *For external application, use as a poultice. Add the shredded herb to a mixture of flour and water to make a paste and apply to the area. Cover.*
- *As a liquid tincture, take 20 drops twice daily after eating.*
- *Mix the shredded herb with honey and hot water for an effective cold remedy.*

POTENTIAL BENEFITS

- *Acts as a mild diuretic*
- *Cleanses the lungs*
- *Acts as an antimicrobial agent*
- *Clears infections*
- *Stimulates digestion*

CULINARY USES

- *Try the fresh leaves in salads or with smoked fish. Roast beef would not be the same without a serving of horseradish sauce.*

ARNICA

Arnica montana

ARNICA ROSE TO fame during the eighteenth century as a cure-all. Although many claims were exaggerated, arnica still holds a special place in herbal medicine today. The plant produces a single, large, yellow flower that lasts throughout the summer. The leaves are picked during the growing season.

Recent studies on arnica have suggested that internal use should be avoided. In the United Kingdom, its external use is widespread. However, short-term internal use, under the supervision of a qualified practitioner, may be helpful for the control of some heart conditions.

When used on the skin, arnica has remarkable properties and can assist the healing process. Bruises, cuts and abrasions all respond very well to arnica cream. Sports injuries, when caught early, improve quickly with an arnica preparation. Arnica liniments are available for the treatment of muscular rheumatism and arthritis.

PARTS USED

- *Leaves*

DOSAGE

- *Internal use should be undertaken with professional guidance only, but homeopathic preparations containing arnica are considered to be very safe. Try using a 4x or 6x strength tincture remedy at a dose of 5–10 drops taken three times a day about a half hour before eating. Take this remedy with water only.*
- *For external application, follow the manufacturer's instructions.*

POTENTIAL BENEFITS

- *Reduces inflammation in tissues*
- *Stimulates the healing process*
- *Reduces muscular spasm and joint inflammation*
- *Soothes irritated skin*

COSMETIC USES

- *Can be made into creams to stimulate the skin's circulation.*

WARNING: Avoid during pregnancy. Do not take internally unless under professional advice as an overdose can prove fatal. External use may cause skin irritation. Never apply to broken skin.

SOUTHERNWOOD

Artemisia abrotanum

THE PLANT'S USE dates back to ancient China, where it was used externally for the treatment of inflamed or burned skin. The herb is very bitter, and its effectiveness can be ascribed to the high concentrations of astringents present in the plant extracts. This plant has a tonic effect on the digestive system. An improved bile and digestive juice flow can be noted after its use. The muscles of the uterus can react strongly to this botanical substance, and menstruation can be induced by taking the extract. For this reason, it must never be taken during pregnancy. This herb has also been reported to help in expelling worms in children.

PARTS USED

- *Leaves*

DOSAGE

- *As a liquid tincture, take 20 drops daily.*
- *For external application, use as a compress for irritated skin.*

POTENTIAL BENEFITS

- *Stimulates digestion*
- *Aids in the flow of bile and, therefore, the digestion of fat*
- *Helps in painful menstruation*
- *Soothes irritated skin*
- *Helps expel worms in children*

WARNING: Avoid during pregnancy.

ASTRAGALUS

Astragalus membranaceus

ASTRAGALUS WAS HELD in high esteem by the Chinese, who incorporated it into many of their medicinal formulas. The herb has a sweet taste and has been used in traditional medicine as an immune system, lung, liver and spleen stimulator. It also stimulates the circulatory system and acts as a heart tonic. Beneficial effects of lowering high blood pressure and blood glucose levels have also been reported.

Herbal practitioners may suggest using this herb during treatment with chemotherapy as it stimulates the immune system, but this approach needs cooperation between the herbalist and doctor and should not be taken without supervision.

PART USED
- *Root*

DOSAGE
- *As a liquid tincture, take 15–20 drops daily.*

POTENTIAL BENEFITS
- *Has a general tonic effect*
- *May help lower blood glucose levels*
- *Stimulates the immune system*
- *Aids the flow of bile and liver function*
- *May help lower blood pressure*

OATS

Avena sativa

OATS CAN BE considered a food as well as an herb. Oats are a rich source of vitamins (especially vitamin E), carbohydrates, and protein.

The heart, nerves and thymus glands all benefit from a dose of oats. The high silica content makes oats a good food to eat if your cholesterol level is high.

As a remedy for exhaustion, oats act as a nutritive nervine or nerve tonic and may help in cases of depression. For eczema, oats form a good poultice, which helps reduce inflammation and irritation.

PARTS USED

- *Seeds*

DOSAGE

- *As a liquid tincture, take 25 drops twice daily.*
- *For external application, use as a poultice. Mix oats into a thick, sticky mass with a little hot water and apply to the skin.*

POTENTIAL BENEFITS

- *Acts as a heart and nerve tonic*
- *Lowers cholesterol levels*
- *May help relieve depression*
- *Eases symptoms of eczema*

COSMETIC USES

- *Use oatmeal for facial scrubs to cleanse the skin*

CULINARY USES

- *Cooked oats are made into oatmeal. Oats can form the basis for pancakes.*

BORAGE

Borago officinalis

A FAMILIAR HERB to cooks, borage has been associated with mood-enhancing effects. The exact constituents of this plant have not been identified, but its reputation for "lifting the spirits" dates back to 1597, when John Gerard included it in his book *The Herball, or Generall Historie of Plantes.* In this book, borage was said to "drive away sorrow and increase the joy of the mind." During this time, the leaves and flowers were often made into wines and given to men and women to make them "glad and merry." Borage has a very high GLA (gamma linoleic acid) content—higher than evening primrose oil (*Oenothera biennis*)—which helps reduce menstrual cramps. Borage tea is said to be good for lowering high temperatures as it has an excellent diaphoretic action. This makes it an ideal remedy for relieving cold and flu symptoms.

PARTS USED

- *Leaves, flowers, oil and seeds*

DOSAGE

- *As a liquid tincture, take 15–20 drops twice daily.*
- *Borage oil can be taken at a dose of 500 mg daily.*
- *As a tea, add about 2 teaspoons (10 ml) of herbs to 2½ cups (600 ml/1 pint) of boiling water and infuse for 5 minutes.*

POTENTIAL BENEFITS

- *Has mood-lifting effects*
- *Helps in cases of premenstrual tension*
- *Helps dermatitis and other skin irritations such as eczema*
- *Lowers high temperatures*

CULINARY USES

- *Try adding chopped borage to vegetables and pasta dishes, or sprinkle the leaves on salads as a garnish.*

CALENDULA

Calendula officinalis

ALSO KNOWN AS marigold, calendula has a long history in herbal medicine. Initially used to dye fabric, as a food and in cosmetics, calendula contains many oils that have health-promoting properties. Used externally, calendula can reduce inflamed skin and sunburn and promote the healing of wounds. It can also be used to relieve cracked

nipples when breast-feeding. The oil can reduce earache.

Its internal use can help stomach ulcers and inflammation. Studies have confirmed the effectiveness of calendula in treating menstrual cramps.

PARTS USED

- *Flower petals*

DOSAGE

- *As a tea, follow manufacturer's directions.*
- *As a liquid tincture, take 15 drops twice daily.*
- *For external application, use as a cream, compress or poultice for wounds and inflamed skin as needed.*

POTENTIAL BENEFITS

- *Reduces inflammation*
- *Eases menstrual cramps*
- *Soothes irritated and damaged skin, such as minor burns*
- *Relieves earache*

COSMETIC USES

- *May be used in a cream to help dry and irritated skin and sore or cracked nipples.*
- *The petals can be used in the bath to cleanse and tone the skin.*

CAYENNE

Capsicum frutescens

THERE HAS BEEN much interest in cayenne since it was shown to reduce sensitivity to pain. Cayenne has the ability to overstimulate nerves and deplete their stores of chemicals that relay information to the brain. In effect, the nerves cannot send pain messages. Cayenne has been used medicinally (externally as a cream) to treat chronic pain syndromes such as post-shingles neuralgia and osteoarthritis. Cayenne contains liberal amounts of vitamins, especially the B complex, and it has more vitamin C than an orange. This herb has beneficial effects on the blood's fat content by reducing the levels of low-density lipoprotein (bad cholesterol) and triglycerides.

Cayenne has the ability to stimulate the circulatory system and can be used to treat varicose veins. This herb is also used to treat asthma and pleurisy. It stimulates the release of adrenaline that opens up the airways. It should always be used with caution and always under supervision.

PARTS USED

- *Fruits*

DOSAGE

- *Take 1 or 2 tablets (100 mg) of dried herb with a meal.*
- *For external application, apply cream daily for no longer than 1 month.*

POTENTIAL BENEFITS

- *Relieves pain in cases of chronic neuralgia (external use)*
- *Reduces pain of osteoarthritis*
- *Stimulates digestion*
- *Stimulates circulation*
- *Protects the heart from excessive cholesterol*
- *May relieve pleurisy*
- *Eases varicose vein symptoms*

WARNING: Do not apply cream to broken skin.

PAW PAW

Carica papaya

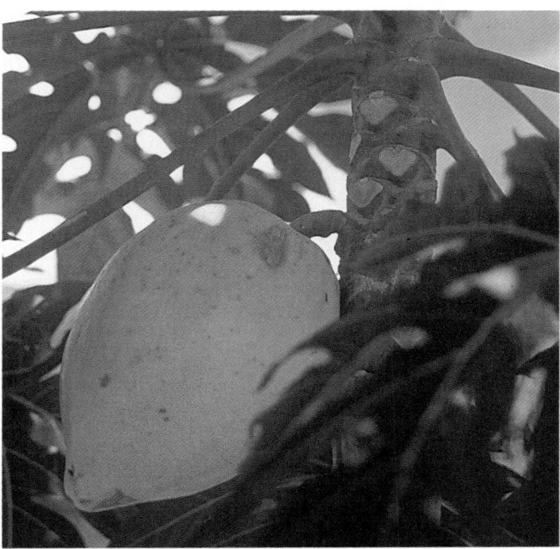

THIS IS NATURE'S very best digestive aid. The enzymes contained in pawpaw break down proteins very efficiently. If you find that you bloat after eating, try some pawpaw after a meal.

As a remedy for intestinal worms (threadworms and roundworms), pawpaw works in almost all cases.

The papain content of pawpaw can help speed wound healing and soften scar tissue.

PARTS USED

- *Leaves, fruits, seeds and sap*

DOSAGE

- *For a worm remedy, take 2 tablets (50 mg) of dried extract daily.*
- *For a digestive aid, take the tablets during every meal or drink fresh juice after each meal.*

POTENTIAL BENEFITS

- *Aids digestion*
- *Relieves abdominal bloating after eating*
- *Helps eliminate worms*

CARAWAY

Carum carvi

THE UNMISTAKABLE SMELL of caraway comes from the high concentration of a volatile oil known as carvone, which makes up 40–60 percent of the oils contained within the seeds. Caraway is well known for reducing colic in babies and flatulence in adults. Its calming effect on the bowels is based on its antispasmodic activity on the bowels' muscular wall. Adding some caraway seeds to an herbal tea will help in fighting a cold or flu. Caraway can also be used to stimulate the flow of breast milk in nursing mothers.

PARTS USED

- *Seeds, leaves, roots and oil extract*

DOSAGE

- *Add a pinch of seeds to an herbal tea.*
- *Add 2 or 3 drops of infant colic formula to each feeding to combat colic.*

POTENTIAL BENEFITS

- *Eases colic in babies*
- *Reduces flatulence and aids digestion in adults*
- *Helps fight colds, flu and bronchitis*
- *Stimulates the flow of breast milk*

CULINARY USES

- *Try adding caraway seeds to cooking water for vegetables. Add to cheese fondues, bread mixes and goulash. It is good when added to lentil dishes.*

CENTAURY

Centaurium erythraea

GROWING IN LARGE numbers in very dry and grassy places, centaury is easily spotted by its characteristic spiky appearance.

All parts of this bitter-tasting plant are used in herbal medicine, especially the stems. A liquid extract of centaury still tastes bitter even after it is diluted 3,500 times!

As a medicine, centaury has general tonic properties, but its most important function is the stimulation of stomach activity and the secretion of gastric juices. It can also be used to relieve dyspepsia, stimulate the appetite and aid in poor digestion. If taken in large doses, it can have a laxative effect.

PARTS USED

- *Whole plant*

DOSAGE

- *As a liquid tincture, take 25 drops before each meal.*

POTENTIAL BENEFITS

- *Stimulates appetite*
- *Aids poor digestion*
- *Helps reduce stomach gas formation*
- *Relieves dyspepsia*
- *Has laxative effects in large doses*

GOTU KOLA

Centella asiatica

FIRST USED BY Ayurvedic healers in India, this herb has played an important role in controlling the symptoms of stress by inducing a state of relaxation by acting on the nervous system. It acts like a nerve tonic.

Similar to ginkgo (*Ginkgo biloba*), gotu kola stimulates the circulatory system, bringing blood to all parts of the body and stabilizing the cells that make up the walls of the blood vessels. This herb has been shown to improve immune function and stimulate resistance to infection.

PARTS USED

- *Whole plant*

DOSAGE

- *Take up to 2 tablets (100 mg) of dried extract daily.*

POTENTIAL BENEFITS

- *Improves resistance to disease*
- *Induces a state of relaxation*
- *Relaxes the nervous system*
- *Stimulates circulation to the entire body*

WARNING: Avoid during pregnancy. Do not use if you have an overactive thyroid gland.

BLACK COHOSH

Cimicifuga racemosa

KNOWN AS SQUATROOT by Native Americans who used it for feminine problems, black cohosh can be traced back to the *sheng ma*, a traditional Chinese medical text (c. 25–200 A.D.). It can be used for digestive problems and to soothe arthritic aches and pains. A stimulant effect on the uterus has been noted, so it should not be used during pregnancy. Other uses include treating bronchitis and nausea associated with headaches.

PARTS USED

- *Rhizome, for medicinal preparations*

DOSAGE

- *Take 1 or 2 tablets (50 mg) of dried herb daily.*
- *As a liquid tincture, take 20 drops twice daily.*

POTENTIAL BENEFITS

- *Reduces muscular discomfort associated with arthritis*
- *Calms menstrual cramps*
- *May be helpful in chronic bronchitis*
- *Reduces nausea associated with headaches*

WARNING: Because of the stimulant effect on the uterine muscles, avoid during pregnancy.

MYRRH

Commiphora molmol

EVER SINCE BIBLICAL times, myrrh has been an essential and standard medicine used in the Middle East for the treatment of wounds, infections and digestive problems. It is especially associated with women's health and purification.

Myrrh has the ability to stimulate healing and reduce inflammation. Its antiseptic properties make it an effective wound cleanser.

Taken internally with echinacea (*Echinacea purpura*), it can speed recovery from infections, especially chest infections, as it has good expectorant and decongestant properties. Myrrh is often taken for relieving colds and bronchitis. When used as a mouthwash, myrrh can strengthen the gums and reduce gum infection and inflammation.

PARTS USED
- *Gum resin*

DOSAGE
- *As a mouthwash, add 5 drops to a little water.*
- *As a liquid tincture, take 10 drops daily.*

POTENTIAL BENEFITS
- *Fights gum infections*
- *Acts as a wound-cleansing agent*
- *Helps fight chest infections*
- *Reduces bruising*

WARNING: Do not take myrrh in high doses during pregnancy.

CILANTRO

Coriandrum sativum

CILANTRO HAS BEEN used as a culinary and medicinal herb throughout the centuries. Taken internally, this herb is used to aid digestion and to stimulate the appetite. It also reduces flatulence and helps relieve colic. Cilantro can be especially helpful in reducing diarrhea in children.

As an external application, the lightly bruised seeds can be used as a poultice to alleviate painful joints and rheumatic symptoms.

PARTS USED

- *Leaves and seeds*

DOSAGE

- *As an infusion, add 1 teaspoon (5 ml) of crushed seeds to 1 cup (250 ml/8 fl oz) of boiling water and let stand for 5 minutes.*
- *To relieve flatulence, drink the tea before eating.*
- *For external application, use the seeds as a poultice for painful joints.*

POTENTIAL BENEFITS

- *Aids digestion*
- *Stimulates the appetite*
- *Relieves flatulence*
- *Reduces diarrhea*
- *Helps painful joints*

CULINARY USES

- *Use fresh leaves on poultry dishes and add to green salads. Alternatively, use as an ingredient in salad dressings. To make chile-and-cilantro vinaigrette, whisk together three green chilies, deseeded and chopped, ½ teaspoon (2.5 ml) of ground cumin, 3 tablespoons (40 ml) of cider vinegar and salt. Slowly pour in ½ cup (125 ml/4 fl oz) of peanut oil, whisking until well emulsified. Stir in chopped cilantro leaves before serving.*

HAWTHORN

Crataegus oxyacantha

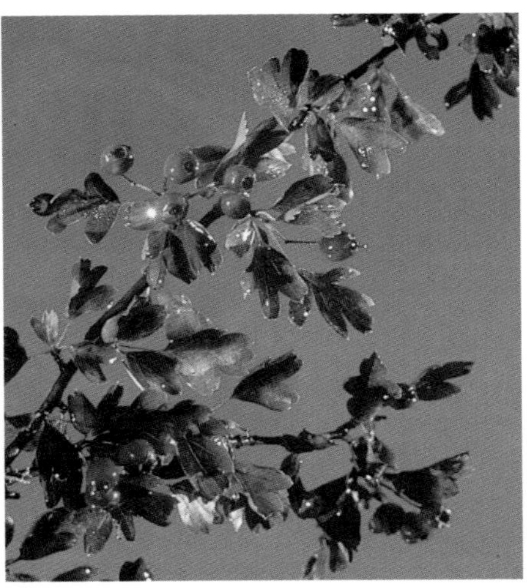

THE BERRIES FROM this plant have been used for digestive problems by herbalists for many years. Its activity on the heart has been likened to that of a heart tonic. The heart benefits in a number of ways. First, the heartbeat is strengthened, which aids a failing heart. Second, the blood vessels are dilated, which reduces the blood pressure and the resultant strain on the heart. Hawthorn has a diuretic action on the body, ridding it of the excess fluid commonly retained by those with heart problems. The hawthorn berries are rich in vitamin C and bioflavonoids—essential factors for blood vessel strength and health.

PARTS USED

- *Fruits*

DOSAGE

- *As a liquid tincture, take 20 drops twice daily.*

POTENTIAL BENEFITS

- *May be used as a heart tonic*
- *Increases efficiency of the heartbeat*
- *Reduces blood pressure*
- *Acts as a diuretic*

TURMERIC

Curcuma longa

THIS IS A classically pungent herb that forms the basis of most curry powders. Its ability to treat stomach problems effectively has been known for centuries in Asia but only recently in the United States and Europe. Turmeric has the ability to stimulate the flow of bile and, therefore, promote the digestion of fats effectively.

Turmeric has beneficial effects on the circulation, increasing peripheral distribution of blood and helping reduce the incidence of clots. It may also help in menstrual problems, especially in congestive types of premenstrual syndrome, by helping the flow of blood.

PART USED

- *Rhizome*

DOSAGE

- *Take 2 tablets (50 mg) of dried herb daily after eating.*

POTENTIAL BENEFITS

- *Increases circulation*
- *Reduces blood clots*
- *May help in menstrual problems*
- *Stimulates bile flow*
- *Aids in fat digestion*

CULINARY USES

- *Forms the basis of most curries and curry powders.*

ARTICHOKE

Cynara scolymus

MUCH PRIZED BY the Romans and Greeks, the artichoke has been used for medicinal purposes for centuries. The discovery of a substance called cynarin, which is contained in the leaves, supported the age-old tradition of taking artichoke for problems relating to digestion. Cynarin appears to improve the flow of bile and thus improve the liver function. A secondary effect is a reduction in cholesterol levels due to the increased flow of bile.

PARTS USED

- *Flower heads, leaves and roots*

DOSAGE

- *As a liquid tincture, take 20 drops twice daily.*

POTENTIAL BENEFITS

- *Stimulates the flow of digestive juices*
- *Increases bile flow*
- *Promotes liver function*
- *Reduces cholesterol levels*

CULINARY USES

- *There is nothing nicer than artichoke vinaigrette. Place an unopened flower head in a pan of boiling water. Reduce the heat and cook for about 15 minutes or until the leaves can be pulled off easily. Drain well, place on a small serving plate and drizzle a vinaigrette dressing over the leaves. Serve immediately.*

ECHINACEA

Echinacea purpura

THE HEDGEHOG-LIKE appearance of the central cone of echinacea, or purple coneflower, gave this herb its name, from the Greek *echinos* meaning "hedgehog." Echinacea is probably one of the most commonly used herbal extracts today. In Germany, the liquid extract is referred to as "resistance drops," owing to echinacea's immune-stimulating effect.

Externally, echinacea can be used to heal minor cuts and scrapes. For all problems relating to bacterial, fungal or viral infection, echinacea should be the first herb of choice.

PARTS USED

- *Roots and rhizomes*

DOSAGE

- *In acute illness, take up to 40 drops (20 for children) of liquid tincture every four hours.*
- *For prevention of colds and flu, take 10–15 drops daily.*
- *In tablet form, take 1 or 2 tablets (50–100 mg) of dried extract daily.*
- *For external application, use as a cream for cuts and scrapes.*

POTENTIAL BENEFITS

- *Stimulates the immune system*
- *Prevents the progression of infections*
- *Relieves symptoms of colds and flu, especially when nasal congestion is a problem*
- *Has a virus killing action*

GINSENG (SIBERIAN)

Eleutherococcus senticosus

THE ACTIVE AGENTS of Siberian ginseng are similar to the *Panax* ginseng form but are considered to be less potent. Siberian ginseng can be taken for longer periods than the *Panax* ginseng form and is thought to be better suited to the treatment of stress when an extended treatment program is needed. It may also be used to improve physical and mental stamina. There are claims that it may reduce cholesterol and blood sugar levels.

PARTS USED

- *Roots*

DOSAGE

- *Take 2 teaspoons (10 ml) of ginseng elixir daily.*

POTENTIAL BENEFITS

- *Improves resistance to stress*
- *Increases mental agility*
- *May reduce cholesterol and blood sugar levels*

WARNING: Generally, ginseng should not be used continuously for longer than 1 month.

HORSETAIL

Equisetum arvense

CONTAINED WITHIN THIS herb is an interesting cocktail of nutrients and phytochemicals. Horsetail is rich in silica and other minerals that facilitate the absorption of calcium from the diet. Nails and hair greatly benefit from this herb, as do the bones and other connective tissues that depend on calcium and trace minerals for their health. Its high silica content may help reduce cholesterol levels.

Horsetail may help regulate the skin's oil production, which in turn may help reduce outbreaks of acne and other congestive skin blemishes.

PARTS USED

Stems

DOSAGE

As a liquid tincture, take 15–20 drops twice daily.

POTENTIAL BENEFITS

- *Adds strength to nails and hair*
- *Supports healthy bone and tissue development*
- *Helps reduce acne in those with oily skin*
- *May help reduce cholesterol levels*

CALIFORNIAN POPPY

Eschscholzia californica

THE WATERY SAP of this plant has a mild painkilling action. The Native Americans often used this to reduce the pain of toothache. The action of this plant appears to be in the central nervous system and is thought to be narcotic in nature. It has also been used as a sedative and may help insomnia.

PARTS USED

- *Whole plant*

DOSAGE

- *As a liquid tincture, take 5–10 drops as needed.*

POTENTIAL BENEFITS

- *Has a painkilling action if applied topically in cases of toothache*
- *Reduces anxiety and tension when used internally*
- *May help insomnia*

EUCALYPTUS

Eucalyptus globulus

THERE ARE MORE than 40 different types of eucalyptus trees, all of which are rich in the volatile oils that are responsible for the aroma.

Traditional aboriginal uses are well-kept secrets, but it was known to help treat dysentery. The extracts from eucalyptus have a great decongestant action due to the high content of aromatic oils. Eucalyptus, also called the blue gum tree, can help in expectoration because it acts as a respiratory stimulant.

Used externally, eucalyptus can help heal sports injuries. Eucalyptus has an antiseptic action that helps reduce muscle spasm. Muscular aches and pains benefit greatly from an application of a eucalyptus-based cream or lotion.

Parts used

❦ *Leaves and essential oils*

Dosage

❦ *As a vapor inhalant, use about 4 drops in a vaporizer and inhale for about 5 minutes.*

❦ *For external application, use as a cream or lotion, as required.*

Potential benefits

❦ *Acts as a decongestant for upper respiratory infections*

❦ *Clears sinus congestion*

❦ *Stimulates the removal of lung congestion*

❦ *Has an antimicrobial activity*

❦ *Can be used as an effective muscle ointment*

Cosmetic uses

❦ *Can be used in a lotion or skin tonic to stimulate the skin's circulation.*

❦ *Add a couple of drops of essential oil to a bath to soothe aching muscles.*

Warning: Do not use on open wounds. Avoid excessive exposure to vapors, as eucalyptus can cause headaches and may aggravate asthma symptoms.

EYEBRIGHT

Euphrasis officinalis

THROUGH THE DOCTRINE of Signatures (if the appearance of the plant or flower looks like an anatomical part, then the herb will help diseases of that area), eyebright became a cure-all for eye problems. The flowers have purple and yellow stripes and spots that resemble the human iris.

The astringent properties of eyebright do make it a useful herb for the treatment of sore and inflamed eyes (conjunctivitis) and other irritant eye problems such as weeping eczema which can occur around the eyes as well as ultra-sensitivity to light.

PARTS USED

- *Whole plant*

DOSAGE

- *For an eye bath, use a commercially made preparation to minimize the risk of infection.*
- *As a liquid tincture, take 1 or 2 drops twice daily.*

POTENTIAL BENEFITS

- *Calms irritated eyes and helps reduce conjunctivitis*
- *Promotes good eye health when taken internally*

WARNING: Avoid high doses of eyebright during pregnancy.

FENNEL

Foeniculum vulgare

FRESH FENNEL DELIVERS a special aroma due to the two oils, anethole and fenchone, which vary from species to species.

Taken internally, fennel aids the digestive process and soothes cases of colic and abdominal discomfort. It can be taken in the form of a tea or as "fennel water," which is very easy to make. It is thought that if this is drunk during breast-feeding it will help reduce colic and act as a general digestive aid. Fennel also has a mild diuretic action and a cleansing action on the kidneys. It can promote the flow of breast milk in nursing mothers.

PARTS USED

- *Leaves, stems, roots and seeds*

DOSAGE

- *As a liquid tincture, take 20 drops just after eating.*
- *As fennel water, put about 2 pinches of fennel seeds in 1 cup (250 ml/8 fl oz) of water and bring to a boil. As the water starts to change color, keep boiling for 1 minute. Strain and cool before drinking. Keep in the refrigerator.*
- *As a tea, add 2 teaspoons of seeds to 1 cup (250 ml/8 fl oz) of boiling water and let stand for 5 minutes.*

POTENTIAL BENEFITS

- *Acts as a digestive aid*
- *Reduces abdominal cramping and colic*
- *Reduces flatulence*
- *Acts as a remedy for infantile colic*
- *Acts as a mild diuretic and kidney cleanser*
- *Promotes flow of breast milk in nursing mothers*

COSMETIC USES

- *The seeds can be used in a lotion to help oily skin.*

CULINARY USES

- *Try fennel seeds in fish dishes or use during the cooking of vegetables. Fresh fennel bulb can be cooked whole and eaten as a vegetable. It has a wonderful aniseed flavor and is a good accompaniment with poultry and lamb.*

WARNING: Avoid during pregnancy.

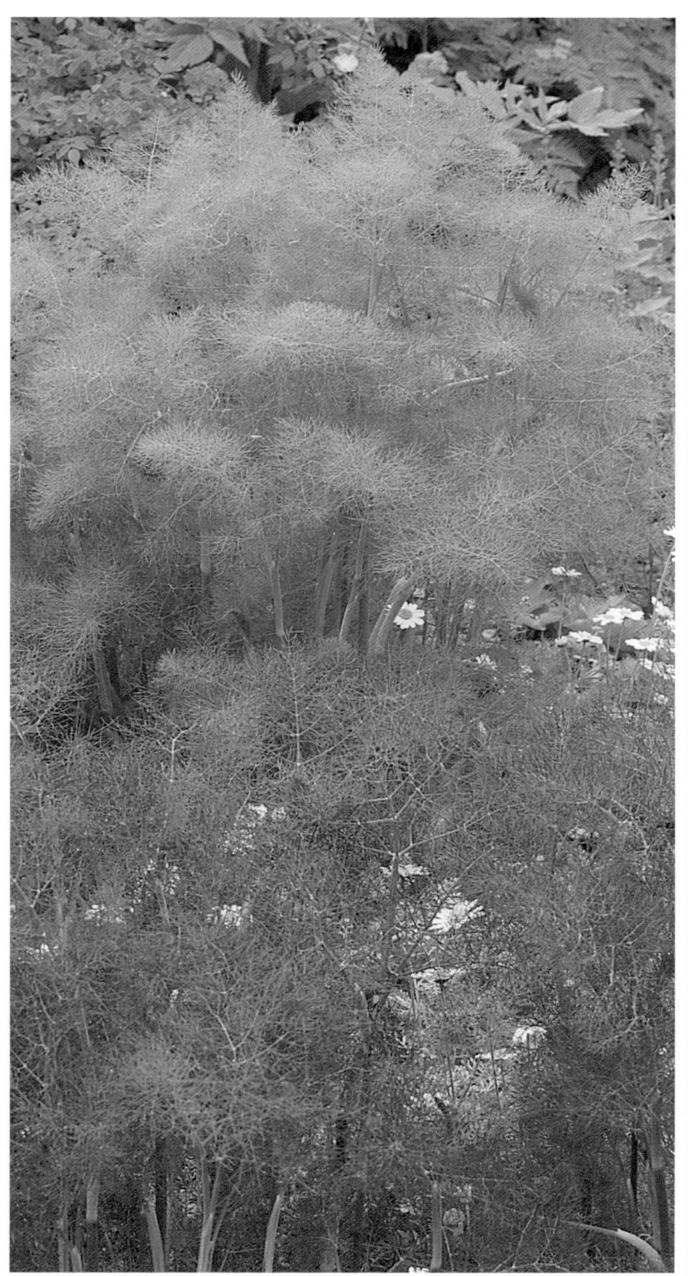

Fennel (Foeniculum vulgare)

AMERICAN CRANESBILL

Geranium maculatum

THIS HERB IS known to be a common medicine used by Native Americans for the treatment of diarrhea and stomach complaints. Analysis of the plant extracts shows a high concentration of astringents. A traditional use of this plant is the control of excessive bleeding associated with menstruation. A topical application of the plant is applied to infected wounds, thrush and hemorrhoids.

PARTS USED

- *Whole plant*

DOSAGE

- *As a liquid tincture, take 20–25 drops twice daily.*
- *For external application, use as a compress for wounds, thrush and hemorrhoids.*

POTENTIAL BENEFITS

- *Has an antiseptic action*
- *Reduces blood flow in menstruation*
- *Soothes hemorrhoid irritation*
- *Reduces diarrhea*

GINKGO

Ginkgo biloba

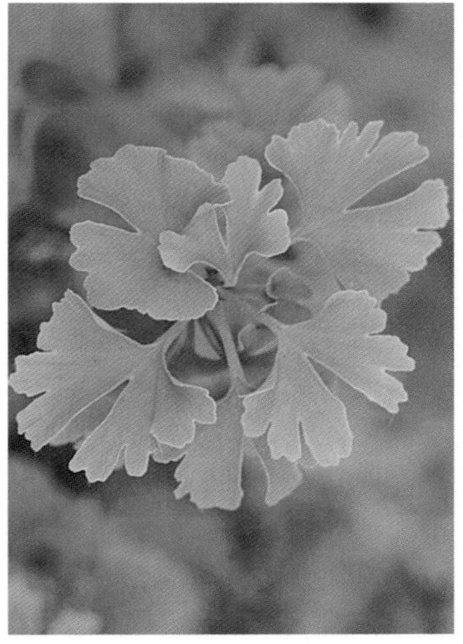

FOSSIL RECORDS SHOW that the ginkgo tree has remained unchanged for millions of years. The trees were present even before mammals walked the earth.

Extracts of the leaves yield a fascinating substance that has profound effects on the allergic response. These chemicals, ginkgolides, act to inhibit platelet-activating factor, a key substance in the allergic response. Other chemicals, ginkgo flavonoids, have a stimulating effect on the blood circulation of the brain and periphery.

Ginkgo has been effectively used for the treatment of asthma, tinnitus, allergic inflammatory conditions and varicose veins. It has also been used to treat reduced brain circulation and Raynaud's disease as this herb improves peripheral circulation. In this disease, peripheral circulation is badly affected, and the hands often turn blue.

PARTS USED

- *Leaves and seeds*

DOSAGE

- *As a liquid tincture, take 20 drops twice daily.*

POTENTIAL BENEFITS

- *Improves blood circulation to the brain*
- *Reduces symptoms of tinnitus*
- *Reduces allergic conditions*
- *Helps in Raynaud's disease*
- *May reduce asthma symptoms*

LICORICE

Glycyrrhiza glabra

THE MAIN CONSTITUENT of licorice is a substance called glycyrrhizin, which is 50 times sweeter than sugar.

Glycyrrhizin reduces inflammation and has been used in treating menstrual irregularities. Taken 14 days prior to menstruation, licorice can suppress the breakdown of progesterone and improve depression, sugar cravings, water retention and breast tenderness.

Taken internally, licorice can help Addison's disease, as glycyrrhizin has a similar effect to an adrenal hormone called aldosterone. Licorice has a detoxifying action on the liver.

An estrogen-like action has been noted, making it a good remedy for the relief of menopausal symptoms. Taken for stomach problems, licorice has a great healing power on the lining of the stomach.

PARTS USED

- *Roots*

DOSAGE

- *Chew 2 or 3 tablets (100 mg) with each meal.*

POTENTIAL BENEFITS

- *Speeds the healing of stomach ulcers*
- *Helps in menstrual irregularities*
- *Detoxifies the liver*
- *Helps in Addison's disease*
- *Relieves the symptoms of the menopause*

WARNING: Because of the sodium content of licorice, avoid during pregnancy. Do not use if you have high blood pressure or kidney disease or if you are taking the heart drug Digoxin.

HOPS

Humulus lupulus

Hops are one of nature's best relaxants. The herb exerts a calming effect on the whole body, relieving nervous tension, irritability and insomnia.

For the treatment of irritable bowel syndrome and a nervous stomach, hops can prove to be a very effective remedy. A good combination is equal parts of valerian (*Valeriana officinalis*) and hops taken about a half hour before bed to induce a natural and restful sleep.

A poultice made from hops can be helpful for cases of eczema and skin ulcerations.

Parts used

Leaves and shoots

Dosage

- *As a soothing agent for irritable bowels, take 2 tablets (50 mg) daily.*
- *As a sedative, try the mixture described above at bedtime.*
- *For external application, use as a poultice for eczema and skin ulcers.*

Potential benefits

- *Acts as a sedative to promote restful sleep*
- *Acts as a calming agent for a nervous stomach*
- *Relieves irritable bowel syndrome*
- *Acts as an anti-stress herb*
- *Relieves eczema and skin ulcerations*

Culinary uses

The young side shoots can be cooked and eaten.

Warning: Avoid if you suffer from depression.

GOLDENSEAL

Hydrastis canadensis

GOLDENSEAL CAN ACT as a double-edged sword. When given for infections of the bowels, it tends to destroy the beneficial bacteria as well as the disease-causing ones. It is recommended, therefore, that its use should be restricted to one month followed by a course of probiotics (capsules containing cultures of good bacteria for the bowel).

Goldenseal can also be used as a laxative. Externally, it can be used for treating irritated skin and conjunctivitis.

PARTS USED
- *Rhizomes*

DOSAGE
- *As a liquid tincture, take 20 drops daily.*
- *For an eyebath, use a commercially made preparation to minimize the risk of infection.*
- *For external application, use as a lotion, compress or cream use as required*

POTENTIAL BENEFITS
- *Reduces constipation*
- *Has an antibacterial action in bowel and gut infections*
- *Helps relieve irritated skin*
- *Acts as a laxative*

WARNING: Do not use for longer than 1 month. Avoid during pregnancy as goldenseal stimulates the uterine muscles.

ST. JOHN'S WORT

Hypericum perfortum

THERE HAS BEEN much interest in this herb since a study found it to be as effective as regular antidepressants but with none of the accompanying side effects. This action was found to be due to the high concentration of hypericin. This herb produces a lovely red pigment when the leaves are crushed between the fingers, and it is the pigment that contains the active agents. St. John's wort has an effective sedative action and can calm nerves and help relieve insomnia.

Another interesting aspect to this herb is its ability to stop the multiplication of certain viruses (retroviruses), meaning it may be used to treat AIDS. Used externally as a lotion, St. John's wort has a powerful healing and anti-inflammatory action and can be used to treat varicose veins, bruises and sunburn.

PARTS USED
- *Whole plant*

DOSAGE
- *As a liquid tincture, take 20 drops twice daily.*
- *For external application, use as a lotion as required.*

POTENTIAL BENEFITS
- *Acts as a remedy for insomnia*
- *Calms nerves*
- *Promotes wound-healing*
- *Has a potential benefit against AIDS*
- *Relieves sunburn*

HYSSOP

Hyssopus officinalis

HYSSOP IS MENTIONED in the New Testament of the Bible as an herb that has purification properties. These are largely due to the high content of camphoraceous oils contained within the herb. Its effectiveness in treating lung infections such as bronchitis can be attributed to this substance. It can also be used to relieve coughs, colds and nasal congestion as well as a gargle for sore throats.

Hyssop has the ability to stabilize low blood pressure and prevent the dizzy spells experienced by people with low blood pressure as they rise from a sitting or lying position.

An external application can be used for the treatment of minor cuts and bruises.

PARTS USED

- *Whole plant*

DOSAGE

- *In tablet form, take 2 tablets (50 mg) of dried herb twice daily.*
- *As a liquid tincture, take 15–20 drops twice daily.*
- *For external application, use as a compress for minor cuts and bruises.*

POTENTIAL BENEFITS

- *Stabilizes low blood pressure*
- *Acts against lung infections*
- *Helps relieve coughs*
- *Helps as a topical application for minor cuts and bruises*

CULINARY USES

- *Try adding a few leaves to meat dishes including beef casseroles. It is also ideal for adding to many legume dishes.*

WARNING: The essential oil must be avoided during pregnancy and by people who suffer from epilepsy.

JASMINE

Jasmine officinale

INITIALLY GROWN FOR the perfume industry, jasmine has many possible health-promoting effects. Jasmine has been successfully used for the treatment of sunstroke, fever, irritant dermatitis and infectious illness including coughs. Emotional upsets, post natal depression, premenstrual tension and headaches all respond well to a dose of jasmine as it exhibits powerful antidepressent properties. Jasmine is also very useful for relieving menstrual cramps, as it has the ability to reduce muscular spasms of the uterus. It is regarded as an aphrodisiac when applied to the body in its oil form.

PARTS USED

Roots, flowers and oil

DOSAGE

As a tea, drink 1 cup of jasmine tea daily.

For external application, use 6 drops of essential oil mixed with 2 teaspoons (10 ml) of almond oil.

POTENTIAL BENEFITS

Improves emotional state

May help reduce dermatitis symptoms

May act as an aphrodisiac

COSMETIC USES

Add 6–8 drops of essential oil for a stimulating bath.

WARNING: Avoid during early pregnancy.

JUNIPER

Juniperus communis

GIN, FLAVORED WITH juniper berries, was created in the 1500s as a diuretic medicine since it was not expensive to produce. For as long as records have been kept, juniper's diuretic action has been noted and used in the treatment of cystitis, inflammation of the kidneys, gout and arthritis. An external application can be helpful for arthritis and rheumatism symptoms. Juniper is also thought to be useful in helping treat oily skin and acne.

PARTS USED

- *Fruits*

DOSAGE

- *As a liquid tincture, take 20 drops twice daily.*
- *For external application, use 6 drops of juniper berry essential oil in 2 teaspoons (10 ml) of almond oil and massage into arthritic joints.*

POTENTIAL BENEFITS

- *Acts as a powerful diuretic*
- *Reduces symptoms of gout*
- *Aids in cystitis*
- *Soothes joint pains associated with arthritis*

COSMETIC USES

- *May be used in a lotion for oily skin and acne.*

CULINARY USES

- *Add some berries to pâtés, relish or sauerkraut.*

WARNING: Avoid during pregnancy because of the stimulant effect on the muscles of the uterus.

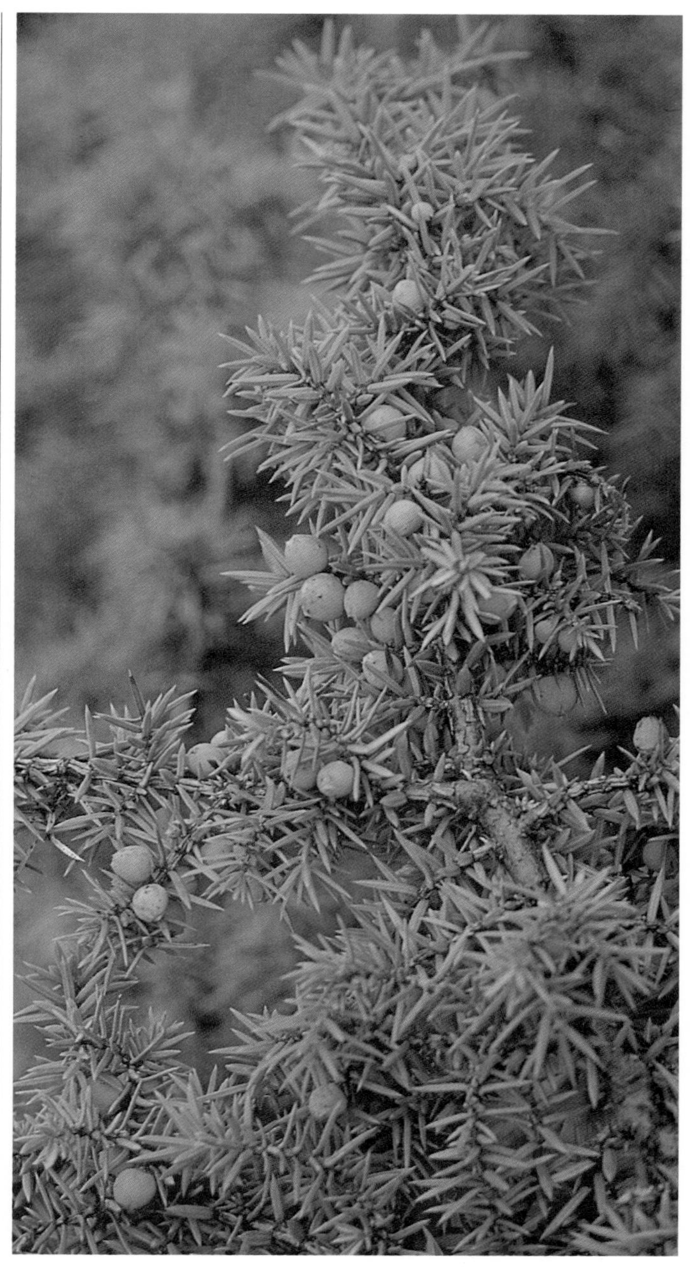

Juniper berries (Juniperus communis)

LAVENDER

Lavandula officinalis

THE ROMANS BROUGHT lavender from the Mediterranean to the United Kingdom. Since then, it has become an essential part of the early monastic and medicinal herb garden.

The aromatic sweet smell of lavender is unmistakable, and it is said to have antidepressant and mood-elevating effects.

As it exhibits powerful sedative and calming properties, lavender has been used for the treatment of digestive problems, anxiety, rheumatism, irritability, insomnia and tension headaches. It has also been found effective for use in migraine headaches. Lavender can be used to treat minor burns, especially sunburn, and rheumatic muscular aches and pains. It is also useful in treating skin problems such as acne. Lavender is one of the most popular essential oils for relaxation.

Melt away all the stresses of the day in a lavender bath.

Parts used
- *Flowers, stems and essential oil*

Dosage
- *For external application, use 6 drops of essential oil mixed with 2 teaspoons (10 ml) of almond oil to treat the affected area.*
- *For a relaxing tea, infuse a commercially prepared tea and drink twice daily.*

Potential benefits
- *Has natural antidepressant effects*
- *Acts as a mood elevator*
- *Reduces anxiety*
- *Helps digestion*
- *Soothes rheumatic muscle and joint pains*
- *May help relieve migraine headaches*

Cosmetic uses
- *Lavender may be used in a lotion for sunburn or in a cream for dry skin.*
- *Add 6–8 drops of lavender essential oil for a relaxing bath.*

Culinary uses
- *Try flavoring preserves with lavender or incorporating it into cake and cookie mixes.*

LINSEED OR COMMON FLAX

Linum usitatissimum

THIS IS GROWN as a farm crop. Contained within this plant are a number of important substances. The oil in the seeds, combined with the plant mucilage, makes an effective laxative. Flax oil on its own has great potential to help reduce the irritation of eczema as it contains high concentrations of essential fatty acids that are needed by the skin. Externally, the crushed seeds can be used in a poultice for treating boils and pleurisy.

PARTS USED

- *Seeds*

DOSAGE

- *As a laxative, chew and swallow 1 or 2 teaspoons (5–10 ml) of seeds at bedtime with a glass of water.*
- *In cases of skin irritation, take 1 or 2 g of flaxseed oil daily after meals.*
- *For external application, use as a poultice made from the crushed seeds for boils and symptoms of pleurisy. Apply to the painful area.*

POTENTIAL BENEFITS

- *Has laxative properties, helpful in chronic constipation*
- *Has an anti-inflammatory action, especially in skin problems such as eczema*
- *Relieves boils*

CULINARY USES

- *Flax flour can be obtained from health food stores and makes great bread.*

DEVIL'S CLAW

Martynia annua

AN EXTRACT OF this herb is used by South African farmers, who note that the locals gain great relief from the symptoms of arthritis and rheumatism after drinking a decoction made from the roots of the plant.

The analgesic effect of this herb is accompanied by its anti-inflammatory action, making it the herb of choice for inflammatory joint problems such as arthritis. The herb has also been noted for its digestive stimulant action.

PARTS USED
- *Tubers*

DOSAGE
- *As a liquid tincture, take 20 drops twice daily.*

POTENTIAL BENEFITS
- *Has a natural painkilling anti-inflammatory action*
- *Soothes symptoms of arthritis and joint swelling*
- *Acts as a mild digestive stimulant*

WARNING: Avoid during pregnancy.

ALFALFA

Medicago sativa

ALFALFA IS AN incredible plant. It can grow in very harsh conditions and transform barren land into a lush pasture. The nutrient content of alfalfa is impressive, comprising vitamins C, D, E, K and the B complex, as well as beta carotene and the minerals potassium, magnesium and calcium. There can be a tendency to consume too much of this herb, but care needs to be taken because it can trigger a flare-up of systemic lupus erythematosus as well as making some people sensitive to sunlight.

Alfalfa is a good laxative and mild diuretic and is used for urinary tract infections. It is given as a tonic for those recovering from any debilitating illness that leaves the patient weak. It has the ability to stimulate the appetite.

PARTS USED

- *Whole plant*

DOSAGE

- *In tablet form, take up to 5 tablets of dried, compressed alfalfa plant daily.*
- *As a liquid tincture, take 15–20 drops twice daily.*

POTENTIAL BENEFITS

- *Acts as a diuretic*
- *Has a laxative effect*
- *Helps recovery from any debilitating illness*
- *Helps relieve the symptoms of cystitis*
- *Stimulates the appetite*

CULINARY USES

- *Seeds can be sprouted and used in salads. Leaves may be eaten raw or cooked.*

WARNING: Do not take if you are suffering from an autoimmune condition such as systemic lupus erythematosus.

LEMON BALM

Melissa officinalis

THIS LEMON-SCENTED herb has powerful antiviral and antibacterial effects, which can be helpful in the treatment of recurrent cold sores. An application of a lemon balm-based cream just as the cold sore is forming can prevent it from erupting.

Taken internally, the herb helps with nervous problems and excitability, especially in children. Those who suffer from panic attacks and heart palpitations may find the extract helpful, as the herb has a sedative action and relaxes the nervous system. For the treatment of depression, try an external application of lemon balm in an aromatherapy massage. Some people may prefer an all-over body massage, while others may prefer to have the upper back and shoulders massaged as an anti-stress technique.

PARTS USED

- *Whole plant*

DOSAGE

- *For external application, use as a cream. Apply enough to cover the area three times a day.*
- *For aromatherapy application, use 6 drops of oil mixed with 2 teaspoons (10 ml) of almond oil. Massage in the usual way.*
- *As a liquid tincture, take 15 drops twice daily.*

POTENTIAL BENEFITS

- *Has antiviral and antibacterial action*
- *Calms the nervous system*
- *Helps panic attacks*
- *Can help relieve depression*

COSMETIC USES

- *Used in cleansing lotions and as an infusion for relaxing baths.*

CULINARY USES

- *Add the leaves to soups, salads and fish dishes. Lemon balm cordial can be purchased. It is similar to an elixir but diluted with water before it is taken. It also forms a vital ingredient in the liqueur Benedictine.*

PEPPERMINT

Mentha piperita

THIS STRONGLY AROMATIC herb has a long history as a decongestant and antiseptic agent and is valuable in the treatment of colds and nasal congestion. The oils contained in the plant have a powerful antispasmodic action on the smooth muscle of the stomach, making it the herb of choice for adult colic, dyspepsia and irritable bowel syndrome.

As a remedy for nausea and morning sickness, the normal internal dose of peppermint is very safe for a pregnant woman. Peppermint is also good for relieving menstrual pain as it has a relaxing effect.

The external application of the oil can help muscular discomfort and neuralgia.

PARTS USED
- *Whole plant*

DOSAGE
- *2 or 3 commercially prepared capsules (2 ml of oil per capsule) taken between meals to relieve bowel spasms.*
- *As a tea, take 1 cup (250 ml/8 fl oz) twice daily.*
- *As an aromatherapy massage, use 6 drops of essential oil mixed with 2 teaspoons (10 ml) of almond oil. Massage in the usual way.*

POTENTIAL BENEFITS
- *Has an antispasmodic agent for bowels*
- *Reduces nausea and sickness associated with early pregnancy*
- *Reduces stiffness when used as a muscle rub*
- *Has a decongestant action*

CULINARY USES
- *Add the leaves to iced tea for a very refreshing drink.*

BASIL

Ocimum basilicum

BASIL IS SOMETIMES referred to as St. Joseph's wort, not to be confused with St. John's wort. Its use dates back to biblical times, when it was seen after the resurrection growing around Christ's tomb. The word "basil" is thought to come from the Greek for "king."

Rich in volatile oils, basil contains over 20 chemical substances, including methyl cinnamate (cinnamon), citral (lemon), thymol (thyme) and camphor. There have been many variants of basil cultivated, each with a different aroma and flavor, making identification of different varieties difficult.

Basil has been taken internally for chills, colds and flu, in which it has a stimulant action. For digestion, basil is of great help in cases of stomach inflammation and helps relieve the abdominal cramps associated with menstruation.

PARTS USED
- *Whole plant*

DOSAGE
- *As a liquid tincture, take 15 drops twice daily.*

POTENTIAL BENEFITS
- *Acts as a stimulant and aids resistance to infection*
- *Soothes an inflamed stomach and aids digestion*
- *Has an antispasmodic action*

CULINARY USES
- *Basil has many uses in cooking. The leaves make a good addition to any salad, adding a special flavor. Basil forms the basis of pesto, a traditional pasta sauce, as well as many stuffings for meat.*

EVENING PRIMROSE

Oenothera biennis

THIS HERB HAS risen to fame as a remedy for premenstrual and menopause symptoms, but there is a lot more to evening primrose than this. It is a very rich source of gamma linoleic acid (GLA), which is an essential fatty acid. GLA is vital for the health of cell membranes and balances the output of hormones. Taking evening primrose oil can block the action of these substances and reduce the discomfort. A dose of this oil can rebalance the hormonal system itself.

The effect on prostaglandins may explain how evening primrose oil can reduce blood pressure and the level of free cholesterol circulating in the blood.

As a remedy for skin problems, evening primrose is safe to use topically on a baby's cradle cap and, should eczema develop, evening primrose can be taken internally.

It is interesting to note that schizophrenia has responded well to evening primrose supplements, although the mechanism behind this is unknown.

Soap containing evening primrose oil is good for moisturizing the skin.

PARTS USED

- *Oil*

DOSAGE

- *For menopausal symptoms, take 2 or 3 capsules (500 mg capsules) every evening with water only.*
- *For premenstrual symptoms, take 3 capsules (500 mg capsules) every evening for about 14 days before the onset of menstruation.*
- *For children, use about 250 mg of oil mixed in food daily.*
- *For cradle cap, massage enough to make the area supple.*

POTENTIAL BENEFITS

- *Balances hormones*
- *Acts as an antispasmodic agent for abdominal cramps*
- *Lowers blood pressure*
- *Lowers cholesterol levels*
- *Helps eczema*
- *Helps schizophrenic symptoms*

WARNING: Do not use if you suffer from epilepsy or migraines.

OLIVE

Olea europaea

THE USE OF olive oil in cooking is well known, but for medicinal purposes, extracts are taken from the leaves as well as the fruits themselves. Leaf extracts can be used for the treatment of high blood pressure and nervous tension, while the oil extracted from the fruits aids in cases of constipation.

The heart's health is greatly improved by the use of olive oil (best taken as the cold-pressed extra-virgin type) in cooking and food preparation.

Olive oil has the ability to reduce the bad cholesterol levels without affecting the beneficial cholesterol levels. Because olive oil is monounsaturated, there is little risk of free-radical generation if food is not cooked at very high temperatures.

PARTS USED

- *Leaves and fruits*

DOSAGE

- *As a laxative, take 2 or 3 tablespoons (30–45 ml) of oil.*
- *For general health, use 1 or 2 tablespoons (15–30 ml) mixed with food daily.*

POTENTIAL BENEFITS

- *Acts as a heart protector*
- *Reduces LDL cholesterol levels*
- *Reduces high blood pressure*
- *Acts to relax nerves and tension-related problems*
- *Helps relieve constipation*

CULINARY USES

- *Use the oil for cooking as you would any other oil, but do not cook at very high temperatures. The oil can also be used instead of butter. Chop and use the fruits in pasta sauces and in bread mixes.*

Olives (Olea europaea)

SWEET MARJORAM

Origanum majorana

THIS IS A popular culinary herb and is used in a variety of dishes. It is used to help digestion and reduce flatulence.

Marjoram is a good antiseptic as it contains a large amount of thymol. It also has a very calming effect on the nerves and is helpful in relieving tension and menstrual cramps. It is helpful when the oil is massaged in an aromatherapy application. Marjoram can be used to soothe sprains and muscular aches and pains. Apply a cold compress to sprains and a hot compress to aches and pains. Marjoram oil can also help with arthritis and rheumatism.

Drinking a marjoram infusion can help fight colds and relieve bronchitis.

Marjoram can give temporary relief from toothache if the leaves are chewed.

PARTS USED

- *Leaves and essential oil*

DOSAGE

- *As an aromatherapy massage, use 6 drops of essential oil mixed with 2 teaspoons (10 ml) of almond oil. Massage into the skin.*
- *As a tea, infuse 2 teaspoons dried leaves in 1 cup (250 ml/ 8 fl oz) of water and let stand for 5 minutes before drinking.*

POTENTIAL BENEFITS

- *Aids digestion*
- *Relieves tension*
- *Helps relieve menstrual cramps*
- *Fights colds*
- *Relieves arthritis and rheumatism*
- *Relieves toothache temporarily*

COSMETIC USES

- *Add an infusion of leaves for a relaxing bath.*

CULINARY USES

- *Add leaves to casseroles, sauces and egg-and-cheese dishes.*

WARNING: Avoid during pregnancy.

GINSENG

Panax ginseng

PANAX IS DERIVED from the word panacea, meaning a treatment for all problems. The Chinese, some 5,000 years ago, attributed to ginseng many properties and cures. When taken internally, ginseng acts as a general tonic by stimulating the central nervous system. It encourages the secretion of hormones to improve stamina. The stimulant effect may be used to treat stress and chronic fatigue.

Ginseng has been shown to reduce the blood concentrations of both glucose and cholesterol as well as stimulating resistance to disease. It also has a reputation for being an aphrodisiac.

PARTS USED

- *Root*

DOSAGE

- *Take 2 teaspoons (10 ml) of ginseng elixir daily for up to two weeks.*

POTENTIAL BENEFITS

- *Stimulates the central nervous system*
- *Improves stamina*
- *Boosts resistance to infection*
- *Reduces blood glucose and cholesterol levels*
- *May act as an aphrodisiac*

WARNING: Ginseng should not be used continuously for more than one month. In some cases it may cause headaches.

PARSLEY

Petroselinum crispum

PARSLEY WAS FIRST recorded in an early Greek herbal as long ago as the third century B.C. It was used in ancient Rome in cooking and in ceremonies. It is rich in vitamins A and C and contains flavonoids that help to reduce allergic reactions, but its main action appears to be detoxification.

An internal dose of parsley can help stimulate the menstrual process and help relieve menstrual cramps. Parsley also acts as an effective diuretic and helps relieve kidney complaints. It also helps reduce inflammation of the bladder as well as the prostate. In the stomach, it can help relieve colic, flatulence and indigestion.

The stimulant effect on the uterus makes this herb one to avoid during pregnancy, but once the baby is born, it may help stimulate lactation and milk flow.

Parsley sprigs can be added to make delicious dressings for salads.

PARTS USED

❦ *Seeds, leaves, roots and oil extract*

DOSAGE

❦ *As a liquid tincture, take 20 drops twice daily.*

POTENTIAL BENEFITS

❦ *Stimulates flow of breast milk*
❦ *Aids menstrual cramps*
❦ *Reduces inflammation in the bladder (cystitis)*
❦ *Stimulates the flow of urine*
❦ *Helps reduce colic and indigestion*

CULINARY USES

❦ *Used as an ingredient in sauces and as a garnish for fish, cheese and egg dishes.*
❦ *Can also be added to dressings and vinaigrettes.*

WARNING: Avoid during pregnancy.

KAVA KAVA

Piper methysticum

Kava kava dealers on the island of Tonga, Polynesia.

THIS INTOXICATING PEPPER was made into a special drink by the Polynesians and given to Captain Cook. The resulting effects led him to name it botanically as "intoxicating pepper." Kava is still made into a drink by the Melanesians during certain rituals, when it is said to enhance mental awareness.

Herbalists today use this herb to stimulate the nervous and circulatory systems. It cures insomnia and nervousness by enhancing restfulness. Kava kava has the ability to reduce the pain associated with muscle spasms and arthritis.

PARTS USED
- *Roots and rhizomes*

DOSAGE
- *Take 2 tablets (100 mg) of dried herb daily.*

POTENTIAL BENEFITS
- *Acts as a remedy for insomnia*
- *Acts as a nerve tonic*
- *Acts as a mental stimulant*
- *Reduces muscle spasms*
- *Helps reduce joint pains associated with rheumatism*

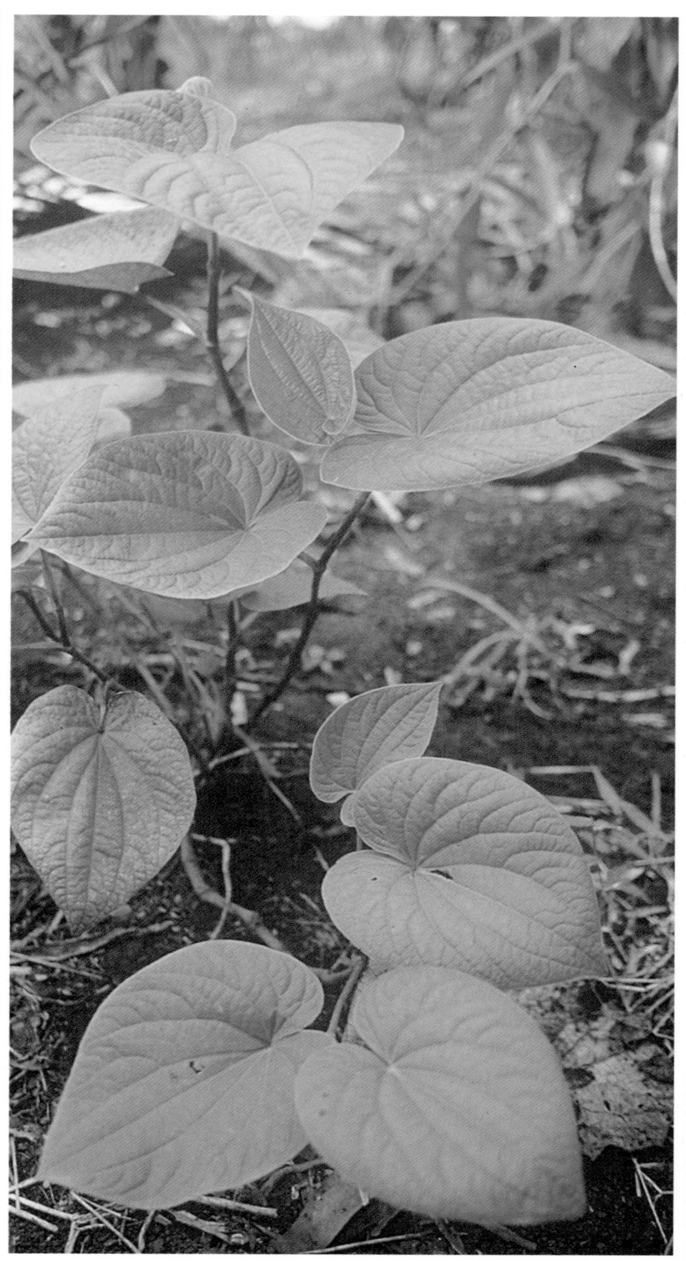

Kava Kava (Piper methysticum)

GREATER PLANTAIN

Plantago major

First discovered in ancient China in about 206 B.C., plantain was a popular medicine of the day. Its astringent properties promote healing and act as an effective expectorant in cases of chest infections. These properties led the herb to be used for cases of diarrhea and bowel inflammation. Externally, the juice can be used for ear infections, wounds, inflammation of the eye and hemorrhoids.

Parts used
- *Leaves*

Dosage
- *As a liquid tincture, take 20 drops twice daily.*
- *For external application, crush the leaves and collect the juice, then apply directly to the affected area.*

Potential benefits
- *Cleanses wounds*
- *Has an antiseptic action*
- *Helps control diarrhea and bowel inflammation*
- *Reduces ear and eye inflammation*

TORMENTIL OR BLOODROOT

Potentilla tormentilla

THIS RATHER UNASSUMING plant has very thick and strong roots that, when cut, reveal a blood-red color—hence the common name of bloodroot.

Tormentil contains a high concentration of astringents, making it an important medicinal plant. The action of this herb is mainly due to tannic acid, which makes it a useful preparation for treating diarrhea and inflammatory problems affecting the mucous membranes of the mouth, throat and stomach. Externally, it can be used to help heal wounds and cuts.

PARTS USED

- *Roots (rhizome)*

DOSAGE

- *As a liquid tincture, take 2 drops twice daily after eating.*
- *For external application, use as a poultice for wounds.*

POTENTIAL BENEFITS

- *Helps treat colitis*
- *Reduces diarrhea*
- *Soothes an irritated throat*
- *Reduces inflammation of the lining of the mouth*
- *Helps heal wounds and cuts*

BLACKTHORN

Prunus spinosa

BLACKTHORN CONTAINS VERY powerful chemicals (anthraquinone glycosides) that stimulate the contraction of the bowel wall, causing nausea, abdominal cramping and vomiting. Storing the herb for a number of years will dramatically reduce this effect.

For this reason, blackthorn has been used as a purgative (to induce vomiting) and, in smaller doses, as a laxative.

PARTS USED

- *Bark and fruits*

DOSAGE

- *As a liquid tincture, take 20 drops daily.*

POTENTIAL BENEFITS

- *Acts as a very effective laxative*
- *Acts as a purgative*
- *Acts as a diuretic*

WARNING: This herb is very strong. Overdosage will cause vomiting and diarrhea.

ROSEMARY

Rosmarinus officinalis

RICH IN volatile oils, rosemary is a very strong antiseptic agent with powerful anti-inflammatory actions. The phenolic acid content of rosemary is responsible for this antimicrobial property. Recent studies have suggested that rosemary may be beneficial in the treatment of toxic shock syndrome, but its historical use as an anti-infective agent is unquestionable.

The internal use of rosemary includes the treatment of depression, fatigue, migraine and tension headaches, poor circulation and digestive disorders including flatulence. Rosemary acts as a good circulatory stimulant and has a balancing and calming effect on the digestive system.

For rheumatism and muscular aches and pains, the external application of rosemary oil can give symptomatic relief. The oil can also be used as an insect repellent and the dried leaves can be used in potpourris and to scent clothes and linen. Traditionally, an infusion of rosemary has been used as a shampoo to stimulate hair growth and as a rinse to lighten blonde hair.

Rosemary (Rosmarinus officinalis)

PARTS USED

❦ *Leaves, flowering tips and essential oil*

DOSAGE

❦ *As an external application, apply 6 drops of essential oil, mixed with 2 teaspoons (10 ml) of almond oil, to the desired area twice daily.*

❦ *As a liquid tincture, take 10 drops twice daily.*

❦ *As a tea, add a teaspoon of chopped leaves to 1 cup (250 ml/8 fl oz) of boiling water and let stand for 5 minutes.*

POTENTIAL BENEFITS

❦ *Acts as an antiseptic agent for cuts and wounds*

❦ *Has an antidepressant activity*

❦ *Reduces headache and migraine symptoms*

❦ *Stimulates circulation and digestion*

❦ *Relieves flatulence*

CULINARY USES

❦ *Especially good with lamb and in soups and stews. Leave a fresh sprig in oil to steep for 1 month to produce a flavored oil, that must be refrigerated and used quickly.*

WARNING: The essential oil should not be used internally.

RASPBERRY LEAVES

Rubus idaeus

RASPBERRIES HAVE FORMED part of the human diet for as long as fossil records date back; they were even mentioned in the writings of Hippocrates (460–370 B.C.).

The astringent properties of this herb can be of use to pregnant women as it tones up the uterine muscles during pregnancy and is often given in preparation for childbirth. It is also given for a couple of months after birth to help restore the tone of the uterus. As a remedy for menstrual cramps, raspberry tea appears to be very effective.

PARTS USED

- *Leaves and fruits*

DOSAGE

- *As a tea, add a teaspoon of raspberry leaves (or use a commercial preparation) to 1 cup (250 ml/8 fl oz) of boiling water and drink twice daily during the third trimester of pregnancy.*
- *As a remedy for menstrual cramps, sip the tea as needed.*

POTENTIAL BENEFITS

- *Aids childbirth labor*
- *Tones up the uterus*
- *Reduces menstrual cramps*

WARNING: The use of this herb during pregnancy should be restricted to the third trimester.

BUTCHER'S BROOM

Ruscus aculeatus

AS FAR BACK as the first century A.D., butcher's broom was known to have medicinal properties, and it was mentioned as a treatment for kidney stones. Modern techniques have now identified the active agent, a steroid-like substance that can effectively reduce inflammation by constricting the veins.

A popular use for this herb is as a mild diuretic. When butcher's broom is taken internally, the circulatory system benefits from its tonic action, and improvements in poor circulation and hemorrhoids have been reported. An external application can be soothing when applied to hemorrhoids.

PARTS USED
- *Young shoots and roots*

DOSAGE
- *As a liquid tincture, take 15 drops twice daily.*
- *For external application, use as a cream, as required.*

POTENTIAL BENEFITS
- *Acts as a circulatory tonic*
- *Has an anti-inflammatory action*
- *Acts as a mild diuretic to reduce swollen ankles*
- *Helps relieve the pain of arthritis*

WARNING: Avoid in cases of high blood pressure.

WHITE WILLOW

Salix alba

SALIX CONTAINS A natural aspirin-like substance, salicylic acid, which was first produced commercially in 1838. The actions of aspirin are well known and include the reduction of fever, improvement in joint stiffness associated with arthritis and rheumatism, symptomatic easing of headache and reduction of inflammation.

It is interesting to note that pure salicylic acid intake is associated with stomach irritation, but that its presence in the white willow is buffered by tannins, which actually protect the stomach.

PARTS USED

❦ *Leaves and bark*

DOSAGE

❦ *As a liquid tincture, take 20 drops twice daily after eating.*

POTENTIAL BENEFITS

❦ *Acts as an anti-inflammatory agent*

❦ *Helps treat arthritis and rheumatism*

❦ *Reduces fevers*

SAGE

Salvia officinalis

SAGE WAS ASSOCIATED with long life in the eighteenth century and was a cherished herb. A wide array of aromas can be noticed coming from freshly cut sage due to the high content of volatile oils present in the plant.

Sage provides us with a readily available antiseptic agent. Fresh sage juice has anti-inflammatory and antiseptic activities. It can be used as a mouthwash and a gargle for tonsillitis and laryngitis. Sage can be used externally in a compress to promote the healing of wounds.

Sage extracts can effectively relax smooth muscles (found in the internal organs), and it has an effect on the female chemistry rather like that of estrogen. This estrogenic effect can actually reduce and suppress the production of breast milk. Sage can, therefore, be taken to control excessive lactation. The estrogen-like stimulation of sage can help relieve menopausal problems, and sage has been used to assist fertility.

People with indigestion and digestive problems such as dyspepsia benefit from this herb.

*Sage (*Salvia officinalis*) tea is useful for combating stress.*

PARTS USED

- *Leaves*

DOSAGE

- *As a liquid tincture, take 20 drops twice daily.*
- *For external application, use as a compress for wounds.*

POTENTIAL BENEFITS

- *Stimulates fertility*
- *Helps relieve menopausal problems*
- *Reduces excessive milk production in lactating women*
- *Has antiseptic and anti-inflammatory effects*

CULINARY USES

- *The leaves can be made into a pleasant tea or used in the traditional manner as a key ingredient in stuffings. Sage can also be used as a garnish for vegetable soup. Use sparingly as it is quite strong.*

WARNING: Avoid during pregnancy as large quantities of this herb are toxic.

CLARY

Salvia sclarea

There are more than 750 different species in the sage family. The term "clary sage" (also known as muscatel) is derived from the folkloric words "clear eye."

The volatile oil is used in aromatherapy massage and has many therapeutic actions. It is very effective as an antidepressant. It has a calming effect and can act as a sedative. Clary is also used as a general tonic for the whole body and helps to relieve menstrual cramps. This oil blends very well with sandalwood (*Santalum album*) and lavender (*Lavandula officinalis*), and it is safe to use on children.

Parts used

- *Essential oil*

Dosage

- *As an aromatherapy application, use 3 drops in 1 teaspoon (5 ml) of almond oil and massage in the usual way.*
- *As a bath for children, add 2 drops in 1 teaspoon (5 ml) of almond oil and mix in the bath.*

Potential benefits

- *Relieves depression*
- *Has a calming effect*
- *Helps reduce menstrual cramps*

Warning: Avoid during early pregnancy. Do not use when drinking alcohol.

ELDER

Sambucus nigra

WHEN A COLD is on its way, drink a hot tea made from elder. This will stimulate an increase in body temperature, which will help your body to speed the killing of the invading bacteria or virus. Elder has very effective decongestant properties and can be combined with many herbs to boost their activity in combating chest infections, nasal congestion and chills. This herb can also help relieve hay fever, bronchial congestion and sinusitis. The fruits of elder can be used in relieving rheumatic joint problems.

An external application of elder can be of great relief to irritated skin, bruises, sprains and minor wounds. It can be applied to the skin as an infusion or ointment. Elderflower water can be used as an effective skin toner, lightener and to fade away any unwanted freckles.

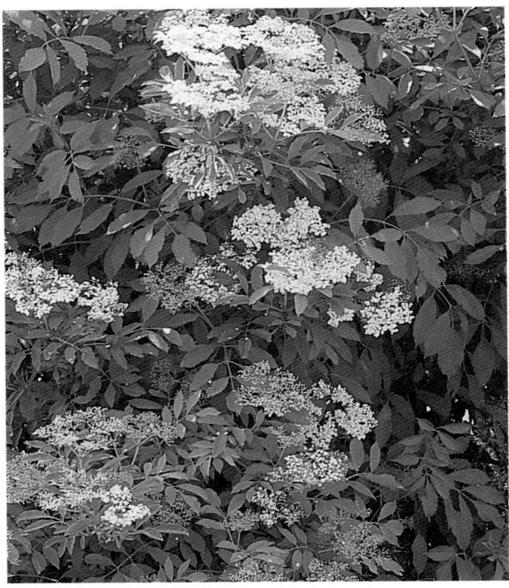

*Elder flowers (*Sambucus nigra*)*

PARTS USED

- *Leaves, bark, flowers and fruits*

DOSAGE

- *A remedy made from elderberry juice boiled with sugar to make a syrup is good taken twice daily for bronchitis and colds.*
- *For external application, use as a cream as required.*

POTENTIAL BENEFITS

- *Helps clear colds and flu*
- *Increases body temperature to assist in the elimination of invading infections*
- *Helps relieve sinusitis*
- *Soothes irritated skin*

COSMETIC USES

- *Can be made into a cleansing milk and lotion to soften the skin*

CULINARY USES

- *Boil the juice from the fruits with a little sugar, ginger and a few cloves to produce elderberry rod (cordial). Preserves and sauces can be made from the fruits.*

WARNING: The seeds from the elder can be toxic and should be avoided. Always cook the fruits first before eating them.

SKULLCAP

Scutellaria baicalensis

FIRST MENTIONED IN Chinese writings dating back to 25–220 A.D., skullcap has been used in medicinal preparations ever since. Its active agents such as certain flavonoids that improve liver function make it an important remedy for all kinds of liver disease. Its anti-inflammatory action makes it an effective treatment for poisonous bites, diarrhea and pharyngitis. Skullcap is also used to treat anxiety, depression and insomnia as it relaxes the nervous system.

The plant was used by the Cherokee, to induce menstruation, but this use has now dwindled.

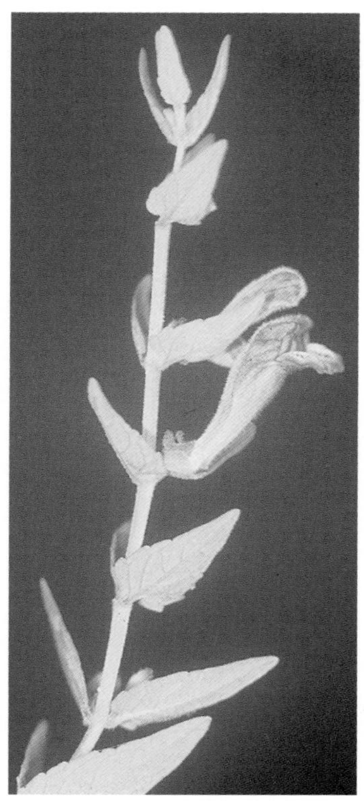

PARTS USED

- *Roots*

DOSAGE

- *As a liquid tincture, take 20 drops twice daily after eating.*

POTENTIAL BENEFITS

- *Can be used to treat liver disease*
- *Reduces inflammation of stomach and bowel*
- *Reduces diarrhea*
- *Helps cases of sore throat*
- *Can help insomnia*

MILK THISTLE

Silybum marianum

THIS POWERFUL HERB can counteract the damage of a lethal dose of the death cap mushroom (*Amanita phalloides*). Liver enzyme systems are protected by the silymarin content of this bitter herb.

Liver function is not only protected by silymarin, but its function also appears to be enhanced and new liver cells can be seen to appear. This action is used to treat liver cirrhosis and hepatitis, both potentially fatal conditions.

PARTS USED

- *Whole plant*

DOSAGE

- *As a liquid tincture, take 20 drops twice daily.*

POTENTIAL BENEFITS

- *Acts as a powerful liver protector*
- *Helps fight hepatitis*
- *May help regenerate damaged liver cells*

COMFREY

Symphytum officinale

COMFREY IS PROBABLY one of the best-known medicinal herbs. Its use by herbalists can be traced back over many centuries and is related to borage (*Borago officinalis*). Comfrey is known under other names including knitbone as it can heal bone fractures. Recent work has isolated an active agent, a pyrrolizidine alkaloid, which is responsible for the healing actions of comfrey, but this substance can induce liver damage and tumors. For this reason, internal usage is not recommended.

Used externally, comfrey has the ability to speed the healing of wounds and comfrey creams are perfectly safe and are very effective remedies for poorly healing wounds, eczema, psoriasis, hemorrhoids and skin ulcers. A comfrey poultice can be used to help heal sprains and severe cuts and to soothe

soothe pain and inflammation. It can also be used to drain boils and abscesses. Comfrey cream has been used for the treatment of mastitis in nursing women, but, because of its possible toxic effects, this should be avoided in case the infant should ingest some of the cream during feeding.

PARTS USED
- *Leaves and roots*

DOSAGE
- *For external application, use as a cream locally as required.*
- *For external application use as a poultice as required.*

POTENTIAL BENEFITS
- *Heals skin*
- *Speeds the healing of wounds*
- *Soothes hemorrhoids*
- *Reduces inflammation associated with eczema and psoriasis*
- *Helps drain boils and abcesses*
- *Helps relieve sprains*

COSMETIC USES
- *Add an infusion of comfrey leaves for a healing bath.*
- *May be used in a lotion to soften the skin.*

*Comfrey (*Symphytum officinalis*) can be used in lip balm to protect the lips.*

WARNING: Do not take internally or use for the treatment of mastitis if breast-feeding.

CLOVES

Syzygium aromaticum

FRESH CLOVES look quite different from the dark twiglike dried herb we are used to seeing. As far back as 600 A.D., the Chinese were documented to use cloves for many different reasons.

The volatile oil contained in cloves, eugenol, gives them their unique aroma. Another active constituent of cloves, methyl salicylate, has been recently identified and may be involved in the painkilling aspects attributed to clove extracts.

For toothache, clove oil should be used. Apply a small amount either directly on the tooth or use a cotton swab for difficult-to-reach areas. It is not recommended to leave absorbent cotton soaked in clove oil for too long in one place because the surrounding tissue of the mouth may suffer. When taken internally, cloves can help an upset stomach, symptoms of nausea, chills and even impotence.

PARTS USED

- *Flower buds and oil*

DOSAGE

- *Apply a few drops of oil to a toothache 2 or 3 times a day.*
- *Add 6 cloves to an herbal tea and let stand for 5 minutes.*

POTENTIAL BENEFITS

- *Helps an upset stomach*
- *Relieves chills and colds*
- *Acts as a toothache remedy*

CULINARY USES

- *Cloves give a special flavor to preserved meats, especially ham. Stud a ham with cloves and wrap well. After a few days the ham will take on a hint of the clove flavor. Whole cloves can be added to an oil base and allowed to steep for a month to produce a flavored cooking oil that should be refrigerated and used shortly. Cloves may also be used in pickling and baking.*

FEVERFEW

Tanacetum parthenium

THERE HAS BEEN much research performed on this powerful herb. Feverfew contains many chemicals, one of which (parthenolide) has the ability to block the action of serotonin, an inflammatory chemical released from special blood cells called platelets. Prostaglandins, hormonelike substances released from white blood cells, can aggravate migraines by affecting the blood circulation to the brain. These actions are blocked by feverfew extracts. Studies have confirmed that feverfew was a migraine cure. Feverfew has the ability to treat minor fevers, rheumatism and arthritis.

PARTS USED

❦ *Leaves and stalks*

DOSAGE

❦ *As a liquid tincture, take 20 drops twice daily.*

POTENTIAL BENEFITS

❦ *Acts as a migraine treatment*

❦ *Helps control minor fevers*

❦ *May be helpful in cases of joint pain and arthritis*

WARNING: Avoid during pregnancy. It is not advised to eat the fresh leaves because these may cause mouth ulcers in sensitive individuals.

TANSY

Tanacetum vulgare

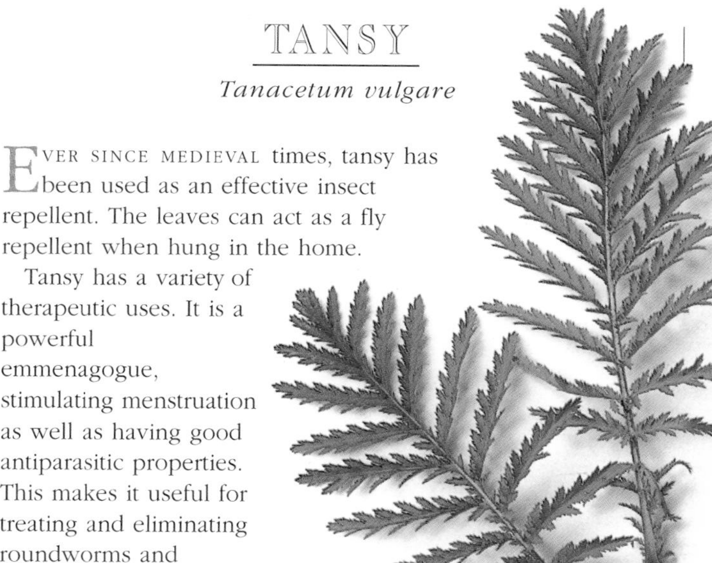

EVER SINCE MEDIEVAL times, tansy has been used as an effective insect repellent. The leaves can act as a fly repellent when hung in the home.

Tansy has a variety of therapeutic uses. It is a powerful emmenagogue, stimulating menstruation as well as having good antiparasitic properties. This makes it useful for treating and eliminating roundworms and threadworms from the digestive tract. This herb also improves digestion and helps relieve dyspepsia.

Applied externally, tansy can be used to treat scabies as well as help with rheumatism.

PARTS USED
- *Leaves*

DOSAGE
- *For external application, use as a compress to treat scabies and rheumatic joints.*

POTENTIAL BENEFITS
- *Stimulates menstruation*
- *Eliminates worms*
- *Improves digestion*
- *Relieves dyspepsia*
- *Helps treat rheumatism*
- *Helps treat scabies*

CULINARY USES
- *Fresh leaves may be used in salads and egg dishes, but only use in small quantities.*

WARNING: Avoid using over a long period of time. Avoid during pregnancy. An overdose of tansy tea or oil can be fatal.

DANDELION

Taraxacum officinale

THE DANDELION FIRST appeared in European medicine in 1480, having been used by the Chinese since 659 A.D.

Dandelion acts as a diuretic, increasing the urine flow so much that early users often called it "wet-the-bed." Its high potassium content is thought to be responsible for this action. High blood pressure has also been reduced by dandelion treatment thanks to its diuretic activity and potassium content.

The liver and gallbladder can benefit from dandelion, which appears to enhance the function of these organs. For this reason it has been used for the treatment of hepatitis, gallstones, gout and skin problems, including eczema.

PARTS USED

- *Whole plant*

DOSAGE

- *As a liquid tincture, take 20 drops twice daily.*

POTENTIAL BENEFITS

- *Acts as a liver-stimulating agent*
- *Increases flow of bile*
- *Helps in skin conditions such as eczema*
- *Lowers blood pressure*
- *Increases urine flow (diuretic)*
- *Is a good source of potassium*

COSMETIC USES

- *Add an infusion of dandelion leaves to the bath to cleanse the skin.*

CULINARY USES

- *Cook fresh leaves like spinach or add to a salad.*

THYME

Thymus vulgaris

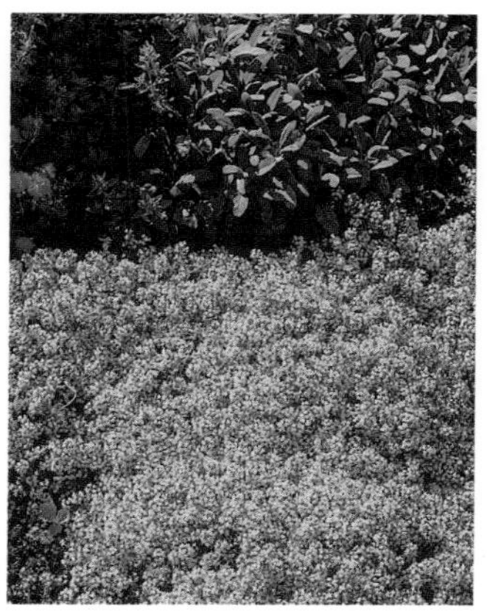

THYME IS ANOTHER herb with valuable antiseptic properties, the active agent being thymol. The aroma of thyme varies among species and depends on the concentrations of oils present in the plant. Thyme is an herb with a long tradition of use in respiratory problems. It is taken internally for coughs and colds or more serious problems such as bronchitis and asthma. The mucus-clearing ability of thyme makes it the appropriate remedy for chronic congestion when inflammation is a problem. Externally thyme can soothe painful joints.

PARTS USED
- *Whole plant*

DOSAGE
- *As a liquid tincture, take 20 drops twice daily.*
- *For external application, use 6 drops of essential oil, mixed with 2 teaspoons (10 ml) of almond oil and apply to the desired area.*

POTENTIAL BENEFITS
- *Clears lung congestion and infections*
- *Helps reduce asthma symptoms*
- *Has an antiseptic action*
- *Relieves colds*
- *Soothes painful joints*

CULINARY USES
- *Thyme is the basis of bouquet garni. Try adding a little to soups, meat and fish dishes. Added to marinades, thyme provides a special flavor.*

WARNING: Do not use the essential oil internally. Avoid during pregnancy.

FENUGREEK

Trigonella foenum-graecum

As far back as 1500 B.C., fenugreek was being used and its effects documented in the writings of the ancient Egyptians. Its ability to reduce muscular spasm made it the herb of choice in menstrual cramps and labor pains. It was even used in ancient civilizations to induce childbirth.

Modern medicine has been interested in extracts of fenugreek since the isolation of two chemicals: trigonelline, a potential cancer treatment, and certain saponins that can be used in contraceptive preparations.

The traditional use of this herb has been in the treatment of non-insulin-dependent diabetes, inflammation of the stomach, digestive problems and menstrual cramps. Fenugreek is also used to stimulate the flow of breast milk in nursing mothers. An external application can help arthritis.

Parts used
- *Leaves and seeds*

Dosage
- *As a liquid tincture, take 20 drops twice daily.*
- *For external application, use as a poultice, mix freshly crushed seeds with a little water and apply as needed.*

Potential benefits
- *Reduces menstrual cramps*
- *Can stimulate the flow of breast milk*
- *Improves digestion*
- *Assists in the balance of blood sugars*
- *Soothes arthritic joints*

Culinary uses
- *Use fenugreek seeds to add a spicy flavor to pea soups and to cooked carrots.*

COLTSFOOT

Tussilago farfara

THE PLANT WAS used as far back as 23–79 A.D., when the leaves and roots were burned over coals and the smoke generated was taken as a remedy for persistent cough. During the classical period, coltsfoot was smoked for the treatment of asthma and lung congestion.

Coltsfoot has a licorice flavor. It is used for the control of spasms involving the respiratory system. As a cough expectorant, coltsfoot is quite effective, but its main application is to reduce inflammation associated with irritated mucous membranes in the respiratory tract. Externally, coltsfoot has a soothing effect on inflamed skin, especially eczema and dermatitis.

PARTS USED

- *Flowers and leaves*

DOSAGE

- *As a liquid tincture, take 20 drops twice daily after eating.*
- *For external application, use as a compress for eczema and dermatitis.*

POTENTIAL BENEFITS

- *Acts as a cough remedy and expectorant*
- *Helps control asthma*
- *Eases symptoms of bronchitis and laryngitis*
- *Has a soothing effect on inflamed skin*

SASSAFRAS LEAVES

Umbellularia californica

A NATIVE PLANT of California, sassafras leaves were found to be a very effective insect repellent. The sassafras plant has a strong camphoraceous aroma, and it has been used as an inhalant for the treatment of headaches and sinus congestion. The leaves have been used traditionally for the treatment of headache and neuralgia, for which they are bound to the painful area in the form of a poultice.

PARTS USED
- *Leaves*

DOSAGE
- *As an infusion, take 2 or 3 cups (475–750 ml/16–25 fl oz) daily.*
- *As a liquid tincture, take 25 drops twice daily.*

POTENTIAL BENEFITS
- *Acts as a headache remedy*
- *Helps in cases of neuralgia*

CULINARY USES
- *Try using in place of bay leaves in meat dishes or stews.*

WARNING: Do not use sassafras roots as they are carcinogenic.

NETTLE

Urtica dioica

NETTLE HAS BEEN used since Roman times for treating rheumatic disease. The Romans would flail the inflamed joints with nettles to induce an inflammatory reaction that would calm down the disease.

Nettles contain a rich source of nutrients, especially vitamins A, B and C, and minerals including silica. The astringent properties of the herb can help reduce the blood flow, control bleeding and reduce blood pressure. It may be used to treat nosebleeds.

Taken internally, nettles can help rebalance the nutritional status of anemia sufferers. It may be helpful in controlling excessive menstrual bleeding. Arthritis, gout and rheumatism can all be reduced by using nettles, probably due to their diuretic action.

PARTS USED

❦ *Whole plant and leaves*

DOSAGE

❦ *As a liquid tincture, take 20 drops twice daily.*

POTENTIAL BENEFITS

❦ *Reduces symptoms of arthritis and rheumatism*

❦ *Supports requirements needed to prevent anemia*

❦ *Controls bleeding*

COSMETIC USES

❦ *Use in shampoo to help reduce dandruff.*

CULINARY USES

❦ *Cook the young leaves like spinach or purée for soups. Nettles can be made into wine or beer. Older leaves can be gritty and should not be used for cooking.*

WARNING: Do not use the uncooked plant for culinary purposes as it is poisonous and can produce kidney damage.

CRANBERRY

Vaccinium macrocarpon

A RECENT REPORT on cranberries estimated their current usage in the United States to be about 400 million pounds (81.5 million kg), which equates to a value of $1.25 billion. Cranberries are certainly popular!

Cranberries contain about 80 percent water and have a high vitamin C content. Their citric acid levels are very high—higher even than that of lemons.

The healing properties of cranberries date back to the seventeenth century, when they were used for the treatment of

*Cranberry (*Vaccinum macrocarpon*)*

stomach and liver problems. Cranberries have become the herb of choice for the treatment of bladder infections. Studies have located a natural polymer, arbutin, that actually prevents the bacteria from sticking to the wall of the bladder and urinary tract. An earlier theory suggested that cranberries made the urine acidic, which killed bacteria, but this theory has been replaced by the finding that bacteria actually lose their foothold on the walls of the urinary system in the presence of cranberry extracts.

Cranberries are delicious added to preserves.

PARTS USED

- *Fruits*

DOSAGE

- *Take 2 tablets (100 mg) of dried berries twice daily in acute phase, reducing to 1 tablet (50 mg) over the following month.*
- *Drink 1 teaspoon (5 ml) of cranberry powder (commercially prepared) in ⅔ cup (150 ml/¼ pint) of water twice daily until symptoms ease, reducing to ½ teaspoon (2.5 ml) for the next month.*

POTENTIAL BENEFITS

- *Acts as a cystitis treatment*
- *Acts as a urinary cleanser*

CULINARY USES

- *The fruits can be added to preserves, desserts and salads.*

BILBERRY

Vaccinium myrtillus

BILBERRY IS FULL of beneficial phytochemicals. Blood sugar levels are improved by the substances known as glucoquinones, while other agents called anthrocyanosides keep blood circulation flowing by dilating blood vessels. The species of bilberry *Vaccinium myrtillus* contains a unique substance (arbutin) that has powerful antiseptic effects on the urinary system and has been used as an effective natural cystitis treatment.

During World War II, Royal Air Force pilots in the United Kingdom received preserves made from bilberry to improve their night vision. It is interesting to note that recent studies have confirmed that bilberry extract can regenerate visual purple (the chemical that keeps night vision healthy) and, therefore, improve vision.

PARTS USED
- *Leaves and fruits*

DOSAGE
- *As a liquid tincture, take 20 drops twice daily.*

POTENTIAL BENEFITS
- *Improves vision*
- *Stabilizes blood sugar levels*
- *Acts as an effective cystitis remedy*

CULINARY USES
- *Bilberry preserves is a common product. The fruits may be added to salads and incorporated into desserts.*

VALERIAN

Valeriana officinalis

THE NAME VALERIAN is derived from the Latin word *valere* meaning "to be well." This herb gives us the opportunity to get well by inducing a restful sleep and relaxation, allowing the body to divert its healing powers to where they are most needed.

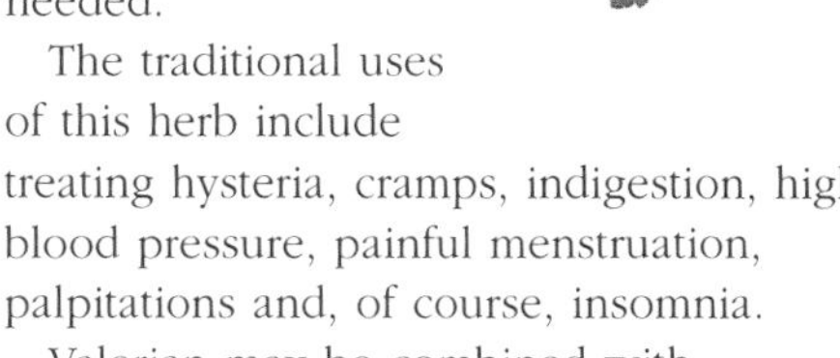

The traditional uses of this herb include treating hysteria, cramps, indigestion, high blood pressure, painful menstruation, palpitations and, of course, insomnia.

Valerian may be combined with passionflower (*Passiflora incarnata*) for a deeper sedative action, or it can be combined with licorice (*Glycyrrhiza glabra*) or hyssop (*Hyssopus officinalis*) and used as a cough expectorant. This herb can also help treat mouth ulcers when used as a mouthwash.

PARTS USED

- *Rhizome, roots and oil extract*

DOSAGE

- *As a sleep aid, take 25 drops of liquid tincture at bedtime.*
- *As a mouthwash, use a cooled infusion.*

POTENTIAL BENEFITS

- *Acts as a calming agent*
- *Induces a restful sleep*
- *Helps in panic attacks*
- *Reduces muscular tension*
- *Aids in menstrual cramps*

MULLEIN

Verbascum thapus

MULLEIN HAS BEEN used in folkloric medicine to treat respiratory disorders including coughs, congestion, and asthma. It was traditionally used to treat serious wasting conditions such as tuberculosis and was associated with witchcraft. It was thought that witches used the hairs on top of the leaves to make potions. The stems were also dipped in tallow and used as torches by the Greeks and Romans. Mullein has good expectorant and anti-inflammatory properties and can be used to soothe dry and irritating coughs as well as help expel phlegm.

PARTS USED

- *Leaves*

DOSAGE

- *As an infusion, add 2 teaspoons (10 ml) of dried leaves to 1 cup (250 ml/8 fl oz) boiling water and let stand for 5 minutes.*
- *Take a liquid tincture made from the flowers for coughs and sore throats.*
- *Take a leaf tincture for eliminating phlegm.*

POTENTIAL BENEFITS

- *Soothes dry and irritated coughs*
- *Acts as a mild sedative*
- *Has a mild diuretic action*
- *Has an expectorant action*
- *Has an anti-inflammatory action*

COSMETIC USES

- *Use the dried flowers infused in water to make a hair rinse to lighten hair.*

VERVAIN

Verbena officinalis

VERVAIN HAS A long history of medicinal uses, especially treating nervous disorders.

Taken internally, vervain can help depression that is often present after an illness and can help treat stress-related headaches and migraines.

This herb contains bitters that stimulate the liver and help relieve hepatitis and jaundice. It also stimulates the digestive system and improves digestion. Vervain has a diuretic action, which makes it useful for relieving fluid retention. This herb is an effective emmenagogue. Taken as a tea at bedtime, it acts as a mild sedative.

Vervain can be used to soothe inflamed eyes. This herb can also be used to treat insect bites and sprains.

PARTS USED

- *Leaves*

DOSAGE

- *As a tea, add 2 teaspoons of dried leaves to 1 cup (250 ml/ 8 fl oz) of boiling water and let stand for 5 minutes before drinking.*
- *For external application, use as a diluted infusion for soothing inflamed eyes.*
- *For external application, use as a poultice for insect bites and minor injuries.*
- *For external application, use as an ointment for eczema.*

POTENTIAL BENEFITS

- *Helps depression*
- *Improves digestion*
- *Alleviates nervous disorders*
- *Helps relieve hepatitis and jaundice*
- *Stimulates menstruation*
- *Has a diuretic action*
- *Has a mild sedative action*
- *Helps soothe inflamed eyes*

WARNING: Avoid during pregnancy as vervain acts as a stimulant to the uterus.

CRAMPBARK

Viburnum opulus

CRAMPBARK AND ITS close relative stagbush (*Viburnum prunifolium*) have been used since colonial times as treatments for painful menstruation. Contained within the plant are botanical substances that relax the uterus and, therefore, reduce the pains associated with menstrual cramps. The plant has also been used in cases of threatened miscarriage and high blood pressure.

PARTS USED
- *Bark*

DOSAGE
- *As a liquid tincture, take 20 drops twice daily.*

POTENTIAL BENEFITS
- *Reduces pains associated with menstruation and uterine cramps*
- *May help prevent miscarriage*
- *Helps lower high blood pressure*

WARNING: Do not eat the uncooked fruits as they are poisonous.

YUCCA

Yucca gloriosa

THE CHEMICAL SAPONIN contained within the yucca has been shown to affect toxins absorbed by the stomach bacteria. It is these toxins that may be responsible for the destruction of joint cartilage, so yucca, in blocking the uptake, may hold possible therapeutic applications in the treatment of arthritis. This observation has been supported by the traditional use of yucca by Native Americans for the treatment of inflamed joints and rheumatism.

PARTS USED
- *Sap*

DOSAGE
- *Take 2 tablets (100 mg) of dried sap daily.*

POTENTIAL BENEFITS
- *Reduces inflammation*
- *Eases symptoms of rheumatism*
- *May be a possible arthritis remedy*

GINGER

Zingiber officinale

GINGER'S ACTIVE AGENT is gingerol. It was a curious observation that dried ginger was more pungent than the fresh root. It turns out that upon drying, gingerols broke down into chemicals called shogaols, which are twice as potent.

Ginger's main effect on humans is to reduce nausea and motion sickness. It has become a popular herb for the treatment of morning sickness associated with pregnancy. Its safety in recommended doses is good, but excessive intake can be dangerous. This herb also promotes gastric secretions and is useful in treating flatulence.

Ginger has been used as a traditional treatment for skin irritations, both externally applied and by internal dosage.

For colds and flu, ginger extract has a warming effect and can boost the immune response to infection. Ginger has a powerful diaphoretic action and induces sweating. It can also be used as a gargle to relieve sore throats.

*A ginger (*Zingiber officinale*) dressing is a delicious accompaniment to fruit.*

Parts used

- *Rhizome and oil extract*

Dosage

- *As a liquid tincture, take 25 drops twice daily.*
- *As a tea, crush a slice of fresh gingerroot and add to the infusion.*

Potential benefits

- *Acts as an antinausea remedy*
- *Helps in morning sickness*
- *Reduces cold and flu symptoms*
- *Induces sweating*
- *Helps relieve flatulence*
- *Boosts the immune response*

Culinary uses

- *Add a couple of slices of freshly chopped gingerroot to a stir-fry, curry or gingerbread mixture for an extra-fresh flavor, or add to salad dressings.*
- *To make a ginger dressing, put ½ cup (50 g/2 oz) of sugar and ⅔ cup (150 ml/¼ pint) of water in a saucepan and heat gently, stirring, until the sugar has dissolved. Bring to a boil, then simmer 1 minute without stirring. Remove from the heat and add ⅔ cup (150 ml/¼ pint) of ginger wine, two pieces of chopped stem ginger, finely grated rind and juice of 1½ limes. Pour over fruit and leave to cool. Chill before serving.*

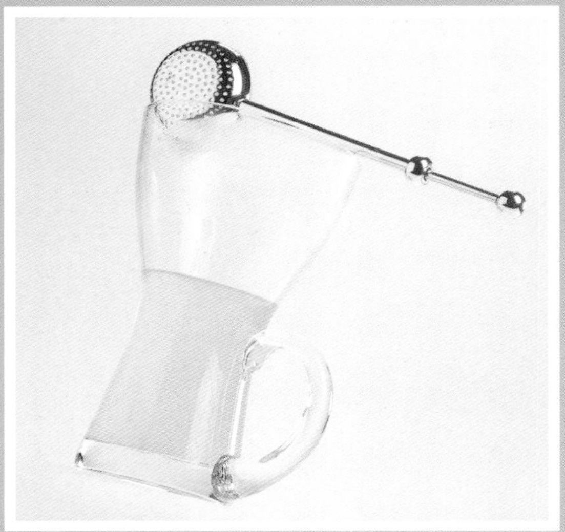

REMEDIES

Cautionary note:

At all times it is recommended that you consult a health-care professional before embarking on a program of self-treatment. Herbal medicines are effective and safe when used in the correct circumstances. This book has been written to educate, and every effort has been made to make the book as accurate and as informative as possible, but the advice contained within is no replacement for professional guidance.

HERBAL REMEDIES FOR CHILDREN

Echinacea (Echinacea purpura) *helps stimulate the immune system.*

Fever

It is important to remember that a fever is not always a bad thing, but keeping a close watch on the child's temperature is important. The average body temperature is 98.6°F (37.0°C). A lower temperature is suggestive of shock or excessive cooling if you are sponging your child down with cold water, or it could be a sign that the temperature is going to increase soon, possibly up to 103°F (39.8°C) or more. Temperatures up to 101°F (38.8°C) are thought of as moderate fever; when this rises to 102° to 104°F (39.2–40.3°C) or more, it is considered to be seriously high, and prompt medical attention is strongly advised.

Basic natural methods are often enough to help your child through most fevers of the mild to moderate variety. If your child has a fever but is not sweating, try to stimulate sweating by using a natural sweat-inducing agent (known as a diaphoretic).
A hot tea made from elder (*Sambucus nigra*) or

Sweat-Inducing Formulation

Make a decoction using 2 tablespoons (30 ml) to 2¼ cups (500 ml/18 fl oz) of water. This tea is taken hot, about 1 or 2 cups (250–475 ml/8–16 fl oz), along with a warm-hot bath.

chamomile (*Anthemis nobilis*) has a considerable stimulatory effect and can break a fever very effectively.

During the entire illness, doses of echinacea (*Echinacea purpura*) should be given at regular intervals to assist in the stimulation of the immune system. Its antiviral and antibacterial properties are other factors that make this the best extract for all illnesses.

Upset Stomach and Diarrhea

All children from time to time suffer from a nonspecific infection and other maladies that tend to induce acute diarrhea and stomach pains often accompanied by a mild fever.

Other causes of upset stomachs in children include food poisoning, new food in the diet (often rich foods), overexcitement and fright, very cold or chilled foods, overeating, too much sun and mental or physical distress.

For diarrhea, try a tincture of dandelion (*Taraxacum officinalis*) or tormentil (*Potentilla tormentilla*). Caution: Diarrhea can be life-threatening. So, if the diarrhea does not appear to improve and the child is becoming dehydrated, seek urgent medical attention. As the upset stomach slowly improves, the appetite may take a little while to return to normal; if this is the case, try a dose of centaury (*Centaurium erythraea*).

Rehydration Formulation

Boil a scant 1 cup (200 ml/ 7 fl oz) of water, and, as it cools, add 1 teaspoon (5 ml) of sugar, a generous pinch of baking soda and a smaller pinch of salt. Stir until all of the ingredients have dissolved and give to the child when the formula is cold.

Common Childhood Diseases

Chicken pox This condition is also known as *Varicella* and is one of the most contagious diseases known today.

For the symptoms of skin irritation, try an application of aloe vera (*Alo barbadensis*) salve or chamomile (*Anthemis nobilis*) lotion. Taking a tea made from yarrow (*Achillea millefolium*), chamomile (*Anthemis nobilis*) or goldenseal (*Hydrastis canadensis*) can be beneficial. A tincture of echinacea (*Echinacea purpura*) should always be taken.

Common Cold There is no cure for the common cold, but by using naturopathic principles, it should be possible to control many symptoms and, with luck, prevent your child from catching colds regularly. A daily dose of echinacea is essential, along with plenty of vitamin–C-rich foods. Supplements are advised if your child is fussy about eating fruits and vegetables. If there is a persistent cough, try sage tea, or for excessive mucus, a tea made from fenugreek (*Trigonella foenum-graecum*) or ginger (*Zingiber offinale*) can be very effective. A tincture of goldenseal (*Hydrastis canadensis*) is advisable during the infectious period to assist in fighting the infection.

A tea made from ginger, fennel and honey is an ideal remedy for colds.

Measles Natural supportive measures include using tinctures of yarrow (*Achillea millefolium*) and echinacea (*Echinacea purpura*). A tea made from yarrow, with the addition of a few drops of echinacea tincture, can be very beneficial. To stimulate the appetite when the worst of the disease is over, try a tincture of barberry (*Berberis vulgaris*).

Mumps There is no specific treatment for mumps, but the glands will settle within 10 days. General naturopathic measures should be followed.

Eczema and Psoriasis

It is interesting that eczema and psoriasis share some key factors. Both skin conditions are aggravated by stress and anxiety. The underlying reason for this is not known, but stress does increase the levels of certain hormones known to stimulate the circulation to the skin, which inflames an already irritated condition. The second common factor lies in the observation that essential fatty acid metabolism and the metabolism of micronutrients such as selenium and zinc appear to be defective.

The irritation can be related to an imbalance in inflammatory chemicals, such as histamines, and dry flakiness. Raised patches of skin occur due to an excessive production of deeper skin layers that rapidly migrate to the surface. Unfortunately, the trigger mechanisms behind such changes are, at present, unknown. Some claim that dietary allergy or chemical contact can start these changes, and in some sufferers, this is definitely the case, but in most there is a coexistent nutritional imbalance. Selenium and zinc, as well as other micronutrients, are needed for healthy skin cell maturation. A corrective daily dose of the nutrients zinc and selenium taken for a month, followed by a lower dose of these minerals for another month or so, should rebalance this situation.

Skin inflammation is best approached by optimizing fatty acid metabolism. There are many essential fatty acids, but the most important to the skin appear to be gamma linoleic acid (GLA) and the omega 3 and 6 oils.

Derived from borage (*Borago officinalis*) seed and evening primrose (*Oenothera biennis*) seeds, GLA is probably the best known of all the essential fatty acids. The only all-natural source of GLA is breast milk, which may go some of the way to explaining the link between eczema and bottle-fed babies. The omega 3 and 6 oils are found in fish and fish oils, linseeds, marine algae and meat from marine mammals such as seals and whales. Flaxseed (*Linum usitatissimum*) oil contains both GLA and the omega 3 and 6 oils in one balanced form.

An interesting herb known as *Plectranthus barbatus* or sometimes *Coleus forskohlii* is showing great promise as a remedy for psoriasis. It is best taken as a dried extract in commercially prepared tablet or capsule form.

Asthma and Hay Fever

It is unfortunate, but both of these distressing conditions appear to go hand in hand. Both may be based in allergies, usually to inhaled triggers, but they may have other aggravating factors such as food sensitivities.

An elimination diet is the most sensible course of action to take when investigating food allergies, but this method is best followed under professional supervision to ensure that a balanced diet is maintained during the testing process.

Herbal remedies such as Chinese skullcap (*Scutellaria baicalensis*), licorice (*Glycyrrhiza glabra*), garlic (*Allium sativum*) and angelica (*Angelica archangelica*) commonly feature in the management of childhood asthma and hay fever.

Chinese skullcap
(Scutellaria baicalensis)

Garlic (*Allium sativum*) has the ability to prevent a special enzyme (lipoxygenase) from working. The enzyme activates an important part of the inflammatory response, which is prevented by supplementation with garlic extract.

Angelica (*Angelica archangelica*) is especially effective in those individuals suffering from allergies to pollen, dust and animal dander. These allergens play an important role in generation of symptoms in hay fever and asthma.

Licorice (*Glycyrrhiza glabra*) also has anti-inflammatory and anti-allergy activity with a cortisone-like action. Steroids are widely used in the long-term management of asthma. Licorice extract has none of the side effects of steroids, but it does have many of the benefits. The inflammatory aspect of asthma can be managed using this extract.

Chinese Skullcap (*Scutellaria baicalensis*) has been used for its anti-inflammatory properties in the management of arthritis for many years. The herb contains high levels of flavonoids that work in a similar way to some anti-asthmatic drugs.

Common Problems and Remedies

Colic
- Extract of dill (*Anethum graveolens*)
- Fennel water (*Foeniculum vulgare*)
- Tincture of ginger (*Zingiber officinale*)
- Tincture of cloves (*Syzygium aromaticum*)

Constipation
- Extract of licorice (*Glycyrrhiza glabra*)
- Tincture of barberry (*Berberis vulgaris*)

Cough
- Elder syrup (*Sambucus nigra*)
- Tincture of plantain (*Plantago major*)
- Tea made from marshmallow (*Althaea officinalis*)

Cough with phlegm
- Tincture of echinacea (*Echinacea purpura*)
- Tea made from ginger (*Zingiber officinale*) and fennel (*Foeniculum vulgare*) with honey

Cradle cap
- Tincture of burdock (*Arctium lappa*)
- Tincture of nettle (*Urtica dioica*)
- Tincture of dandelion (*Taraxacum officinale*)
- Plantago ointment (*Plantago major*)
- Olive oil *(Olea europaea)*

Diaper rash
- Zinc and castor oil cream
- Calendula ointment (*Calendula officinalis*)

Earache
- Tincture of hops (*Humulus lupulus*)
- Tincture of St. John's wort (*Hypericum perforatum*)
- Tincture of goldenseal *(Hydrastis canadensis)*
- Tincture of echinacea (*Echinacea purpura*)
- Tincture of plantain (*Plantago major*)

Nasal congestion
- Tea made from hyssop (*Hyssopus officinalis*)
- Tincture of hyssop (*Hyssopus officinalis*)
- Tincture of goldenseal (*Hydrastis canadensis*)
- Extract of garlic (*Allium sativum*)

Sleeping problems
- Tincture of lemon balm (*Melissa officinalis*)
- Tea made from lemon balm *(Melissa officinalis)*
- Tincture of valerian (*Valeriana officinalis*)
- Tincture of hops (*Humulus lupulus*)

Sore throat
- Tincture of marshmallow (*Althaea officinalis*)
- Tincture of plantain (*Plantago major*)
- Tincture of elder (*Sambucus nigra*)
- Tincture of echinacea (*Echinacea purpura*)

Teething
- Tincture of chamomile (*Anthemis nobilis*)
- Marshmallow syrup (*Althea officinalis*)

HERBAL REMEDIES FOR YOUNG PEOPLE AND ADULTS

Premenstrual Syndrome (PMS)

Tension is probably one of the most common symptoms reported by women who suffer from a menstrual dysfunction. It has been estimated that up to 75 percent of women suffer from some form of premenstrual anxiety. Other symptoms such as food cravings, weight gain and depression also occur to varying degrees. There are many safe, natural ways to conquer PMS that do not have dangerous side effects.

Anxiety is a common problem. This tends to be due to a hormone imbalance, namely excessive estrogen and low progesterone levels. The high estrogen has a blocking effect on vitamin B_6, inhibiting the liver production of serotonin and altering the ability to balance blood sugar levels. A rise and fall of sugars is partly responsible for mood elevation and depression.

Herbal extracts of dandelion root (*Taraxacum officinalis*) contain the plant chemical inulin (not to be confused with the hormone insulin), which has a balancing effect on blood glucose levels. This can be used alongside the trace mineral chromium to help control fluctuating sugar levels associated with premenstrual problems.

Depression is suffered by about 30 percent of women with PMS. This might be an effect of disordered brain chemistry (namely, serotonin) or a dysfunction of other brain chemicals.

The exact cause is not known, but there appears to be a link with estrogen levels. The extract from St. John's wort (*Hypericum perforatum*) is very effective at relieving this type of depression. In one study, more than 65 percent of those treated improved while using St. John's wort extract. The active agent, hypericin, was standardized in these tests.

It is not uncommon for women to gain more than 3 pounds (1.4 kg), mostly due to water retention. The hormone to blame is aldosterone, which appears in excess in the premenstrual phase of the cycle, again linked to the estrogen imbalance. A dose of uva-ursi (*Arctostaphylos uva-ursi*) taken from the time of ovulation (day 14 of the cycle) will increase the urine flow and control fluid retention.

*Uva-ursi (*Arctostaphylos uva-ursi*)*

Natural Considerations Adjust the types of food to include complex carbohydrates such as pasta, potato and rice and reduce the intake of animal fats. Eat simpler foods such as vegetables and fruit.

The essential fatty acids contained in evening primrose oil can help with menstrual cramps and pain as well as help to balance hormone levels. A dose of 500–1,000 mg taken at bedtime with water is recommended.

Substances such as feverfew extract (*Tanacetum parthenium*) have been able to stop prostaglandins from being produced, and this is important for those who suffer menstrual discomfort.

Cystitis

Cystitis is a common problem. Most cases are due to an infection traveling up from the vagina into the bladder. Flare-ups often occur after sexual intercourse, when the infection is reintroduced into the bladder.

Cystitis in men results from an infection traveling to the bladder from the urethra or from the prostate gland, which may itself be harboring a bacterial infection. The most common symptoms in both men and women are pain and urgency—a constant sensation of the need to pass urine. Blood may be passed in the urine indicating the severity of the bladder infection. It is important to remember that the infection can travel up from the bladder into the kidneys and this requires urgent medical treatment.

Three-Step Treatment for Cystitis

For most people, the following steps can be followed, and a successful treatment for cystitis can be achieved.

Step 1 Increase fluid intake. Few people drink enough water to keep themselves hydrated. We lose about 6¼ cups (1.5 liters/2½ pints) of water daily through our breath, sweat, urine and feces, so to remain in balance, you need to drink that amount daily. This does not take into account activity levels that cause us to sweat, body type, temperature, food consumption, stress levels etc. As a rule, 8 cups (2 liters/3⅓ pints) of water (preferably bottled water) are recommended.

Step 2 Try to locate, or better still, make, unsweetened cranberry (*Vaccinium macrocarpon*) juice and drink 2 cups (475 ml/16 fl oz) daily. Cranberry powders and capsules are available. The dose for powders is 2 teaspoons (10 ml) taken in the morning and evening or two capsules taken twice daily. If you cannot obtain unsweetened cranberry juice, take the capsules or powders. Increasing your sugar intake will just encourage excessive bacterial growth in the bladder.

Step 3 Increase general health and boost immunity. It is advisable to check that your diet contains the correct balance of foods. Taking echinacea (*Echinacea purpura*) extract has been shown to elevate white blood cell activity and stimulate the immune response. Take 25–30 drops of liquid extract twice daily or take 2 capsules twice daily.

Irritable Bowel Syndrome (IBS)

It has been estimated that more than half of the abdominal problems are diagnosed as IBS. Because it is common, you may think there is a simple cure, but in a case of IBS you need to take a holistic view of health in order to plan an individual treatment program. Each sufferer may have similar symptoms, but it is not uncommon to find different aggravating factors ranging from food sensitivities to stress.

One popular theory suggests that there is an imbalance in the body's nervous system. A specialized division of the nervous system (the autonomic nervous system) controls the internal running of our bodies such as the beating of the heart, and plays a vital role in the coordinated activity of the digestive system. The stomach and bowels are at work 24 hours a day digesting food, absorbing water and nutrients, killing invading bacteria and collecting waste matter. This activity needs to be controlled on a subconscious level, leaving the brain free to conduct day-to-day business.

In times of stress, the body brings the "fight-or-flight" mechanism into play. During this, we prepare ourselves, biologically, to fight or run away from danger. In either case, adrenaline is released, and nervous activity is stimulated. The bowel cannot contract and move normally and symptoms such as abdominal bloating, pain and cramping, fatigue, alternating bouts of constipation and diarrhea, passage of mucus in the stool, flatulence and nausea are common. Another common finding is that the pain of IBS is often relieved by the passing of stools while some find that certain foods induce the pain.

It is important to seek professional advice when bowel symptoms are experienced, since other conditions may mimic IBS—conditions such as lactose intolerance, celiac disease, diverticular disease and bowel cancer. These conditions have their own special collections of symptoms that must be ruled out before IBS can be diagnosed.

IBS needs an individual treatment program, but some guidelines can be followed that may give relief.

Dietary Fiber Increasing the intake of soluble dietary fiber from vegetables, fruits, oat bran, beans and psyllium husk can be beneficial. However, this must be done slowly since the bowel in IBS tends to be hyperactive and may respond unfavorably with an unaccustomed dose of fiber.

Bowel Spasms For the symptomatic control of bowel spasms, the use of peppermint (*Mentha piperita*) oil capsules offers relief. Peppermint oil has relaxing effect on the smooth muscle that forms the bowel wall. Capsules that are coated pass through the stomach undigested and open up in the lower bowel. Generally, 0.2-ml capsules are used at doses of two or three capsules taken between meals.

Other antispasmodic agents are the herbs valerian (*Valeriana officinalis*), rosemary (*Rosmarinus officinalis*), chamomile (*Anthemis nobilis*) and lemon balm (*Melissa officinalis*).

Diarrhea When diarrhea and irritation are the main symptoms, an old preparation called Robert's formula has survived. It combines marshmallow (*Althaea officinalis*) root, cabbage (*Brassica oleracea*) extract, echinacea (*Echinacea purpura*), goldenseal (*Hydrastis canadensis*), okra (*Hibiscus esculentis*) and slippery elm (*Ulmus fulva*) to produce a remedy for the bowels. Modern preparations of Robert's formula are available in capsules and should be taken at a dose of one or two capsules between meals.

Nausea The nausea experienced by sufferers may be helped by taking ginger (*Zingiber officinale*). Studies have documented how effective ginger can be in treating motion sickness and

Ingredients in Robert's Formula

Cabbage extract
(*Brassica oleracea)* 100 mg
Marshmallow root
(*Althaea officinalis*) 100 mg
Okra
(*Hibiscus esculentis*) 75 mg
Slippery elm
(*Ulma fulva*) 75 mg
Echinacea
(*Echinacea purpura*) 25 mg
Goldenseal
(*Hydrastis canadensis*) 25 mg

nausea. Ginger used in cooking or taken as a dietary supplement will not upset sensitive bowels, and it may calm the spastic nature of IBS as well as reduce the nausea.

Psychological Aspects Finally, the psychological aspects of IBS must not be forgotten. Almost all sufferers complain of fatigue, anxiety, depression, feelings of hostility or sleep disturbances. These problems need attention and can be overcome with the correct help.

Common Problems and Remedies at a Glance

Acne

- Tincture of echinacea (*Echinacea purpura*)
- Tincture of goldenseal (*Hydrastis canadensis*)
- Tincture of dandelion (*Taraxacum officinalis*)

Candidiasis *(Yeast infection)*

- Tincture of goldenseal (*Hydrastis canadensis*)
- Tincture of echinacea (*Echinacea purpura*)
- Extract of garlic (*Allium sativum*)

Chronic fatigue

- Tincture of echinacea (*Echinacea purpura*)
- Tincture of goldenseal (*Hydrastis canadensis*)
- Licorice root extract (*Glycyrrhiza glabra*)
- Extract of panax or Siberian ginseng (temporary measure only) (*Panax ginseng*)

Hypertension

- Extract of garlic (*Allium sativum*)
- Tincture of hawthorn berry (*Crataegus oxyacantha*)
- Tincture of mistletoe (*Viscum alba*)

Inflammatory bowel disease

- Marshmallow root extract (*Althaea officinalis*)
- Extract of cabbage (*Brassica oleracea*)
- Tincture of echinacea (*Echinacea purpura*)
- Tincture of goldenseal (*Hydrastis canadensis*)
- Extract of slippery elm (*Ulmus fulva*)

Migraine

- Tincture of valerian (*Valeriana officinalis*)
- Tincture or extract of feverfew (*Tanacetum pathenium*)

Obesity

- Tea made from dandelion (*Taraxacum officinalis*)

Sinus infections

- Tincture of echinacea (*Echinacea purpura*)
- Tincture of goldenseal (*Hydrastis canadensis*)

Sports injuries

- Extract of turmeric (*Curcuma longa*)
- Witch hazel ointment (*Hamamelis virginiana*)

HERBAL REMEDIES FOR PREGNANT AND BREAST-FEEDING WOMEN

WARNING: No pregnant woman should take any preparation without consulting with her health-care practitioner.

Morning Sickness

There have been many ideas to help explain morning sickness, but the trigger is still shrouded in mystery.

Teas made from fennel (*Foeniculum vulgare*), peppermint (*Mentha piperita*) or ginger (*Zingiber officinale*) can give relief from symptoms. Taking a nighttime cup of chamomile *(Anthemis nobilis)*, lemon balm (*Melissa officinalis*) or hops *(Humulus lupulus)* tea will help you get a restful sleep. There has been suggestions that ginger may be toxic during pregnancy, but all of the reviews state that the intake obtained via a tea is safe. The problem can arise when multiple concentrated extracts are taken in capsule or tablet form.

Emotional Problems

During pregnancy, moods may swing, and emotions become unbalanced. It is important to relax and have a good soak in a warm bath using a few drops of essential oils. Lavender *(Lavandula officinalis)* and chamomile *(Anthemis nobilis)* oil can be very relaxing. A tincture of rosemary *(Rosmarinus officinalis)* can also help.

Heartburn

As the baby grows, it will take up a lot of space within your lower abdomen. This causes the stomach to become pushed up, and its contents occasionally leak into the lower part of the food pipe causing heartburn. Attention to diet is vital, as is taking digestive aids such as dill *(Anethum graveolens)* or caraway *(Carum carvi)*. These can be chewed or made into a tea and sipped during or between meals. Powdered slippery elm bark *(Ulmus fulva)* can give relief from the irritation of stomach acid.

Varicose Veins and Hemorrhoids

To prevent these, you will need to include garlic *(Allium sativum)* in daily meals to keep the circulation strong. Try a tea made from dandelion *(Taraxacum officinalis)*. Extracts of St. John's wort *(Hypericum perforatum)* can be made into a tea and taken two or three times daily.

To strengthen the walls of the veins, drink a tea made from fresh ginger *(Zingiber officinale)*. If the skin is irritated, try making a compress from comfrey *(Symphytum officinale)* and marshmallow *(Althaea officinalis)*, plantain *(Plantago major)*. For an intensive treatment of hemorrhoids that may be bleeding, apply a comfrey cream directly to the area.

Lactation

Remedies used to encourage the flow of breast milk have been used for centuries and do offer help. Infusions of milk thistle *(Silybum marianum)*, nettle *(Urtica dioica)*, fenugreek *(Trigonella foenum-graecum)* and hops *(Humulus lupulus)* are all safe to use during this time. These herbs may also help reduce the risk of colic in the baby.

Mastitis

If caught early, this condition can be reversed without antibiotics. As soon as mastitis is suspected, express your milk by hand or use a breast pump, and take a dose of flaxseed *(Linum usitatissimum) oil*, 1–3 tablespoons (15–45 ml) daily. If there is no improvement within 48 hours, seek medical advice.

Sore Nipples

The application of comfrey *(Symphytum officinale)* cream has been questioned by those who consider that accidental intake

Herbs to Avoid in Pregnancy

Yarrow
(Achillea millefolium)
Angelica
(Angelica archangelica)
Camomile
(Anthemis nobilis)
Celery
(Apium graveolens)
Bearberry
(Arctostaphylos uva-ursi)
Arnica
(Arnica montana)
Wormwood
(Artemisia absinthium)
Southernwood
(Artemisia abratanum)
Calendula
(Calendula officinalis)
Gotu kola
(Centella asiatica)
Black cohosh
(Cimicifuga racemosa)
Myrrh
(Commiphora molmol)
Eyebright
(Euphrasis officinalis)
Fennel
(Foeniculum vulgare)
Licorice
(Glycyrrhiza glabra)
Goldenseal
(Hydrastis canadensis)
Hyssop
(Hyssopus officinalis)
Juniper
(Juniperus communis)
Devil's claw
(Martynia annua)
Nutmeg
(Myristica fragrans)
Pennyroyal
(Mentha pulegium)
Sweet marjoram
(Origanum majorana)
Parsley
(Petroselinum crispum)
Poke root
(Phytolacca americana)
Raspberry leaves
(Rubus idaeus)
Rye
(Ruta graveolens)
Sage
(Salvia officinalis)
Clary
(Salvia sclarea)
Feverfew
(Tanacetum parthenium)
Tansy
(Tanacetum vulgare)
Thuja
(Thuja occidentalis)
Thyme
(Thymus vulgaris)
Vervain
(Verbena officinalis)

of the cream from the nipple when feeding the baby is dangerous. Keeping in mind its long history and the lack of reports of toxic reactions, there is little risk, but if you wish to avoid this cream, use a yarrow *(Achillea millefolium)* -based cream. Do not use yarrow if you are pregnant.

HERBAL REMEDIES FOR MENOPAUSE SYMPTOMS

It has been reported that up to 75 percent of women suffer unpleasant menopause symptoms due to decreasing levels of hormones. For the majority, the symptoms may be short-term (lasting for two to three years), but for others they may persist for more than five years, making life intolerable.

Menopause symptoms are likely to occur at about 50 years of age, unless surgery (hysterectomy) brings on symptoms earlier. Over this transition, menstruation usually becomes irregular until it stops altogether. Menopause is a normal and natural phase of a woman's life, and for many it can herald the start of a special era. With the family grown up, attention can be focused on the woman—so long as she feels well!

Emotions may alter, and the person may become more forgetful. The sleep pattern could change, especially if night sweats are troublesome. Other symptoms may include hot flashes; joint stiffness; vaginal dryness; loss of sexual interest; anxiety; recurrent urinary tract infections; changes in hair, nail and skin quality; and loss of self-esteem.

Many of these problems are short-term, but other symptoms may not appear until much damage has been done. These include osteoporosis and the effects of heart disease and elevated blood cholesterol.

Look very carefully at diet and learn a little about some very interesting plant extracts that have a phytoestrogen activity (an estrogen-like activity but extracted from a plant) in the body. Foods naturally high in phytoestrogens include soy, fennel (*Foeniculum vulgare*), celery (*Apium graveolens*), parsley (*Petroselinum crispum*), flaxseed oil (*Linum usitatissimum*), nuts and seeds. Because of this alternative activity, such herbal extracts are often prescribed for hormone-excess conditions (premenstrual syndrome) as well as hormone-deficiency problems (menopause).

A high-dose vitamin E and C supplement can be of great help. It has been shown that vitamin E helps reduce hot flashes and vaginal problems compared to placebo treatment.

*Licorice (*Glycyrrhiza glabra*)*

Many herbs have been used in traditional folk medicine as uterine tonics, formulated to relieve menopause symptoms. The classic example is black cohosh *(Cimicifuga racemosa)*, but licorice *(Glycyrrhiza glabra)*, chaste berry *(Vitex anguscastus)* and ginseng *(Panax ginseng)* are considered to be good sources as well.

Black cohosh has a history of use dating back to when Native Americans used it as a remedy for menstrual cramps and menopause symptoms. Studies have concluded that the plant has an estrogen-like effect by virtue of its ability to rebalance hormone levels.

Historically, licorice has been used for the treatment of feminine disorders, an application that is now supported by scientific research, which can confirm a mild estrogen-like activity.

Panax ginseng (also known as Korean ginseng) was viewed as a masculine "tonic" until its estrogen-like activity was demonstrated. This action can be so strong that in high doses, the extract may induce postmenopausal bleeding.

The following daily formulas are recommended as part of a natural treatment program. Use one or the other.

Formulas for Menopause

Formula 1

Licorice extract
(Glycyrrhiza globra) 25 mg
Black cohosh
(Cimicifuga racemosa) 25 mg
Chaste berry extract
(Vitex anguscastus) 25 mg
Fennel seed extract
(Foeniculum vulgare) 12 mg

Formula 2

Vitamin E 150 IU
Flaxseed oil
(*Linum usitatissimum*) 300 mg
Gamma-oryzanol 100 mg

HERBAL REMEDIES FOR THE ELDERLY

Arthritis

There are many types of arthritis; some result in extreme inflammation and joint deformity, while others cause long-term pain, stiffness and a less severe degree of joint deformity. Osteoarthritis is the most common type of joint condition. The underlying process is one of joint degeneration whereby the smooth joint coverings lose their ability to provide frictionless motion. The cartilage starts to develop patches where its surface has become eroded. This acts as a focus for more erosion, and what was once a small patch soon expands into a much larger area of degeneration. The visible signs of arthritis are a thickening of the tissue and the appearance of nodules around the edges of the joint.

Natural diuretic herbs can

Golden Grass Tea (Dried Herb)

40% Goldenrod *(Solidago virguaria)*
30% *Betula alba*
15% Birch *(Polygonum avicularea)*
10% Horsetail *(Equisetum arvense)*
5% Pansy *(Viola tricolor)*

help in the elimination of toxic substances such as uric acid by increasing the flow of urine. The two formulas listed below have a safe and effective action on the kidneys, and they are best combined with a special herbal tea, known as golden grass tea.

Formulas for Arthritis

Formula 1 (tincture)
50% Goldenrod
(Solidago virguaria)
14% Silverweed
(Potentilla anserina)
13% Birch
(Betula alba)
5% *Ononis spinosa*
5% Pansy
(Viola tricolor)
5% *Polygonum aviculare*
4% Horsetail
(Equisetum arvense)
4% Juniper
(Juniperus communis)

Formula 2
(solid extracts)
Bearberry
(Arctostaphylos Uva-ursi) 100 mg
Lespedeza capitatae 50 mg
Boldo
(Peumus boldo) 50 mg
Goldenrod
(Solidago virguaria) 50 mg

To support the elimination process and assist in the reduction of inflammation, a combination herbal tincture remedy can be very effective.

Massage given by a qualified therapist can be a great relief when applied to the muscle structures that surround the degenerated joint. Massage increases circulation, aids in the drainage of tissue fluids and stimulates the release of healing substances. Aromatherapy can also be helpful. Useful aromatherapy oils for arthritis include eucalyptus *(Eucalyptus globulus)*, ginger *(Zingiber officinale)*, lavender *(Lavandula officinalis)* and rosemary *(Rosmarinus officinalis)*.

A selection of massage oils

Common Problems and Remedies at a Glance

It is recommended that you consult a health-care professional before embarking on a program of self-treatment.

ALZHEIMER'S DISEASE
- Tincture or capsules of ginkgo (*Ginkgo biloba*)

ANGINA
- Tincture or capsules of hawthorn (*Crataegus oxyacantha*)

ATHEROSCLEROSIS
- Extract of garlic (*Allium sativum*)
- Extract of alfalfa (*Medicago sativa*)
- Tincture or capsules of ginger (*Zingiber officinale*)

BRONCHITIS
- Extract of licorice (*Glycyrrhiza glabra*)
- Tincture of echinacea (*Echinacea purpura*)
- Extract of garlic (*Allium sativum*)

DIABETES
- Extract of aloe vera (*Alo barbadensis*)
- Extract of bilberry (*Vaccinium myrtillus*)
- Extract of fenugreek (*Trigonella foenum-graecum*)
- Extract of garlic (*Allium sativum*)
- Tincture or capsules of ginkgo (*Ginkgo biloba*)
- Tincture of burdock (*Arctium lappa*)
- Tincture of dandelion (*Taraxacum officinalis*)
- Tincture of artichoke (*Cynara scolymus*)

GLAUCOMA
- Tincture or capsules of gingko (*Gingko biloba*)

PROSTATE DISEASE
- Tincture of nettle (*Urtica dioica*)

VARICOSE VEINS
- Extract of bilberry (*Vaccinium myrtillus*)
- Tincture or capsules of ginkgo (*Ginkgo biloba*)
- Tincture of horse chestnut (*Aesculus hippocastanum*)
- Tincture of hawthorn (*Crataegus oxyacantha*)

Herbal Tincture

15% *Polygonum aviculare*
15% Goldenrod *(Solidago virguaria)*
10% Butterbur *(Petasites officinale)*
10% Silverweed *(Potentilla anserina)*
10% Yarrow *(Achillea millefolium)*
10% Birch *(Betula alba e folium)*
10% Mistletoe *(Viscum alba)*
10% Horsetail *(Equisetum arvense)*
5% *Colchicum autumnale*
5% Peppermint *(Mentha piperita)*

HERBAL REMEDIES FOR TIMES OF STRESS

Herpes Simplex and Cold Sores

There is no sign like an eruption of cold sores to indicate that the body is under stress. The immune system becomes suppressed, and opportunistic diseases such as herpes simplex make their appearance.

Lemon balm *(Melissa officinalis)* has been known as an herbal remedy for more than 2,000 years. During the 1960s, the dried extract was reported to exhibit antiviral activity in a number of studies. The efficiency of cream containing lemon balm depends on starting the therapy within eight hours of the onset of symptoms. And to be effective, the cream needs to be very concentrated, containing a 70:1 lemon balm extract with 1 percent allantoin.

Common Problems and Remedies at a Glance

Exhaustion
- Tincture of oats (*Avena sativa*)
- Extract of ginseng (*Eleutherococcus senticosus*)

Fatigue
- Tincture or tablets of hyssop (*Hyssopus officinalis*)
- Extract of ginseng (*Eleutherococcus senticosus*)

Headache
- Tincture of valerian (*Valeriana officinalis*)
- Extract of butterbur (*Petasites hybridus*)

High blood pressure
- Tincture of mistletoe (*Viscum alba*)
- Extract of garlic (*Allium sativum*)

Insomnia
- Tincture of passionflower (*Passiflora incarnata*)
- Tincture or capsules of valerian (*Valeriana officinalis*)

Irritability
- Tincture of oats (*Avena sativa*)
- Tincture of lemon balm (*Melissa officinalis*)
- Tincture of hops (*Humulus lupulus*)
- Tincture of valerian (*Valeriana officinalis*)
- Tincture of passionflower (*Passiflora incarnata*)

Migraine
- Extract of butterbur (*Petasites hybridus*)
- Tincture of lemon balm (*Melissa officinalis*)

Palpitations
- Tincture of hawthorn (*Crataegus oxyacantha*)
- Tincture of passionflower (*Passiflora incarnata*)

Poor memory
- Tincture or capsules of ginkgo (*Ginkgo biloba*)

HERBAL REMEDIES FOR EMOTIONAL PROBLEMS

St. John's wort (Hypericum perforatum)

Depression

It has been estimated that nearly one in four people experiences some degree of depression at some time in their lives, with women tending to be at a slightly higher risk than men. The biochemistry of mood and mood disturbance is complex, but it is known that many nutritional and environmental factors play a vital role in psychological health. There has been no single factor identified as the cause of depression.

An herbal substance that shows promise in the battle against depression is St. John's wort (*Hypericum perforatum*). This shrubby plant is native to Europe and has been used medicinally for centuries. Studies in Germany have found that the active agent, hypericin, alters brain chemistry and improves mood. Hypericin appears to be able to increase the brain's production of dopamine, an effect similar to many prescription drugs dispensed for depression. Other studies have shown that a standardized extract of St. John's wort is more effective than prescription antidepressants such as amitriptyline that are associated with significant side effects. The use of St. John's wort does not lead to any significant side effects.

The dose of St. John's wort taken in these studies was 300 mg (containing 0.125% hypericin). St. John's wort preparations are available in 300-mg capsules (standardized to contain 0.3% hypericin) and should be taken at the dose of two to three capsules daily.

Other herbs that may help in this condition include ginkgo *(Ginkgo biloba)* and Siberian ginseng *(Eleutherococcus senticosus)*.

Common Problems and Remedies at a Glance

ANXIETY

❦ Extract of kava kava (*Piper methysticum*), as needed

❦ Extract of Korean ginseng (*Panax ginseng*), as needed

PANIC ATTACKS

❦ Valerian (*Valeriana officinalis*) capsules, as needed

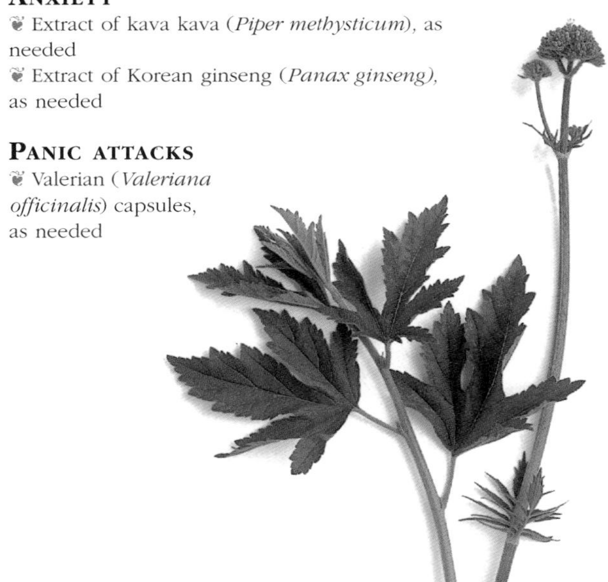

HERBAL FIRST AID KIT

Keeping an accessible collection of essential natural remedies around the house will encourage their use over their potentially more toxic pharmaceutical counterparts. The first aid kit can include bandages, arnica liniments, scissors, herbal-based creams, essential oils and gels. The following chart shows what you need in the basic first aid kit.

Basic First Aid Kit

Echinacea (*Echinacea purpura*) tincture or capsules
Arnica (*Arnica montana*) and comfrey (*Symphytum officinale*) creams
Arnica tincture or tablets
Essential oils: tea tree (*Melaleuca alternifolia*), chamomile (*Anthemis nobilis*) and lavender (*Lavandula officinalis*)
Ginger (*Zingiber officinale*) capsules or tablets
St. John's wort (*Hypericum perforatum*) oil
Aloe vera (*Alo barbadensis*) gel

USING HERBS IN A BUSY LIFE

It is an unfortunate fact of life that most of us lead hectic lifestyles and, as much as we would like to slow down, the pressures of day-to-day living forbid it! Herbal medicine can help keep our bodies in balance.

Growing herbs for home use can be great fun and an enjoyable hobby, but the preparation of medicines—although possible at home—needs much time and effort, especially if you need to maintain a home supply of medicinal remedies for regular use.

For this reason, the use of prepared tinctures and encapsulated dried extracts has become a popular alternative to the home production of medicinal remedies. The herbs listed in the following section, Recommended Over-the-Counter Remedies, are available worldwide as single-tincture preparations or as combination remedies. Most are developed

according to strict production codes of practice, with organically grown herbs prepared to a pharmaceutical grade, but always read the label carefully. Using such remedies allows the user to maintain their remedy intake while minimizing the fuss of home production.

RECOMMENDED OVER-THE-COUNTER REMEDIES

Each remedy listed will support and stimulate the itemized function or system, and in the case of vaginal thrush *(Candida albicans)*, the aim is to eliminate the condition.

Adrenal function

- Korean ginseng *(Panax ginseng)*
- Siberian ginseng *(Eleutherococcus senticosus)*
- Licorice *(Glycyrrhiza glabra)*

Bladder health

- Cranberry *(Vaccinium macrocarpon)*
- Uva-ursi *(Arctostaphylos uva-ursi)*

Bowel function

- Fenugreek *(Trigonella foenum-graecum)*
- Ginger *(Zingiber officinale)*
- Marshmallow *(Althea officinalis)*
- Peppermint *(Mentha piperita)*

Eye function

- Bilberry *(Vaccinium myrtillus)*

Heart and circulation

- Cayenne pepper *(Capsicum frutescens)*
- Garlic *(Allium sativum)*
- Ginkgo *(Ginkgo biloba)*

Hormone (female) function

- Fennel seed *(Foeniculum vulgare)*
- Licorice *(Glycyrrhiza glabra)*

Hormone (male) and prostate function

- Ginkgo *(Ginkgo biloba)*
- Korean ginseng *(Panax ginseng)*

Immune system

- Echinacea *(Echinacea purpura)*
- Goldenseal *(Hydrastis canadensis)*

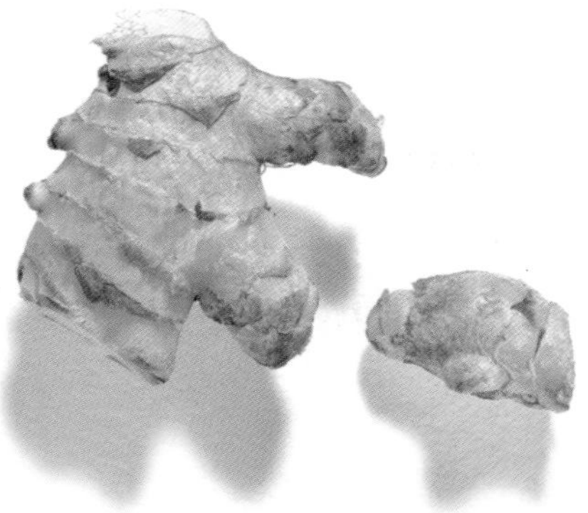

JOINTS
- Butterbur *(Petasites hybridus)*
- Horsetail *(Equisetum arvense)*
- Peppermint *(Mentha piperita)*
- Yarrow *(Achillea millefolium)*

KIDNEY FUNCTION
- Uva-ursi extract *(Arctostaphylos uva-ursi)*
- Boldo extract *(Peumus boldo)*
- Goldenseal extract *(Hydrastis canadensis)*
- Horsetail *(Equisetum arvense)*
- Juniper *(Juniperus communis)*

LIVER FUNCTION
- Boldo *(Peumus boldo)*
- Dandelion *(Taraxacum officinale)*
- Licorice *(Glycyrrhiza glabra)*
- Peppermint *(Mentha piperita)*

LUNG FUNCTION
- Fenugreek *(Trigonella foenum-graecum)*
- Garlic *(Allium sativum)*
- Marshmallow *(Althaea officinalis)*
- Thyme *(Thymus vulgaris)*

LYMPHATIC SYSTEM
- Goldenseal *(Hydrastis canadensis)*

NERVOUS SYSTEM
- Chamomile *(Anthemis nobilis)*
- Hops *(Humulus lupulus)*
- Passionflower *(Passiflora incarnata)*
- Valerian *(Valeriana officinalis)*

SKIN HEALTH
- Chamomile *(Anthemis nobilis)*
- Horsetail *(Equisetum arvense)*
- Rosemary *(Rosmarinus officinalis)*
- Sage *(Salvia officinalis)*

VAGINAL THRUSH
- Goldenseal *(Hydrastis canadensis)*
- Oregano *(Origanum vulgare)*
- Peppermint *(Mentha piperita)*
- Thyme *(Thymus vulgaris)*

THE SPICE COMPANION

The Culinary, Cosmetic and Medicinal Uses of Spices

RICHARD CRAZE

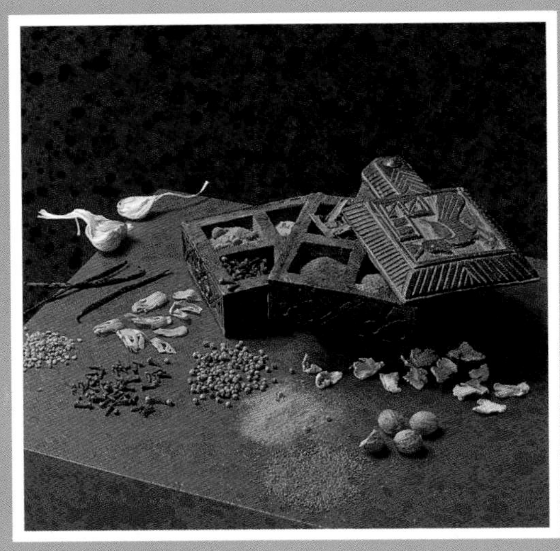

INTRODUCTION

Spices are, strictly speaking, the dried parts of aromatic plants—the seeds, flowers, leaves, bark or roots—although a few are used fresh. But there is something evocative about spices that goes way beyond their culinary or medicinal uses. Who can hear the words "Spice Islands" without feeling a shiver of excitement, a call of adventure and discovery? Wars were fought over spices; empires were lost in their cause. Explorers set out to find the strange and exotic lands that they came from—names that still stir the imagination—Egypt, China, Arabia, Persia, India, Greece, Zanzibar.

Some spices are worth more than precious metals and gems; both frankincense and myrrh were considered so valuable that they were included in the three gifts the Wise Men brought to the baby Jesus.

Spices are essential ingredients in any good cook's kitchen. They are also used in the manufacture of incense,

A precise definition of spices is difficult. Is garlic a spice?

oils, cosmetics, preservatives and flavorings. Their history is a fascinating and rewarding subject.

In this guide you can learn all about them—their history and cultivation, their uses and preparation. Exploring more than 50 spices from around the world, this authoritative and exhaustive guide is an illustrated directory of the essential properties of the world's most widely used and popular spices.

Star anise (Illicium verum)

But what exactly is a spice? A precise definition is difficult because some plants are regarded by some people as spices, while other people would argue that they are not. Take garlic, for instance. Is it a spice? It is certainly aromatic and spicy tasting—but it does not grow in the tropics, which is where most spices come from. The word "spice" usually means the dried seeds of certain hot aromatic plants—but what about sweet peppers? We certainly use their dried fruit in paprika, but we also use the fresh flesh—as we do for chilies. Maybe it is all in the taste. But then we would have to discount turmeric, which has little in the way of a spicy taste but nevertheless is regarded the world over as a spice; certain dishes would be lost without its brilliant yellow color. In this guide we have included all the traditional spices—as well as a few you may never have heard of but that are still regarded as important in their own countries.

Measurements

All recipes are given in U.S. Customary units with metric measurements.

Abbreviations used are the following: tsp (teaspoon), tbsp (tablespoon), ml (mililiter), l (liter), g (gram), oz (ounce), fl oz (fluid ounce), kg (kilogram), m (meter), F (Fahrenheit), C (Celsius).

Any recipes that include a cup of ingredients refer to a standard cup holding 8 fl oz (250 ml), which is the equivalent of just under ½ pint in British Imperial measurement. Also 500 ml = 2 cups (approx.). A teaspoon is 5 ml and a tablespoon is 15 ml.

All weights are given in grams or kilos. 5 g (approx.) = 2 tsp (approx.) 10 g = 4 tsp = 20 ml. And 40 g = 5 tbsp = 80 ml.

For any recipes using eggs, medium-sized eggs are used unless otherwise specified. And a pinch or dash of spice means exactly that—the merest pinch or dash, not a handful.

Oven temperatures are not usually given because they can vary so much. However, we would recommend a moderate heat of 350°–375°F (180°–190°C).

> **Caution**
>
> Any medicinal uses are given purely for information. Any conditions that require medical attention should be referred to a qualified medical doctor. No attempt should be made to treat any serious conditions at home.

The Spice Directory

The directory contains the most important, common, exotic and unusual spices from around the world. It includes well-known and commonly used spices such as black pepper, mustard and caraway as well as not-so-well-known ones such as java galangal and asafetida. The directory for each spice includes its history, where it is grown, its medicinal and culinary uses and its principal properties. At the beginning of this directory, you will find an alphabetical index of the spices by their common name.

Black pepper in classic vinaigrette—an essential ingredient.

Cooking With Spices

Here are all the tips any cook will need to prepare and use spices. Also included are recipes for spicy butters, oils, drinks, salad dressings, bouquet garni, chutneys (relishes of fruits, spices and herbs), pickles, curries, puddings and spicy ice cream.

Garam masala is one of the better-known spice combinations.

Spice Combinations

We have included some of the more commonly known spice combinations such as curry powder, garam masala and Chinese five-spice, along with some that are less well-known such as alino criolo and sambal.

Chilies come in a variety of shapes and sizes.

The Sweet Peppers

Sweet peppers contain just about the highest concentration of vitamin C you can get. Here you will find some unusual and tasty recipes for preparing and cooking juicy red and green sweet peppers.

The Chilies

We all, quite rightly, associate chilies with some of the hottest spices known to cooks the world over. Here you will find information about how to prepare and cook them—and recover afterward.

Cutting the Mustard

Mustard is one of the oldest and most popular spices. In this section you will learn the differences between some of the best-loved mustards including Dijon, English, American and German.

Spices add extra zest to pickles and relishes.

Spice Vinegars

Do you know how to make ginger vinegar or a very spicy vinegar? Now you can learn how to make spicy vinegars quickly and easily to spice up your vinaigrette dressing—and you will find a recipe for Worcestershire sauce.

Spices for Beauty, Relaxation and Health

Since the very earliest times, ancient people have used spices for cosmetics, soaps, incense, potpourri and perfumes. In this section you will find some unusual and interesting things to do with spices—to make yourself and your home beautiful. While we urge caution against using spices as general medicinal treatments and recommend that you consult a qualified medical doctor, the warming and stimulating properties of some spices are worth knowing about.

THE HISTORY OF SPICES

World history without the history of spices would be impossible. Spices have been directly responsible for wars, trade routes, the discovery of America, papal edicts and decrees, medicinal cures, cosmetic preparations and religious rituals, not to mention some of the most tasteful cuisine. And they have been traded and used for longer than most people would think.

SPICES AND CHINA

At least 5,000 years ago in China, Emperor Shen Nung was writing a medical treatise extolling the virtues of ginger, cassia, anise and turmeric. He founded spice markets, and his longevity is attributed to the vast amounts of spices he used in his own food. Confucius, around 550 B.C., was advising his disciples not to eat any food that had not been prepared properly with spices.

ARAB TRADERS

At about the same time, the Arab world was trading spices with India. The Indian spice ports on the Malabar Coast were doing a roaring trade in cardamom, ginger, turmeric, peppers, sesame and cumin. Their ships carried pots of growing ginger to ward off scurvy. And the Arabs bought spices from other places—

Spices have been traded for thousands of years.

cinnamon from Sri Lanka; mace, nutmeg and cloves from the East Indies; myrrh from East Africa—as well as produced their own frankincense. The trade routes were long and arduous—traveled by camel caravan from Calcutta or by sea through the Persian Gulf. It was a profitable and lucrative trade, and naturally the Arabs kept the exact location of the spice lands to themselves—and even invented fantastic and ludicrous stories of where the spices came from to throw others off the trail. The Arab traders were the importers and exporters of the spice world. They bought from and sold to places such as Egypt, Persia, Afghanistan and the whole of the Mediterranean—and from there to Europe.

Greece and Rome

In ancient Greece and Rome, spices were considered so valuable and important that they were used to flavor just about everything. The Greeks and Romans also wrote extensively about their cosmetic and medicinal applications, but they wasted them too—Nero is said to have burned a year's supply of cinnamon at his wife's funeral (consisting not just of his own personal supply but also the supply for the whole of Rome).

The Greeks liked their food plain and unadorned, and the philosopher Epicurus maintained that although pleasure was what life was all about, it should be simple and enjoyed in moderation. It was he who gave us the word "epicurean." By the time the Greek civilization fell into decline, the Greeks were spicing their food as much as anyone.

The Visigoths Demand Pepper

As the Roman Empire spread throughout Europe, the Romans took their spices with them and introduced them to the indigenous populations—some of whom already had their own spices. And as the Roman Empire collapsed and the Romans retreated to Rome, they left behind a rich legacy of spices. When the Visigoths blockaded Rome in 408 A.D., one of the ransoms they demanded was 3,000 pounds of pepper.

The Dark Ages

With the sacking of Rome came 700 years of darkness in Europe. The spice trade continued in the Middle and Far East, but the art of spices was lost in Europe until the crusaders returned from Palestine in the twelfth century with the beginnings of a new trade. Europe woke up again, and the spice trade flourished once more.

The Italian Renaissance

Venice and Genoa became rich as they capitalized on the new trade, and, from the profits of that trade, the Italian Renaissance was born. Medieval cooking took on a new emphasis and originality—everything had to be spicy and highly colored despite the fact that the spices were so expensive. At one time a horse was valued at the same price as a pound of saffron, while a sheep could be bartered for a pound of ginger or a cow for two pounds of mace. Pepper was so highly valued that its price was measured in individual peppercorns, and they were used as currency to pay taxes and rent. Later, when peppercorns became less valuable, tenants who were still allowed to pay their rent in peppercorns were considered extremely lucky, and "peppercorn rent" came to mean the exact opposite of what it did originally.

Peppercorns were once used to pay taxes and rent.

Marco Polo traveling in a caravan (from a Catalan map).

Marco Polo

But the Arab world still controlled the flow and trade of spices and kept prices high. At the beginning of the thirteenth century, Marco Polo set out from Venice to find a new route to the Far East—one that would bypass the Arab traders. When he returned 25 years later, he brought with him fabulous wealth and treasures from the court of Chinese Emperor Kubla Khan—and spices of course. In fact, nobody back in Venice believed that he had actually made such a fantastic journey until he cooked a magnificent meal for his friends with the new and exotic spices he had brought back with him.

But it would be another two centuries before the Europeans decided that they had had enough of the exorbitant prices and that they really had to do something about it.

Henry the Navigator

Because it was Venice's trading agreements with the Arab world that kept the prices artificially high and provided the Venetians with much of their wealth, it wasn't going to be a Venetian who would seek alternative routes. Enter Prince Henry of Portugal, known as "Henry the Navigator." He financed and equipped expeditions to sail around Africa to find a route into the Indian Ocean. This was in the days of primitive sailing ships that had never before left the sight of land. Prince Henry died without seeing a successful voyage. By 1480 the Portuguese had learned how to sail before the wind, had sailed around Africa and were able to sail to India itself. They reached India in 1497—but not before their great rivals, the Spanish, had become increasingly worried that they might lose out.

Vanilla was brought to Europe by Columbus.

Christopher Columbus

The Spanish-employed and unknown Italian Christopher Columbus claimed he could reach India ahead of the Portuguese—not by sailing around Africa, but by sailing westward into the unknown Atlantic. He set sail in 1492 and three months later landed in the West Indies. He was, of course, disappointed. He had set out to find India and instead found America. He returned with allspice from the West Indies, chilies from Mexico and vanilla from Central America.

So almost simultaneously, the two routes opened up, and the spice trade wars really got going. The Spanish and Portuguese found so many ways to interfere with each other's spice trade that the pope was obliged to issue an edict dividing the world into two spice halves—Spain could have everything to the west of an imaginary line in the Atlantic Ocean, while Portugal could have everything to the east.

Magellan

The Spanish employed Magellan (who was Portuguese) to sail westward with five ships and more than 200 sailors to find another route to the Moluccas and the island of Bandaas. They argued that if they approached from the west, they would be within their sphere of influence—and so would not upset the pope, but they would be able to capture the clove and nutmeg market. Magellan did not make it back, but some of his crew and one ship did by rounding the coast of South America.

The British and the Dutch

The British and Dutch entered the market in a big way. The Dutch founded the Dutch East India Company to trade directly with India for spices—and the British financed Francis Drake to sail around the world to find another passage to China. War broke out between England and Spain over trade routes. This led to the defeat of the Spanish armada and the British formation of the East India Company.

In 1658 the Dutch fought and beat the Portuguese for the cinnamon trade of Ceylon—and added the pepper ports of Malabar and Java. By 1690 the Dutch had a monopoly on the clove trade—only because they burned all the clove trees growing on any other island except Aboyna. They fiercely kept this monopoly for 60 years until a Frenchman managed to smuggle a ripe fruit off the island and took it to the French colonies, where it was successfully planted.

By the end of the eighteenth century, the British had ousted the Dutch from India, and London briefly became the center of the world's spice trade. But that was not to last for long.

The Americans

During the American Revolution, the Americans (or colonists, as they were then called) developed swift sailing warships—clippers—to defeat the might of the British navy. After the Americans won the war, these ships sat idle for only a short while before they were put to use sailing to the East Indies—Britain's spice monopoly was broken before it had really begun.

Spices Today

After the ferocious spice trading that went on during the last 600 years, the situation today may seem a little tame. Spices seem to have gradually gone out of favor—no longer do we seek new spice routes or wage war over them. Maybe we have grown used to the less-than-fresh, commercially prepared spices that can be bought in any supermarket. Perhaps it is time to grind a few for ourselves and reawaken our taste buds to the rich aromas and pungent qualities of fresh spices. Or maybe, thanks to the introduction of the refrigerator into virtually every household in

Chilies are native to the Americas.

the Western world, we have so much fresh food that we no longer need spices to mask the taste of less palatable food. Spices, however, are worthy of far more than acting as a cover up—they provide a varied and scintillating range of tastes and experiences.

The current cultivation and distribution of spices is fascinating. Who would have thought that the chilies discovered in Mexico would have been brought to India and incorporated into curries? This has occurred to such an extent that most people today believe that Indian chilies are native to India rather than to the Americas. What is more, who would have thought that Canada would become the world's largest mustard producer?

Spices are no longer regarded as wonders of medicine, but they still play an important part in the manufacture of many cosmetics and perfumes and are grown commercially for their coloring and preservative properties.

Nutmeg is grown on a large scale in Grenada.

Nutmeg and mace are no longer the main crops of the Moluccas, but instead are grown on a large scale on the West Indian island of Grenada.

Cloves, however, still come from Madagascar and Zanzibar—names that are still evocative and romantic and hint strongly of spices.

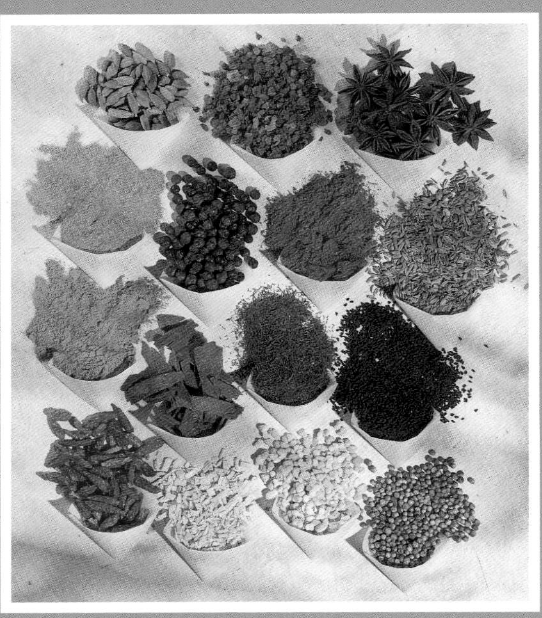

THE SPICE DIRECTORY

Cautionary note:

At all times it is recommended that you consult a health-care professional before embarking on a program of self-treatment. Spices are effective and safe when used in the correct circumstances. This book has been written to educate, and every effort has been made to make the book as accurate and as informative as possible, but the advice contained within is no replacement for professional guidance.

Spices have been in use for as long as humans have been cooking their food and as long as herbal medicine has been around, which may be even longer. There is a myth that spices were originally used to disguise the flavor of rancid or less-than-fresh meat, but there seems to be little truth in this. Our taste buds need stimulation and new experiences—and what could better provide this than the spices gathered together for you in the following pages?

We looked at the history of the spice trade earlier, but perhaps a forgotten essential in the use of spices was the invention of the cooking stove. No longer did humans need to cook everything in one pot; they could use several pans—and this meant variety, experimentation and a vast explosion in the use of spices. As the Spanish explorers returned from the New World, they brought not only gold but also new spices—spices never heard of before—and they spread across Europe quickly. There would have been no need for this if spices were used only to flavor meat on its way to going bad—there were already sufficient spices to do that. They spread because people the world over like their food to have a taste, to deliver a surprise, to be interesting and rich.

Now they are the indispensable ingredients in all types of dishes, adding and enhancing existing flavors while at the same time aiding digestion. They complement almost any type of meal, from salads, casseroles and soups to sweet dishes, cakes, pickles and drinks.

The Spice Directory is a comprehensive photographic reference, in alphabetical order by botanical name. It

A pepper mill can be used to grind spices.

covers both common and lesser-known spices, from ginger, cinnamon and pepper, spices that we're all familiar with, to allspice, elecampane and quassia. The directory shows the many different forms in which the spices are available—fresh, dried or ground, in many cases accompanied by a photographic reference of the spice growing as a plant in its native habitat.

Try all or any of the following spices. One or two may need to be used with some caution—especially the chilies. You can experiment and discard any you do not like, but there will not be many of those. These are the best spices the world has to offer. These are spices to improve the dullest cookery; spices to blend and try; spices to find out about and perhaps use for the first time. Most people have the ubiquitous black pepper mill in the kitchen. Now is the time to go out and buy several more—and grind your own spices in them.

We have included the traditional medicinal uses of spices, but you should refer any ailment or condition to a qualified medical doctor before attempting to treat anything yourself at home. We have also included culinary uses, the history of each spice and its origins. There may even be a recipe or two to delight and surprise you.

Have fun and spice it up a bit.

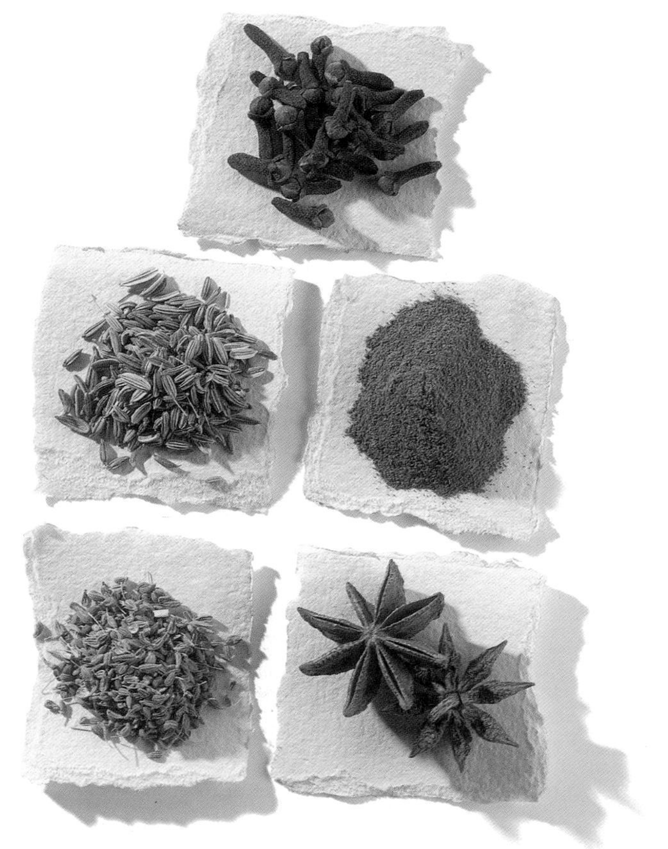

SPICE LIST BY COMMON NAME

Allspice	*Pimento officinalis*	282
Aniseed (Anise)	*Pimpinella anisum*	284
Asafetida	*Ferula assafoetida*	256
Capers	*Capparis spinosa*	224
Capsicum (Sweet peppers)	*Capsicum annuum*	226
Caraway	*Carum carvi*	236
Cardamom	*Elettaria cardamomum*	252
Cassia	*Cinnamomum cassia*	238
Cayenne pepper	*Capsicum longum*	230
Celery	*Apium graveolens*	218
Chilies	*Capsicum frutescens*	228
Cilantro	*Coriandrum sativum*	242
Cinnamon	*Cinnamomum zeylanicum*	240
Cloves	*Eugenia caryophyllus*	254
Coriander	*Coriandrum sativum*	242
Cubeb	*Piper cubeba*	286
Cumin	*Cuminum cyminum*	246
Curry leaf	*Murrya koenigii*	268
Dill	*Anethum graveolens*	216
Elecampane	*Inula helenium*	264
Fennel	*Foeniculum vulgare*	258
Fenugreek	*Trigonella foenum-graecum*	298
Galangal	*Alpinia officinarum*	214
Ginger	*Zingiber officinale*	304
Grains of paradise	*Aframomum melegueta*	210
Horseradish	*Armoracia rusticana*	220
Java galangal	*Alpinia galanga*	212
Juniper	*Juniperus communis*	266
Lemongrass	*Cymbopogon citratus*	250
Licorice	*Glycyrrhiza glabra*	260

GRAINS OF PARADISE

Aframomum melegueta

The western African tree Amomum melegueta *produces orchidlike, trumpet-shaped flowers in a beautiful yellow or pink with a yellow flash, which in turn produce brilliant scarlet fruits. It is from these that we get the tiny brown seeds of grains of paradise, which are a very unusual, almost pyramid-like shape. They are also known as melegueta pepper and Guinea grains. Related to cardamom, this spice was once used in place of pepper when the price of pepper became too high.*

Grains of paradise

ORIGINS & CHARACTERISTICS

Originally from western Africa, grains of paradise are widely used in both African and Caribbean cooking. The tree grows only about 8 feet (2½ m) tall and is related to both ginger and cardamom. Grains of paradise were certainly known and used in ancient Rome as well as medieval Europe as a pepper substitute. In Britain they were banned by King George III (1760–1820), who believed that peppers or any such hot spices were bad for a person's health.

Culinary Uses

Because the flavor of grains of paradise is hot, spicy and aromatic, they can be used to flavor any dishes in which you would traditionally use black pepper. They can be used in a pepper mill to make an unusual condiment. If you are able to buy the whole seeds from a West Indian or African grocery store, you can then grind them yourself.

Medicinal Uses

In western Africa the seeds are used internally for a wide range of ailments including painful menstruation and excessive lactation. The root of the tree is cooked and used as a treatment for infertility. The best-known use for the seeds is as an aphrodisiac—but you will have to try them out yourself to see if they work.

Recipe

Spicy Jarlsberg Bake

There are several species of grains of paradise. *A. angustifolium* is one of them, and you can cook meat with this pepper.

You will need:

- 2 lb (800 g) any meat
- handful of grains of paradise
- 2 cups (500 ml) Jarlsberg cheese
- ⅓ oz (10 g) French mustard
- 1 tsp (2 g) cloves
- ½ cup (125 ml) heavy cream (double cream)

Place the meat in thin slices in a baking tray and sprinkle with ground grains of paradise. Mix the cheese, mustard, cloves and cream and spread over the meat. Bake at 400°F (204°C) for 10 minutes (or until meat is cooked), then grill until golden brown. Serve hot.

JAVA GALANGAL

Alpinia galanga

Galangal originated in China, where it is called Liang-tiang. However, the Java variety, greater galangal is slightly different from lesser galangal (Alpinia officinarum). *It is a much bigger plant, growing 10 feet (3 m) tall, with roots more than 3 feet (1 m) long. Java galangal is cultivated in Indonesia and Malaysia, where it is used in cooking to produce a gingerlike flavor in curries and savory meat dishes. In Indonesia it is known as laos and in Thailand as khaa. In Oriental shops it may be sold under any of these names. It is also known as galingale and Siamese ginger.*

Greater galangal

ORIGINS & CHARACTERISTICS

The rhizomes (underground stems of the plant) are harvested in the autumn and washed and dried before use. Knobbly and very like those of ginger in appearance, they have a pungent taste and smell like roses. They are lifted, cleaned and then processed in a similar way to both ginger and turmeric. The powdered root is then often mixed with other powdered spices.

Rhizomes

Ground galangal can be added to curries.

CULINARY USES

You can add the powdered root to curries and stews. Because it is subtler than lesser galangal (see page 214), it has a more delicate flavor and is suitable for people who prefer a milder curry. It can be used to flavor sausages. The oil can be extracted and used to flavor soft drinks, liqueurs and bitters. The powdered root can be used in any dish in which you might traditionally use fresh ginger.

MEDICINAL USES

Java galangal is a warming digestive and is used as a remedy for diarrhea, gastric upsets and incontinence. In Asia it is used to treat respiratory problems and congestion, and a drink of grated galangal mixed with lime juice is regarded as a tonic in Southeast Asia. The English variety of galangal, *Cyperus longus*, is used, according to the English physician Nicholas Culpeper (1616–1654), for "expelling wind, strengthening the bowels, helping colic, provoking urine and preventing dropsy." It is also said to be good for fainting spells.

RECIPE

Java Galangal Tea

You will need:

- 1 oz (25 g) powdered root
- 2 cups (500 ml) boiling water

To make Java galangal tea, place the powdered root in a pot and add the water. Steep for half an hour, then strain and let cool. Sip 2 tbsp (30 ml) at a time. This is thought to be a good remedy for liver complaints such as hepatitis and cirrhosis and stomach and digestion upsets.

GALANGAL

Alpinia officinarum

This is the strong Chinese variety of galangal. Its taste and effects are much less subtle, and it is a smaller plant than the Java galangal, growing only to around 5 feet (1½ m) tall. It has been an essential ingredient in Chinese herbal medicine since at least 500 A.D. and is also known as lesser galangal and China root. In China it is called sa leung geung, while its Southeast Asian name is kencur.

Ground galangal

ORIGINS & CHARACTERISTICS

The lesser galangal has spikes of wonderful orchidlike white flowers with red streaks. The roots are washed and dried before they are powdered; they are brown on the outside and orange on the inside. Galangal has been known to the West since the time of the crusades, when the knights brought the root back in the thirteenth century. In Tudor and medieval times, it was used extensively in cooking and as an ingredient in perfume, but it fell out of favor by the eighteenth century. Today it is valued in the West only as a medicine, although in China it is still an important ingredient in soups and stews—it is valued for its warming, gingerlike effect.

Culinary Uses

You can add the powdered root of galingal to any savory dish in which you would use fresh ginger—the taste and effect are very similar. It makes a useful substitute if you cannot get fresh ginger.

Medicinal Uses

It is taken internally for chronic gastritis, digestive upsets and gastric ulcerations and to relieve the pain of rheumatism. The powdered root can be used to make a poultice to relieve the itch and irritation of skin infections. A tea thought to relieve the pain of gum disorders and mouth ulcers can be made by adding 1 oz (25 g) to 2 cups (500 ml) of hot water and letting it stand for an hour. A tablespoon at a time can be used as a gargle and mouthwash. This tea can be drunk, a tablespoon at a time, to relieve flatulence and indigestion.

Recipe

Spinach and Galangal Bhaji

You will need:

- 1¾ lb (800 g) cooked spinach
- 1 medium onion
- 4 tbsp (60 ml) butter
- 4 dried red chilies
- 1 tsp (5 ml) cumin seeds
- 2 tsp (10 ml) ground galangal powder
- salt

Chop then fry the onion in the butter and add to the spinach. Then add the chilies, cumin seeds and galangal powder and cook over low heat for 10 minutes. Add salt to taste.

DILL

Anethum graveolens

The name for dill comes from the old Norse word dilla, *which means "to lull"—and dill's mild sedative effect certainly lulls. Dill water, known as gripe water, has been used for centuries to soothe colicky and fretful small babies. It was once, in medieval times, thought to be a magic herb and, as such, was used to combat witchcraft. It was also used in love potions for the same reason. Both the seeds and the leaves are used. Dill was not introduced to the United States commercially until the nineteenth century. Nowadays it is mostly grown in the Northern Hemisphere.*

Dill seed

Dill weed

Origins & Characteristics

Dill is a native of northern Europe and Russia but is now cultivated throughout the world. It is a tall, spindly plant that grows nearly 6½ feet (2 m) tall, with slender stems and fine leaves. The tiny yellow flowers turn into winged seeds at the end of the summer. Both the flowers and seeds are harvested.

Culinary Uses

Dill seeds are strong tasting and warming. They taste similar to caraway, and they can be used to flavor cakes and desserts. You can also use them as a pickling spice for vinegars. The leaves have a less strong flavor and are slightly less bitter. You can add the finely chopped fresh leaves to any fish dishes, salads and sour cream sauces. If you use the leaves in any hot dishes, add them near the end of the cooking time to preserve the flavor.

Medicinal Uses

Dill is rich in sulfur, potassium and sodium and is considered by herbalists to be a completely safe plant. To make gripe water, steep a teaspoon of partly crushed seeds in a glass of hot water for two hours. Strain and add honey for flavor. Make sure it is completely cool before giving it to a baby and give only a teaspoon at a time. Adults are also said to benefit from gripe water if they have upset stomachs because dill is a good aid to digestion; it may also stimulate appetite and help promote milk production in nursing mothers. The seeds can be chewed raw to sweeten the breath and can also act as a digestive aid.

Harvesting & Storage

Pick the fresh leaves at any time to add to your cooking, but to harvest the seeds, pick the flower heads when they are part flower and part seed. Hang the heads upside down in a dry place over a cloth to catch the seeds as they fall. Sow the seeds in a sunny but sheltered garden. Do not plant them near fennel because the two can cross-pollinate.

Dill (Anethum graveolens)

CELERY

Apium graveolens

From the little wild celery known as smallage that grows wild throughout Europe in river estuaries and salt marshes, we get the cultivated celery from Italy that we have known since the seventeenth century. Smallage, once used as a medicine, would taste very bitter to the modern palate, but the Romans found it useful as a flavoring. They also associated it with bad fortune and death and used the leaves in wreaths. The crisp stems and leaves of cultivated celery can be used in salads and cooked with meat stews and casseroles, but the seeds of the wild celery are used as a spice. They are warming and aromatic but quite bitter.

Celery stalks

ORIGINS & CHARACTERISTICS

Seeds from the wild celery have been found in the tomb of Tutankhamen, and Culpeper says that the seed "helps the dropsy and jaundice and removes female obstructions" and that the leaves are of the same nature and "eaten in the spring sweeten and purify the blood and help the scurvy."

Celery salt

Culinary Uses

The seeds of the wild celery are quite strong and bitter, so you need very small quantities. They can be used whole to flavor soups and stews or ground and mixed with salt and used as a condiment. To make a warming and spicy tea, grind ½ tsp (2½ ml) of seeds and add to 1 cup (250 ml) of hot water. Allow to stand for 10 minutes and drink it while it's still warm. The juice of cultivated celery stalk can be extracted in a food processor and drunk cool. Celery salt, a salt-based seasoning flavored with the essential oil, is more widely available but soon develops a stale taste.

Medicinal Uses

A poultice for external use can be made from celery leaves to relieve fungal infections, and the seeds taken internally in small quantities are said to be good for relieving gout, arthritis and inflammation of the urinary tract. Eating the seeds of raw cultivated celery, either by chewing or swallowing them whole, is said to lower blood pressure, to stimulate digestion and to treat rheumatism.

Growing

To grow your own wild or cultivated celery, plant the seeds in rich, damp soil in a sunny but sheltered position in the spring. The plants do not like frost and will not flower until their second year. Once they have flowered, they will produce seeds readily. The stems of the cultivated celery are best picked and used in the autumn, traditionally after the first frost.

Caution

The seeds sold for cultivation should not be used for medicinal purposes because they may well have been treated with fungicides.

Celery (Apium graveolens)

HORSERADISH

Armoracia rusticana

Horseradish originated in eastern Europe and is a good kitchen garden plant because its root can be used in a variety of ways to season food. It does need to be contained, however, as it spreads rapidly and, once established, can be a nightmare to eradicate. The root has an extremely powerful flavor. It is used to make the well-known horseradish sauce, in which the combination of ingredients brings out the root's qualities to the best advantage. A homemade sauce is much more flavorful than the commercial variety.

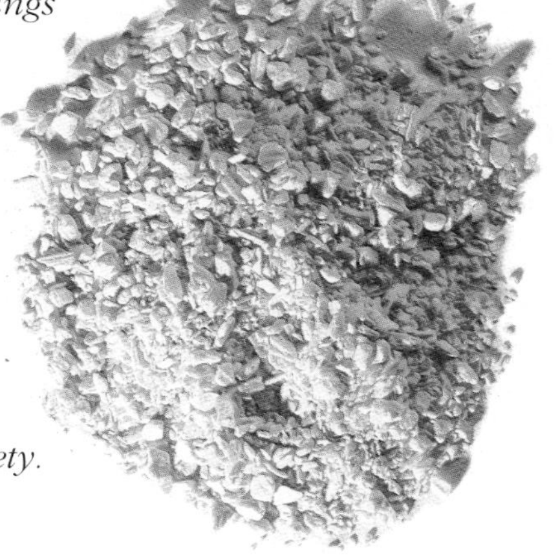

Ground horseradish

Origins & Characteristics

Horseradish is a perennial, dark green plant with white flowers. The young leaves can be used for flavoring, but it is the root that most people associate with horseradish. The root has to be dug up fresh because it does not store or keep well.

Horseradish sauce

Culinary Uses

The fresh root has a strong eye-watering pungency (overpowering for some people) and a powerful and stimulating flavor. The fresh root should be grated—carefully to prevent any juice from getting into the eyes—and then added to cream and vinegar to make a sauce that can be used to add zest to fish and, traditionally, roast beef. It makes a good accompaniment to hard-boiled eggs and smoked mackerel. You can make the root a little milder by adding apple to it when you are grating it. You can warm the sauce, but do so very gently because too much heat destroys the oils that give it its pungency.

Medicinal Uses

Horseradish is a diuretic, which increases urinary flow. It increases perspiration as well, which can be good for some fevers, and it can be made into a poultice to be used externally for wound infections, arthritis and pleurisy. The considerable warming effect of horseradish can cause skin irritation in certain circumstances, and if too much is taken internally, it can cause vomiting and may provoke allergic reactions. Taken internally, it can relieve gout and arthritis as well as urinary and respiratory infections. It should not be given to anyone with stomach ulcers or thyroid problems.

Horseradish (Armoracia rusticana)

MUSTARD

B. nigra, B. juncea, B. hirta

There are so many varieties of mustard and so much can be made from this one plant that cooks may not need any other kitchen spices. Brassica nigra *is the black mustard, now only grown in peasant economies, which has been replaced in large-scale farming by* B. juncea, *brown mustard. Indian mustard is similar to black mustard—it is also brown and is known as brown mustard. In medieval times mustard was the only spice that the general populace could afford. Mustard has given us some interesting language—"as keen as mustard," "cutting the mustard" and, from the Bible, "The kingdom of heaven is like to a grain of mustard seed."*

Black mustard seeds

Brown mustard seeds

Origins & Characteristics

Mustard has been grown for so long that its origins are lost, but it probably came from the eastern Mediterranean, where it grows as a weed and is used for feeding horses. It is a spindly plant that grows around 3 feet (1 m) tall, with bright yellow flowers. The seeds are usually brown or reddish. Real mustard was originally made with fresh grape juice, or the must, from the Latin word *mustum*, hence its name.

Mustard in vinaigrette dressing

Culinary Uses

The young leaves can be cooked as a vegetable, and the flowers can be added to summer salads. The seeds are ground and used as a fiery spice for making mustard, which accompanies many dishes from cold meats to cheeses and is used in sauces for hot dishes. It is also used in vinaigrette dressing. You can use it to add a certain piquancy to sauces for macaroni or baked cauliflower with cheese. Dry mustard powder releases its pungency when it comes into contact with cold liquid. If you use hot liquids, the pungency is reduced or even eliminated altogether—so always make your mustard with cold water. The whole seeds can be used for especially hot curries and for pickling. (See page 340 for additional information—Cutting the Mustard.)

Medicinal Uses

Traditional mustard plasters were applied as poultices to relieve rheumatism, muscular pain and chilblains. You can soak your feet by wrapping the plaster, soaked in mustard, around them to ease aches and strains. Mustard plasters may also provide relief for headaches and colds. Remember to use cold water to maximize the heating effect.

Mustard (Brassica nigra) *in flower*

Caution

People with sensitive skin should take care when using mustard plasters because they can cause blistering. In large doses mustard causes vomiting.

CAPERS

Capparis spinosa

In southern Europe the pickled caper has been used as a condiment for at least the last 2,000 years. The characteristic flavor comes from the capric acid that develops when the flower buds are pickled in vinegar. Capers are used widely in North African cooking as well as in cooking throughout the whole of the Mediterranean—they are especially loved in Sardinia. Increasingly used in the West, they can make a surprising and useful addition to salads or be used as pizza toppings.

Capers

The flower of Capparis spinosa

ORIGINS & CHARACTERISTICS Capers grow wild throughout the Mediterranean, where they are regarded as weeds. The plant has thick, shiny leaves and short-lived flowers that have purple stamens and fringed white petals streaked with pale pink. It is a beautiful plant and can be grown in temperate climates if it is grown under glass in well-drained soil.

Culinary Uses

The whole pickled caper buds are used in casseroles, stews and lamb dishes as well as in ravigote, tartar and remoulade sauces. They are a good complement to any oily fish and are especially good eaten with salty foods such as salted meat or fish. Capers add an unexpected but refreshing taste to food. They can be added to parsley and sprinkled over beef. They are an essential ingredient in tapenade, which is an olive paste made in the Mediterranean, and in caponata, which is a Sardinian salad of eggplants and tuna.

Capers are an essential ingredient in tapenade

Medicinal Uses

Capers can increase digestion and appetite and induce a general feeling of well-being and vitality. They are thought to be good for gastrointestinal infections and diarrhea. The flower buds can be infused in a tea to ease coughs.

Storage

Capers should be kept in a tightly lidded glass jar. Always make sure that they are kept immersed in the vinegar in which they were pickled; otherwise, they will dry out and lose their flavor. It is also best to keep them stored in a dark place.

Recipe

Caper Sauce

You will need:

- 1 tbsp each flour and butter
- 1 cup (250 ml) milk
- 1 tbsp (15 ml) chopped capers
- 1 tsp (5 ml) vinegar in which capers were pickled

Melt the butter in a small saucepan and gradually beat in the flour with a wooden spoon. Add the milk little by little, stirring all the time until the sauce is of a medium thick consistency. Then add capers and vinegar.

CAPSICUM (SWEET PEPPERS)

Capsicum annuum

Like chilies, these too are named from the Latin word capsa, *meaning "box," and a pepper is a "box" of seeds. They are milder and more flavorful than chilies and can be eaten raw without any ill effects or burning sensations. They are fresh and juicy with a clear tangy texture and are also known as pimentos.*

Sweet peppers

ORIGINS & CHARACTERISTICS

Sweet peppers are originally from tropical America but are now cultivated the world over in warm climates. They grow on bushes about 3 feet (1 m) tall, with white flowers. The fruits start off green and slowly turn red or yellow as they mature, but the green, immature ones can be used in the same manner as the red or yellow ones.

Culinary Uses

Sweet peppers can be sliced and added raw to salads or used as a salad vegetable on their own. They can be sliced and fried to add to meat sauces. The seeds should be removed before using. The dried and ground flesh of sweet peppers is made into paprika (see page 232). Before cooking sweet peppers, check them for freshness because they go bad easily. Feel for any soft spots and notice any patches of black or brown discoloration. Peppers are excellent pickled or in chutneys and are one of the main ingredients, along with zucchini and eggplant, in French ratatouille (eggplant, zucchini, peppers, tomatoes, etc. cooked in olive oil). The red peppers are sweetest, and the green ones can be quite bitter. You can blanch them for two or three minutes before using to improve the flavor. Peppers can be grilled until they blister and then eaten as a side dish.

Sweet peppers
(Capsicum annuum)

Medicinal Uses

Sweet peppers contain large amounts of vitamin C, so they are very good for you. They also have revitalizing and antiseptic qualities and are used to stimulate the digestive system.

Recipe

Andalusian Gazpacho

You will need:

- 4 green peppers
- 4 large tomatoes
- ½ seedless cucumber
- 5 oz (150 g) white bread crumbs
- 1 cup (250 ml) olive oil
- 4 cups (1 l) water
- salt and black pepper
- 2 garlic cloves, crushed
- 1 tsp (5 ml) white wine vinegar

Finely chop the peppers, tomatoes and cucumber. Add to the bread crumbs with a large helping of olive oil. Leave for one hour in water. Put through a food processor or blender. Add salt and pepper to taste. Add the garlic to the vinegar, and pour over the mixture and refrigerate until well chilled. Serve cold.

CHILIES

Capsicum frutescens

Although related to sweet peppers, there is a considerable difference—mainly the heat. The Latin word capsa *means "box," and a chili is a "box" of seeds. Chilies range in color from red to purple, cream, yellow, green and even black. There is an old saying that the smaller they are, the hotter they are, but be careful—some of the larger ones are really very hot indeed.*

Chilies come in a wide variety of colors.

ORIGINS & CHARACTERISTICS

Chilies were brought to Europe by Spanish explorers returning from South America and are now cultivated throughout the world. There is evidence that they have been grown and used in Central and South America for at least 9,000 years. They can be grown in temperate climates, but they need artificial heat. They grow 6½ feet (2 m) tall, with tiny slender fruits that, when dried, are used as the main ingredient in cayenne pepper and Tabasco sauce. The fresh fruit itself is used in Mexican cooking; generally the seeds are taken out before use. Chilies are best used fresh.

Dried, crushed chilies

Dried bird's eye chilies

A selection of chili relishes

Culinary Uses

Fresh chilies are used in guacamole, mole poblano and Yucatan soup. They can be grilled until the flesh begins to smoke and blister and then eaten hot—but caution should be used because the fumes can be an irritant. Chilies should be washed under cold water to reduce their fieriness. Indian chilies are used in curries to give them that extra hot quality. Chili powder is cayenne powder (a blend of small, ripe chilies of various origins) mixed with cumin and marjoram or garlic.

Medicinal Uses

Chilies are used to revive the body, and they are said to help digestion and have a strong stimulant effect. They are warming for colds and chills, and they have good antibacterial properties.

Chili peppers are the fruit of Capsicum frutescens.

Caution

Chilies are a very powerful eye and skin irritant—use thin rubber gloves whenever you are handling them fresh. If any of the juice gets on your skin, wash it off immediately with large amounts of cold milk or soap and water. If it should get in your eyes, flush them with generous amounts of cool water. Taken in excess, chilies cause damage to the mucous membranes, as well as digestive and renal problems.

CAYENNE PEPPER

Capsicum longum

If you dry fresh chilies and grind them up, you have the makings of cayenne pepper—from which you can make hot sauce and chili powder. Also known as lal mirch in India and pisihui in Southeast Asia, cayenne is also added to ointments for the treatment of neuralgia, chilblains and lumbago. This is because the chilies contain capsaicin, which is a chemical found to increase blood circulation on contact. As their name suggests, Capsicum longum *are long and thin and very hot.*

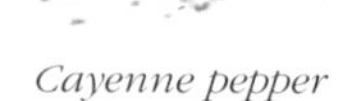
Cayenne pepper

Origins & Characteristics

The usual story told about cayenne pepper is that it was used by the cooks of chuck wagons on the cattle drives across the Texas plains to flavor some pretty unsavory meats—such as rattlesnake. A lot of the cooks sowed seeds of various plants along the cattle trails so that they could have fresh herbs and spices in later years. This is why there has been such a spread of spices growing wild in the United States. Some of these may well have originally not been native plants.

Culinary Uses

Cayenne pepper is used in hot dishes such as chile con carne. Cayenne can be added to any savory meat dishes in which you want to add heat without necessarily adding extra flavor. You can also add the merest pinch to cheese sauces and spicy mayonnaise (instead of mustard) to give them added color.

Medicinal Uses

You can infuse cayenne to make a hot, fiery tea thought to stimulate the appetite, relieve stomach and bowel pains and ease cramps. A poultice of cayenne is said to relieve rheumatism and lumbago.

Recipe

Chile con Carne

You will need:

- 14 oz (400 g) kidney beans
- 1 small onion
- ⅓ oz (10 g) butter
- 1 garlic clove, crushed
- 1¾ lb (750 g) ground beef (minced beef)
- 8 oz (200 g) chopped tomatoes
- 2 tsp (10 ml) cayenne

Whether chile con carne should have beans in it and whether it can include cayenne or only fresh chilies, is debatable, but you can decide which you prefer. Soak the kidney beans overnight and then rinse and boil for 10 minutes; rinse again and boil in salted water until tender, drain and let cool. Chop the onion and fry in the butter and garlic. Add the ground beef and fry together until the beef is browned. Add the tomatoes, kidney beans, cayenne pepper and salt and black pepper to taste. Let simmer for two hours until very thick.

Caution

A poultice of cayenne may cause a reaction in people with sensitive skin.

PAPRIKA

Capsicum tetragonum

Paprika is made from sweet peppers that have been dried and ground. Ideally only the dried fruit should be used. It has more flavor—lightly pungent and rather sweet—and a lot less heat than cayenne pepper. Instantly recognizable by its bright red color, paprika is the traditional ingredient in Hungarian goulash and in many other dishes from that country. It makes a colorful addition to a wide variety of food including meat, vegetables and barbeque spice mixtures. It is also used as an ingredient in Cajun seasoning.

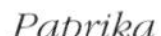

Paprika

ORIGINS & CHARACTERISTICS

Although most people consider Hungary as the natural place for paprika to have originated, it was actually introduced there by the Turks. "Paprika" is, however, a Hungarian word, and paprika is the national spice of Hungary, where it is treated with almost religious fervor. It is made only from red sweet peppers, and most paprika outside of Hungary has little in the way of hotness. Its bitterness depends on how much seed is used—ideally only the dried fruit should be used to make good paprika, and the lighter in color the red peppers, the hotter the spice.

Paprika is used to color many dishes.

Culinary Uses

Paprika is used throughout Europe, especially in Portugal and Spain, but the Hungarians use paprika the most—to flavor and color many dishes including soups, vegetables, chicken, fish and meat. But it is mostly known throughout the world as the key ingredient in Hungarian goulash, a beef stew. Paprika doesn't keep very well, so it should be bought in small quantities. You can also use it to garnish canapés and in sauces for shellfish and shrimp. It also makes an excellent sauce to serve with lobster or crab.

Medicinal Uses

It was in 1926 that a Hungarian chemist by the name of Szent Gyorgi first isolated vitamin C—from paprika. It is ironic to think of the sailors on the spice routes getting scurvy, which is caused by a lack of vitamin C, when they had access to fresh peppers all the time. Paprika has warming qualities that are thought to make it effective against cold symptoms, and paprika is a rich and valuable source of vitamin C and, as such, appears to be the perfect antidote to winter.

SAFFLOWER

Carthamus tinctorius

Because it is often called bastard saffron, you might think that safflower is the poor relation of saffron, but in reality it is an important spice in its own right. However, the more unscrupulous traders will try to sell it as saffron. It has a slightly duller color than saffron and is more orange—in fact this is the spice that produces the bright orange dye used for Buddhists' robes—they really ought to be called safflower robes. The flowers produce a yellow dye if they are processed in water and a red dye if alcohol is used. Safflower will add color to food but won't flavor it.

Safflower

ORIGINS & CHARACTERISTICS

Safflower has been cultivated for so long that it is impossible to say exactly where it originated. It has been found in Egyptian tombs dating back to at least 3500 B.C. and has been used in traditional Chinese herbal medicine for a very long time. The flowers are a bright orange-yellow and are used for making tea and as a saffron substitute. The oil processed from the seeds is used as a cooking oil, and the seeds themselves can be ground and used as a spice.

Culinary Uses

The oil made from safflower is low in cholesterol, so it is very good for anyone on a low-cholesterol diet. You can use the flowers in any recipe in which you would use saffron—they have a slightly more bitter taste but are considerably less expensive.

Safflower tea has many benefits.

Medicinal Uses

The flower petals can be infused to make a tea that is said to be good as a laxative and to induce perspiration and reduce fevers. Safflower taken as a tea is also good for coronary artery disease and menopausal and menstruation problems, although it should not be given to pregnant women. It may help to reduce the symptoms of jaundice and measles. A poultice made from the flowers is used for reducing skin inflammation and for easing bruises and sprains. Applied externally the flowers are also said to relieve painful and swollen joints.

> **Caution**
> Avoid saffron if you are pregnant.

Storage

The flowers only keep for about a year, so they should be used when they are fairly fresh for the best benefit. They will add a gorgeous color to potpourri, earning their keep despite their lack of aroma.

> Recipe
>
> **Safflower Tea**
>
> You will need:
> - 1 tsp (5 ml) safflower flowers
> - 1 cup (250 ml) hot water
>
> For an infusion, steep the flowers in the water. Taken hot, it may induce perspiration. Taken cool, it is said to soothe hysteria.

CARAWAY

Carum carvi

You may not think that such a small, nondescript plant could have so many uses or could be so highly prized as a charm against witchcraft and demons. It was also once believed that anything containing caraway could not be stolen, so it was fed to pigeons to stop them from straying. Caraway was also believed to cure venomous serpent bites, prevent hair loss and restore eyesight. It was thought that if a wife placed a few of the seeds in her husband's pockets, he could not have his heart stolen away.

Caraway seed

Caraway (Carum carvi)

ORIGINS & CHARACTERISTICS
Caraway grows wild throughout Europe and Asia and has now been naturalized in the United States and Canada. It is cultivated in the Netherlands and Russia on a large scale. It grows only about 8 inches (20 cm) tall, with white or pink flowers.

Culinary Uses

The leaves can be eaten fresh in salads or added chopped to freshly cooked vegetables. You can add the chopped leaves to cream sauces for a warming, mild flavor not unlike parsley. The leaves and stems can be cooked in stews and soups. If the flowers are picked off early enough, the tap roots will grow larger and can be cooked as a vegetable—they taste like parsnips. The seeds are used to flavor caraway candy, and the oil of the caraway is used to make liqueurs such as kummel. The ground seeds are used in curry powder as well as in flavoring for cakes, breads and biscuits. Caraway is very popular in German and Scandinavian cooking. The gently fried seeds can be eaten with apples or cheese. The seeds are even dipped in sugar and eaten as a confection known as sugar plums.

Medicinal Uses

The seeds are chewed for immediate relief of indigestion and colic as well as menstrual pains and cramps. The leaves are used to make a tea that may reduce intestinal and uterine spasms as well as relieve gas and indigestion.

Recipe

Satay Sauce

You will need:

- 1 medium onion, chopped
- 2 cups (200 g) roasted peanuts
- 3 garlic cloves, crushed
- 1 tsp (5 ml) caraway seeds
- 4 tsp (20 ml) coriander seeds
- 3 tsp (15 ml) turmeric
- ½ tsp (2½ ml) cayenne pepper
- 2¾ cups (250 g) coconut flakes
- 2 tbsp (30 ml) soy sauce

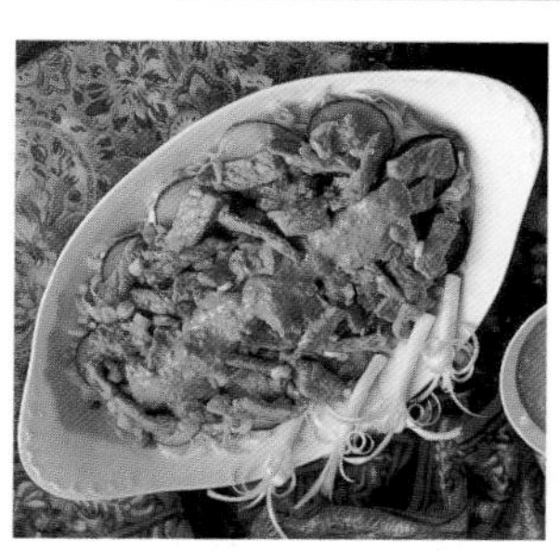

- 1 tsp (5 ml) honey
- 2 cups (½ l) water

Blend everything; simmer until it thickens. Let stand for half an hour before using as a dip or to marinate meat.

CASSIA

Cinnamomum cassia

The bark of cassia, also known as Chinese cinnamon, is a form of cinnamon. Indeed, in the United States, it is used and sold simply as "cinnamon," and in many countries, cassia and cinnamon are used interchangeably. They are closely related, but their taste does differ, cassia being less delicate. It is one of the oldest spices used as a medicine. It was first used in China in 2700 B.C. and in Egypt in 1600 B.C. In Chinese herbal medicine it is known as gui zhi. It is native to Assam and northern Burma.

Cassia bark

ORIGINS & CHARACTERISTICS

Cassia grows in most Asian countries, and the bark is dried in quills for powdering and for using in infusions and tinctures. The twigs and leaves are distilled for their oil—cassia oil contains around 85 percent cinnamaldehyde, which is an important product in the pharmaceutical and food industry. It is also used in the manufacture of cosmetics. The buds are harvested and dried for use as a flavoring in the food industry—they look like cloves.

Culinary Uses

In the United States cassia is used as a sweet spice for flavoring cakes and pastries, while in Asia it is used as a flavoring for curries and savory meat dishes. It is one of the five ingredients in Chinese five-spice (the others being anise, star anise, cloves and fennel seeds). This mixture is used to flavor roasted meats, poultry and marinades. The predominant flavor, however, is star anise.

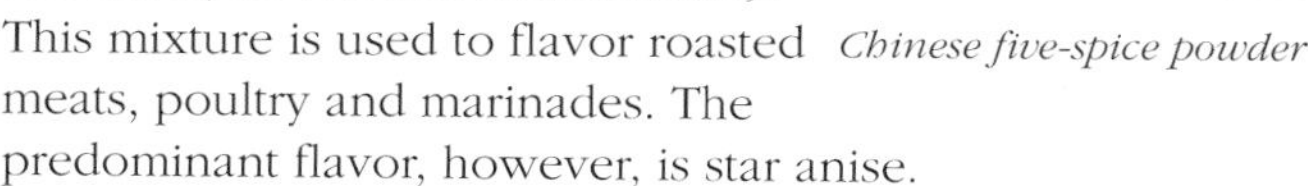

Chinese five-spice powder

Medicinal Uses

In Chinese herbal medicine *gui zhi* is used to treat diarrhea, poor appetite, coldness, rheumatism, angina, palpitations and digestive complaints. In the West cassia is a major ingredient in cold remedies, and it is also used to treat dyspepsia, flatulence and colic.

Other Uses

Making a potpourri mixture

Cassia is sometimes regarded as a poor substitute for cinnamon. However, it has a stronger taste than cinnamon, and some people find that it tastes sweeter and prefer it to flavor mulled wine and sweets. The flowers and dried bark can be used in potpourri. In America cassia is called cinnamon, and in France both barks are known by only one name—*cannelle.* Cassia is much thicker and rougher than true cinnamon and often comes in unrolled lumps, whereas cinnamon usually comes in sticks.

CINNAMON

Cinnamomum zeylanicum

Since ancient times the fragrant, dried inner bark of the cinnamon tree has been a valued spice. The Phoenician traders probably brought it to the Middle East, where it has been used as a perfume since Old Testament times—Moses used it as an ingredient in the anointing oil in the tabernacle. Since the ninth century it has been widely used in Europe, and most of the cinnamon that is used today comes from Sri Lanka.

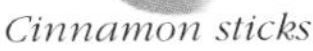

Cinnamon sticks

ORIGINS & CHARACTERISTICS

In its native habitat this bushy evergreen tree can grow very tall indeed. The deeply veined fragrant leaves are long and dark green with lighter undersides. The flowers are yellow and small and turn into dark purple berries. The bark is the part that is used. Cinnamon can be cultivated from seed or by taking cuttings from a plant. The shoots are cut back every two to three years, and the bark is peeled off and left to dry for a day. The outer bark is stripped away, and the inner bark rolls itself into tight sticks as it dries.

Ground cinnamon

Culinary Uses

For spicing hot drinks such as punch and mulled wine, whole cinnamon sticks are used. They can be used with stewed or fresh fruit and fruit punches. You can use the sticks to stir the flavor of cinnamon into other hot drinks.

Medicinal Uses

Cinnamon is a strong stimulant for the glandular system and is used to relieve stomach upset. It is very warming, so it is good for relieving the symptoms of colds, flu and sore throats.

Cinnamomum zeylanicum *grows very tall.*

Storage

Cinnamon is best when bought in sticks, but it can also be bought ground. Ground cinnamon actually tastes stronger, but it should be kept stored in screw-topped glass jars because it loses its smell fairly quickly. The highest quality cinnamon is made from the thinnest bark, which has the best taste and fragrance.

CORIANDER

Coriandrum sativum

Cilantro is a small annual herb that grows wild throughout the Mediterranean. The name cilantro is used to refer to the leaves of the plant, and coriander, the spice, refers to the seeds. It was introduced to China around 600 a.d. and called hu, *meaning "foreign." It is now cultivated in most parts of the world, including the United States, as an important ingredient in the food industry because it is high in linalol (70 percent), which is used as a flavoring for vegetables, pickles, seasonings and curries. The name coriander comes from the Greek word* koros, *meaning "bug" or "insect," because the fruit has an unpleasant fetid smell before it has ripened.*

Cilantro

ORIGINS & CHARACTERISTICS
Cilantro grows well in any well-drained soil as long as it is sunny. It grows about 2 feet (70 cm) tall with delicate pink and white flowers. It will bolt if left to dry at the seedling stage. Cilantro grown in warmer climates has much larger fruit than that grown in more moderate regions.

Ground coriander

Culinary Uses

In the Middle East and Asia, especially China, the leaves are used to flavor savory dishes and the seeds are used as a pickling spice. In Thailand the root is cooked with garlic. The whole seeds can be used in cooking fish as well as in breads and cakes. The ground seeds can be added to sausages to give them more flavor, to curries and to roasted meat. In India the seeds are usually lightly toasted before they are ground. The seeds are slightly sweet and have a citruslike taste.

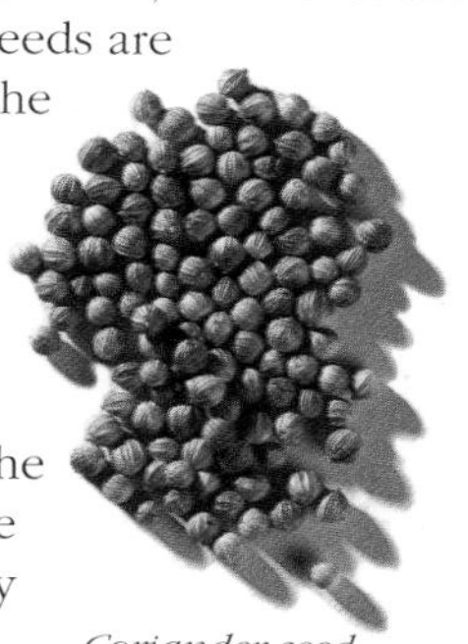
Coriander seed

Medicinal Uses

Cilantro leaves are used as a remedy for minor digestive problems, and the seeds can reduce the painful stomach spasm effect of some laxatives. Coriander ointment is used externally to relieve the symptoms of hemorrhoids and painful joints. It also stimulates the appetite and is a mild stomach relaxant.

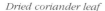

Dried coriander leaf

Cosmetic Uses

A good aftershave can be made by infusing coriander seed in alcohol and adding some honey and orange-flower water. If the seeds are harvested in late summer and dried before they are used, the perfume is drawn out. The longer the seeds are kept, the better the scent.

Coriander (Coriandrum sativum)

SAFFRON

Crocus sativus

At times in its history, saffron has been more expensive than gold, and it still is the most expensive spice in the world. It has the same color as well—a deep, dark orange-gold. The slender stigmas of the plant are very light and are handpicked, which accounts for saffron's high value. Luckily very little of the spice is needed to impart its wonderful, slightly bitter taste to cooking.

Saffron

Origins & Characteristics

Saffron is made from the dried stigmas of a blue-flowered crocus, which are handpicked in their native Turkey. The plants also grow in surrounding countries, and the very best saffron is said to come from Valencia. A lot of stigmas (around 200–500) are needed to make a tiny amount (1 g) of saffron; that is why it is so expensive.

Purchased saffron comes in two varieties—threads and ground. Ideally you should purchase threads because any artificial dying or coloring is easier to spot in threads. Safflower stigmas are often passed off as saffron, but they are redder in color and don't have the same taste. Turmeric is also sold as saffron, but it is easy to spot because it has quite a different color and taste.

Culinary Uses

Saffron has been used to both flavor and color food since ancient times. It is an essential ingredient in paella, bouillabaisse and risotto Milanese, and, of course, saffron cakes. You can use saffron in a variety of dishes. It flavors shellfish and fish well, and it is a useful ingredient in sauces and rice. Saffron threads should be broken up and infused in a little hot water; the strained liquid should then be added to the dish according to the recipe instructions. You can dry the threads in the oven first and then crumble them into the recipe. The threads should be dark orange with no white streaks. Ground saffron should also be infused before it is used. A mere pinch is enough to flavor rice for four people.

Saffron makes an effective dye.

Medicinal Uses

You can infuse saffron to make an herbal tea that is taken as a warming, soothing drink to clear the head. It is also believed to shake off drowsiness and bring on menstruation.

Other Uses

Saffron is also highly effective as a dye. Just a small amount will turn cloth a beautiful light gold color.

Caution

Make sure only the stigmas from *Crocus sativus* are used—the unrelated plant, the autumn crocus, *Colchicum autumnale*, is very similar but poisonous.

The flower of Crocus sativus

CUMIN

Cuminum cyminum

Cumin is a native of the Middle East. It is grown for its seedlike fruit, which is a pungent and aromatic spice slightly similar to caraway. It is mentioned often in the Bible and is a staunch favorite in Greek, Turkish and Arab cooking. The ancient Romans used cumin as a condiment much like we would use black pepper today, but it is probably best known for its role in Indian cuisine—especially curries and chicken roasted in a tandoor *(clay oven).*

Cumin seed

Origins & Characteristics

Cumin will grow in any warm, sunny position in rich, well-drained sandy loam. It grows about 2 feet (60 cm) tall, with very slender stems and tiny pink or white flowers. Indian cumin comes in two varieties—white (*safed*) and black (*kala*). The black cumin has a more subtle flavor but is somewhat expensive and hard to come by outside of India. The fruits are picked before they are fully ripe and left to dry—these are then used ground or whole.

Ground cumin

CULINARY USES

Cumin is used in the spice blend garam masala and is an important ingredient of couscous (cracked wheat steamed and served with meat, vegetables, chickpeas and raisins), which is made throughout the Middle East and North Africa. Cumin is used to flavor meats and cheeses—such as Dutch Edam and the German Muenster. In the Middle East the seeds are often roasted and added to lamb dishes as well as to side dishes of cucumber and yogurt.

MEDICINAL USES

Cumin is taken internally for minor digestive disorders; it is believed to settle stomach upsets that cause migraines. It is a warming appetizer stimulant.

STORAGE

Ground cumin doesn't store well, so it should be bought in small quantities. Whole seeds are difficult to grind with a mortar, so buy both whole seeds and the ground powder.

RECIPE

Spicy Drink with Cumin

A digestive drink is made in India by mixing mint, ginger, salt, sugar, tamarind water and lemon juice with ground cumin. You will need:

- sprig of mint
- pinch of ginger
- pinch of salt
- 1 cup (250 ml) tamarind water
- lemon juice
- sugar
- ground cumin

Mix ginger, cumin and salt into the tamarind water. Add the lemon juice and sugar to taste. Garnish with the mint.

TURMERIC

Curcuma longa

Turmeric is a relative of ginger and, like ginger, the spice is obtained from the roots, which are a brilliant orange, and harvested and processed in the same way as ginger. However, turmeric is always traded whole and ground in the consuming country. The roots are boiled, dried, peeled and then ground to produce the bright yellow spice that is used to flavor curries and color mustards, butter, cheeses, drinks and pickles.

Root turmeric

ORIGINS & CHARACTERISTICS

Turmeric grows about 2 feet (50 cm) tall, with large broad leaves and yellow flowers. It is a native of India, but it is now cultivated throughout the world, especially in China, Java, Peru—and India, of course—where some 12,000 tons of it are produced annually. Most of this is exported.

Ground turmeric

Culinary Uses

Turmeric is one of the principal ingredients of curry powder. Although its very strong color is its main attraction, it does have a distinctive taste—like a mild curry flavor, slightly bitter but fragrant. Turmeric is often added to cooking rice to color it a delicate yellow—rice pilaf. Its name comes from the Arabic word *kurkum*, which means "saffron," but the two should not be confused. Saffron is much more expensive and has a different flavor altogether. Turmeric is the flavoring used for Worcestershire sauce as well as the mustard relish piccalilli.

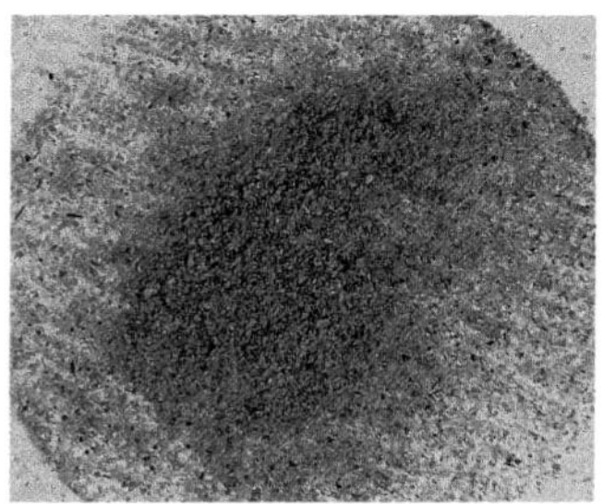

Turmeric is an important ingredient in curry powder.

Medicinal Uses

Taken internally turmeric is thought to be good for digestive upsets and skin disorders. It is said to improve poor circulation and ease menstrual problems and is used in Indian herbal medicine for treating liver disorders, uterine tumors and jaundice. It is a strong stimulant of the digestive and respiratory systems and also has anti-inflammatory and antiseptic properties. Externally it can be applied in a poultice to sores and wounds and can be used for ringworm.

Turmeric (Curcuma longa)

Storage

Turmeric is almost always sold as a ground powder because the root is very hard to grind. Only small quantities should be bought because it loses its flavor, but not its color, very quickly.

LEMONGRASS

Cymbopogon citratus

Although lemongrass is a relatively new spice to the West, it should now be available in most supermarkets. Oriental stores sell both fresh and dry lemongrass, sometimes under the Indonesian name "sereh." Its rich lemony flavor and fragrance make it a tangy, spicy addition to many foods. It is a principal ingredient in Thai, Malaysian and Indonesian cooking and curries.

Lemongrass stalks

Origins & Characteristics

Lemongrass comes from Southeast Asia and is a tender perennial tropical grass, which can grow nearly 6 feet (2 m) tall. It is densely tufted with long, thin leaves that, when crushed, are extremely fragrant—this is what gives it its name. The flowers are greenish with a red tinge, and they appear in clusters in the summer. You could try growing it yourself—it needs a temperature of at least 55°F (13°C), so that may mean a greenhouse. The leaves, when crushed, add a delightful fragrance to soaps and perfumes.

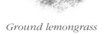

Ground lemongrass

Culinary Uses

The tender stalks can be chopped, and the leaves, once peeled, can be used in the same way as scallions to flavor stews, casseroles and curries. It should be finely chopped and added just before serving. The base of the leaves is used in sereh, which is a currylike powder used in Southeast Asian cooking, especially with fish and meat. You can make an infusion of the dried leaves to be drunk as an herbal tea. And the finely chopped fresh leaves can be floated on summer drinks.

Cosmetic Uses

Lemongrass is used extensively in the manufacture of oils used in making scented soaps because it contains a semidrying property that is excellent for cleansing oily skin.

Lemongrass is used in scented soaps.

Storage

The essential oil (citral) loses its effectiveness if it is stored in the light, so it should be kept in a dark cupboard. It will not store for very long, so it should be bought and used fresh.

Medicinal Uses

Lemongrass is taken internally as a digestive aid for small children and is also used for mild feverish complaints. It is a valuable insecticide and works well externally as a remedy against ringworm, scabies and lice. It is also believed to be an effective treatment for athlete's foot.

Lemongrass
(Cymbopogon citratus)

CARDAMOM

Elettaria cardamomum

There are several varieties of cardamom, each related to ginger and each having a slightly different flavor, but the most common and widely used variety is grown in southern India. Cardamom is both one of the oldest and also highly valued spices in the world—it is the most expensive spice after saffron and vanilla. The Normans brought cardamom to Britain in the eleventh century, and it was very popular in medieval and Tudor recipes. Cardamom is mainly used to flavor curries.

Dried cardamom pods

Origins & Characteristics

The best cardamom comes from the rain forests of Malabar, where it grows as a shrub about 6 feet (2 m) tall, with blue-streaked flowers with yellow tips, and it grows wild throughout India in the tropical mountain forests. It is cultivated in Sri Lanka and Thailand as well as in Central America.

Brown cardamoms

CULINARY USES

In addition to its use in curries, cardamom is used to flavor sausages, breads, cakes and pastries. In the Arab world it is added to coffee as a sign of hospitality because it is one of the most expensive spices—there is also some evidence that it reduces or eliminates the effect of the caffeine in coffee. In northern Europe, especially the Scandinavian countries, it is used mostly as a flavoring for breads and cakes and as a pickling spice, while in Asia it is used as a hot spice for curries, and the whole pods are used as a vegetable. Cardamom is used in India to flavor pilau and curries.

Ground cardamom

STORAGE

Cardamom loses its flavor very quickly, so only very small quantities should be bought. When it is fresh or freshly ground it has a eucalyptus aroma that quickly fades—that is how you can tell if it is fresh. If you buy ground cardamom and it smells of camphor you have been sold a cheap substitute. It is best to buy the whole pods and grind them yourself rather than to buy it already ground (it loses its flavor so quickly when ground that it will already have deteriorated before it can be sold).

The flowers of Cardamom (Elettaria cardamomum) *are white.*

MEDICINAL USES

Cardamom taken internally may settle upset stomachs and counteract the effects of dairy product allergies. Its warmth is believed to help respiratory disorders, and it is used to revitalize the kidneys.

CLOVES

Eugenia caryophyllus

The name "clove" comes from the Latin word clavus, *meaning "nail," which describes its shape. Cloves are the dried flower buds of the clove tree, which is a relative of myrtle. Cloves became known to Europeans by the fourth century as they passed along the spice routes from the East. The Romans and Greeks used cloves extensively in herbal remedies, and there is evidence that cloves were one of the earliest plants used in Chinese herbal medicine.*

Cloves

Origins & Characteristics

The clove tree originally came from the Molucca Islands, but cloves are now cultivated in many countries including the West Indies, Zanzibar and Madagascar. The tree is an evergreen with bright red flowers. It grows very tall—more than 50 feet (15 m). The flower buds are dried, and they turn reddish brown. The dried cloves can be used whole or ground, and the taste is extremely strong, pungent and aromatic, so they need to be used sparingly.

Ground cloves

Making orange-and-clove pomanders

CULINARY USES

Clove is one of the spices used in garam masala, and it can be used to flavor curries, stocks, sauces, pickles, mulled wine, apple dishes, spiced cakes, mincemeat and marinades for meat and fish dishes. It is a very versatile spice and can be used as an ingredient in sauces as well as to flavor fruit punches. Cloves can be used to give a room a pleasant aroma. Stick several in an orange and hang it up. Cloves also repel insects, so it can be used in your wardrobe instead of mothballs.

OTHER USES

Orange-and-clove pomanders make wonderful aromatic decorations. Pierce the orange with the cloves, pushing them in place in quarter segments of the orange. Dip the orange into a bowl of mixed spices, cover and leave in a dark cool place for a few days, so that they draw in the fragrance.

STORAGE

Fresh cloves should ooze oil if you press the stalk with a fingernail. Because they are so aromatic, they should be kept tightly sealed in lidded glass jars. And remember that you need very few of them—only half a dozen in an apple pie are enough to flavor it.

Cloves are the dried, unopen buds of Eugenia caryophyllus.

MEDICINAL USES

A whole clove clamped between the teeth is said to relieve toothache. Cloves are also useful for stimulating the digestive system as they are a warming stimulant. They can be taken internally for gastroenteritis and nausea, gastric upsets and impotence.

ASAFETIDA

Ferula assafoetida

Asafetida is an Asiatic spice that may be known more commonly in the West as devil's dung, or stinking gum. It is hardly surprising, therefore, that it is little known outside India. The name derives from the Persian word aza, *meaning "resin," and the Latin word* fetida, *meaning "stinking." It is a resin collected from a perennial plant that grows wild in Afghanistan and eastern Iran. The resin hardens and is sold in lumps, which are ground to a powder and added to vegetables as a delicious flavoring. It also goes well with fish—fresh or salted.*

Ground asafetida

Origins & Characteristics

The plant grows around 8 feet (2½ m) tall and is quite foul-smelling, with thick roots. It carries pale yellow-green flowers. The stems are quite thick and are cut to the root, and the milky sap that flows out is collected as a resin, which then hardens. Although it looks like a giant fennel, it is unrelated. In Iran and Afghanistan the leaves and stems are cooked as a vegetable, and the smell, caused by sulfurous compounds, disappears on boiling.

Culinary Uses

Asafetida is mainly used in vegetarian curries, but it can also be used to flavor gravies and stews. The merest pinch added to any fish dish seems to bring out the flavor of the fish and adds an interesting flavor of its own. A little can also be added to relishes.

Storage

The ground resin is bright yellow and has a trufflelike flavor when cooked. The ground powder has an unpleasant, strong, garliclike odor and should only be used in minute quantities. Naturally, it should be kept quite separate from other spices in airtight, screw-topped glass jars, or its smell will dominate the aromas of other spices and ingredients.

Medicinal Uses

Asafetida is believed to clean and restore the digestive tract and relieve stomach pains and colic. It is considered a useful treatment for flatulence, constipation and dysentery. It is said to encourage coughing and, in the East, is given as a remedy for whooping cough and bronchitis. It is sometimes given raw—in pill form to disguise the taste—as an antispasmodic and expectorant.

Ferula assafoetida *in bloom*

FENNEL

Foeniculum vulgare

There are several different types of fennel—from Florence fennel to the sweet fennel—but they are all similar in taste and characteristics, and all of them can be grown in your garden. The leaves of the plant are feathery, making it a decorative addition to the border. The Roman (or vulgar fennel), which tastes like aniseed, has been known for thousands of years as a healing and culinary herb, and the Romans used the shoots as a vegetable, but it is the seeds of the fennel that make an interesting and tasty spice.

The fat bulb root

Origins & Characteristics

Because fennel grows wild in so many temperate places, it's difficult to say where it originated. It was known and used by the ancient Chinese, Romans, Greeks, Britons, Indians, Egyptians and Persians. They all used the young shoots as a vegetable, dried and ground the seeds as a spice, dried the leaves as a tea and used them fresh as a salad. It was used as an herbal remedy for sore eyes, as a charm against witchcraft and as an antidote for snake bites. The oil was used as a laxative and as a rub for bronchial congestion.

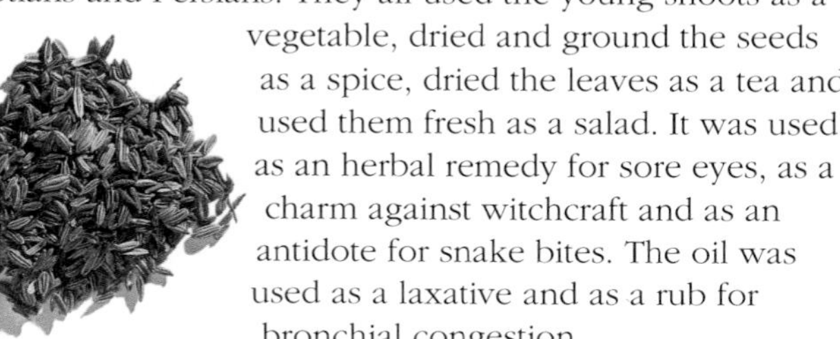

Fennel seed

Baked fennel

Culinary Uses

The leaf bases have a taste like aniseed and can be added to salads. The seeds, dried and bruised, can be used to make a refreshing tea or can be added to fish dishes. The seeds are often sprinkled on the top of bread and cakes. The stems can be dried and chopped and put inside a roasting chicken for flavor. Alternatively, fennel baked on its own is delicious. Fennel seeds are very warming and can be used for adding to any winter stews. You can also finely chop the leaves and add them to yogurt or hummus as an alternative to mint.

Medicinal Uses

Culpeper says that the leaves or seed "boiled in barley water are good for [nursing mothers] to increase the milk, and make it more wholesome for the child." Fennel is thought to relieve digestive disorders and reduce inflammation. It can be used as a mouthwash and gargle for sore throats.

Fennel (Foeniculum vulgare)

Recipe

Spicy Herbal Tea

You will need:

- 1 tbsp (15 ml) fresh fennel seeds, crushed
- 1 cup (250 ml) hot water
- honey

Add the seeds to water. Leave to steep for five minutes. Sweeten with a little honey and drink while still hot. For colic and to settle upset stomachs, make a decoction by boiling ½ tsp (2½ ml) of fresh crushed seeds in 1 cup (250 ml) of milk.

LICORICE

Glycyrrhiza glabra

Licorice grows widely in the Mediterranean and all the way to China. Its name means "sweet root," and it is cultivated for its flavor and medicinal properties throughout Europe, especially in Italy. It was once used as a cooking sweetener because it has 50 times the sweetening power of ordinary sugar, but since the advent of sugar plantations, it has fallen into disfavor and is now regarded mostly as a weed. This is a shame because it still has a valuable role to play in cooking and medicine.

Licorice sticks

Origins & Characteristics

The extremely individual flavor of licorice comes from the root, which is harvested, boiled and filtered and from which the juice is extracted. As it cools, it solidifies into a black, sticky cake. The best of these cakes were always said to be made in Pontefract in northern England, where they still make licorice-flavored candies called Pontefract cakes.

Ground licorice

Culinary Uses

Licorice can be used to add a very strong flavor to beers and liqueurs, or it can be added to pipe tobacco to give it an unusual flavor. Its most common use is as a candy for children. You can buy commercially produced licorice in its sticky black cake form or as a fresh rhizome (the underground stem of the plant). You could always try to grow your own and harvest it yourself.

Licorice (Glycyrrhiza glabra)

Medicinal Uses

Licorice has a surprising number of uses as a medicinal plant. The dried licorice root or the black extract is used as a vehicle and diluting agent. The root can be chewed or sucked to relieve sore throats and ease other cold symptoms. Licorice is also said to reduce inflammation and spasms, and it is soothing for the lungs because it can expel phlegm and soothe the bronchials If you suffer from indigestion, try licorice; it is also used for treating heartburn and is a gentle, natural laxative. In addition, it may lower blood cholesterol and relieve stomach ulcers. Because of its pleasant, sweet taste, licorice is often added to cough mixtures to mask the bitter taste of some of the other ingredients.

Caution

Under some circumstances licorice can lead to a rise in blood pressure, so its use should be kept to a minimum if you have high blood pressure. Avoid licorice if you are pregnant.

STAR ANISE

Illicium verum

One of the most instantly recognizable spices, star anise is easy to see how star anise gets its name—the shape of the fruit is that of an eight-pointed star. Although unrelated to aniseed, its essential oil is virtually the same, so both plants have the same aroma. Star anise is the fruit of an evergreen tree that originated in the East Indies but is now cultivated widely in China, where it is used as a food seasoning and in Chinese herbal medicine. In the West it is often added to fish stews. Its essential oil, which is known as oil of aniseed, is used to flavor liqueurs such as pastis in Italy, Germany and France. Its beautiful shape makes it a welcome addition to potpourris and many decorative projects.

Whole star anise

ORIGINS & CHARACTERISTICS

Star anise is related to the magnolia. The fruits have eight brown seeds and are first harvested when the tree is six years old. By the tree's fifteenth year, it is capable of being cropped three times in a single year, and it continues to be fruitful for many years.

Star aniseed

Culinary Uses

The Chinese use star anise in many savory dishes, especially duck and pork recipes, and they often add the ground seeds to coffee and tea to enhance their flavor. The oil is used to flavor drinks. If you need a strong aniseed flavor in cooking, it is even better to use star anise than aniseed.

Star anise enhances coffee and tea.

Other Uses

The bark can be ground and used as an incense. The Japanese star anise (*Illicium religiosum*) is regarded as a sacred plant, and the tree, which is smaller than star anise, is often planted around temples and near graves. The seeds of star anise can be chewed to sweeten the breath.

Medicinal Uses

Star anise is a diuretic and appetite stimulant and is also used for relieving flatulence and nausea. In Chinese herbal medicine it is recommended for lumbago, constipation, bladder problems, relieving colic and easing the symptoms of acute rheumatism. It is also used to flavor cough medicines.

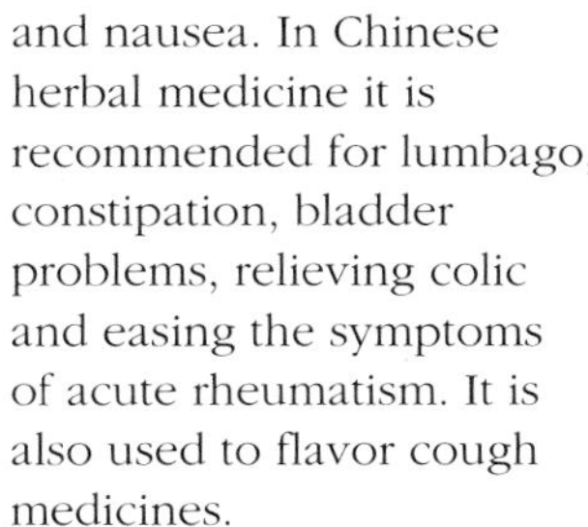

Storage

Keep the seeds in a screw-topped glass jar to preserve their flavor. You will find the spicy, sweet taste is stronger than anise.

Star anise (Illicium verum)

> **Caution**
>
> Do not confuse with Japanese star anise (*Illicium religiosum*). Its fruit is poisonous. But you can tell the difference by the smell—Japanese star anise smells like turpentine.

ELECAMPANE

Inula helenium

This delightfully pretty wild plant grows anywhere in temperate climates that can provide places with the dampness it likes, especially ditches and wet fields, where it can be found in abundance. It is also known as wild sunflower (because of its flowers' similarity to the larger plant), scabwort and horseheal—the latter two names give some indication of its healing properties when applied externally. It is cultivated widely in the Balkan peninsula.

Elecampane

Elecampane (Inula helenium)

ORIGINS & CHARACTERISTICS
Native to central Asia, elecampane was said to have sprung from the tears of Helen of Troy—hence its Latin name. The rayed yellow flowers look like small sunflowers, and it is a tall, rather attractive plant with oval, downy leaves.

Elecampane is used to flavor vermouth.

Culinary Uses

The flower stems must be removed to encourage root growth, and the roots are harvested after two years, when they are scraped and dried in the sun. They then have a strong, bitter, warm taste. The leaves can be added to salads or used to make a tea that stimulates appetite. The roots can be boiled in water, sliced and used in salads. Elecampane is used to flavor liqueurs such as vermouth. It can be candied to be eaten as a confection. The leaves can be dried and used to make an herbal tea that is said to be good for stimulating the appetite in invalids and sickly children. You can steep the root in wine to make a pleasant cordial drink that is said to cause mirth.

Medicinal Uses

Elecampane's warming qualities may make it useful as an expectorant to treat bronchitis, asthma and other pulmonary infections. When applied externally as a poultice, the leaves are said to cure scabies, herpes and other skin disorders. It has long been used as a treatment for horse wounds and sores. It is also said to help bring on menstruation and to treat anemia. Soak 3½ tsp (7 g) of the dried root in 4 cups (1 l) of water overnight, then boil for 30 minutes and allow to cool. A small cupful three times a day is said to aid digestion. This mixture can also be used as a gargle and mouthwash. You can also chew the fresh root raw as a breath freshener.

JUNIPER

Juniperus communis

There are many different forms of juniper—from the common juniper to the red cedars of North America. Some such as the common juniper are used medicinally and in cooking, while others such as Juniperus sabina *contain an oil—podophyllotoxin—that is considered too poisonous to use. Juniper has long been considered a magic plant that wards off evil and evil spirits. It was often burned in rooms occupied by the sick, both to fumigate the air and to drive out the demons. Nowadays it is well-known as the spice that flavors gin and other cordials. Juniper berries can be gathered in the wild.*

Juniper berries

Origins & Characteristics

Juniper is widespread throughout the world. It grows as a small evergreen shrub or a tree of only about 9 feet (3 m) tall. It carries cones, the females of which turn into berries. The berries start off green and slowly turn black over a three-year period, which is how long they take to ripen.

Juniper is used for flavoring gin.

Culinary Uses

The Latin word *Juniperus* comes from the Dutch word *genever,* which gave us the word "gin." And that is one of the best uses for juniper—flavoring gin. Dried juniper berries are added to patés, game, venison and marinades. They will add flavor to potatoes, sauerkraut, sausages and casseroles. Traditionally they have been used with game because they help to remove some of the stronger "gamey" taste, which some people do not like. Fresh berries are used to make a conserve to accompany cold meats. The leaves can be used fresh or dried with grilled fish, and the wood and leaves can be used on a barbecue to give a subtle flavor to meat.

Juniper (Juniperus communis)

Medicinal Uses

Juniper is used for urinary tract infections as well as for gout and rheumatism. It can stimulate the uterus and reduce inflammation of the digestive system.

Caution

Avoid juniper if you are pregnant.

Recipe

Juniper Conserve

You will need:

- juniper berries
- water
- sugar

Cover the berries with water and cook until soft. Crush the pulp and add sugar to the equivalent of three times the weight of the pulp. Beat together vigorously and let cool and set.

CURRY LEAF

Murrya koenigii

In India and Sri Lanka curry leaf is added to curries to strengthen their curry flavor, and it is grown throughout Asia for this purpose; the fresh leaves are widely available. Curry leaves come from a small, ornamental tree that grows wild in the Himalayan foothills. In the West only dried leaves are commercially supplied, and by the time they arrive, they have lost most, if not all, of their flavor. However, there is a Western equivalent, although it is a completely different plant—the curry plant Helichrysum angustifolium. *This is also used as a tea in Africa—Hottentot tea.*

Curry leaves

Origins & Characteristics

Curry leaf grows only in tropical regions, so it is not really suited to temperate climates unless it is grown in a greenhouse. Curry plants will grow in any moderate, well-drained soil as long as they get full sun.

Curry leaf is the essential ingredient in Madras curry powder.

Culinary Uses

Curry leaves should be added fresh to curries and spicy meat dishes. The leaves look like bay leaves. They are the essential ingredient in Madras curry powder and give it its unique aroma and flavor. The leaves should be removed before serving. The dried leaves have almost no flavor, but the powdered leaves can sometimes be bought in shops specializing in Indian food. Good storage preserves its flavor. Curry leaves should be added to dishes as a fresh sprig. They are excellent for steamed vegetables to give them a faint curry flavor. They can also be used to flavor rice, soups and stews. The sprig should be removed before it is served. Curry plants give off a very strong aroma of curry.

Other Uses

Curry plants can be used to give potpourri an aromatic and spicy aroma; the plant has a relative, *H. bracteatum*, which is known as an everlasting flower. Its dry petals will add color to any flower arrangement. It can also be used for garlands and wreaths.

Curry leaf (Murraya koenigii)

Medicinal Uses

The bark of curry plants is used internally for digestive problems, and the leaves are used as an infusion for constipation and colic. The curry plant has little value as a medicinal plant.

MACE

Myristica fragrans

Mace is the bright red, shiny fiber that covers the nutmeg seed inside the fruit of the nutmeg tree. It is a weblike form of flesh that, when dried, becomes brittle and turns from red to brownish yellow. Nutmeg and mace, though they both come from the same tree, have different aromas, tastes and uses and should be regarded as two separate spices. Indonesian mace is usually orange-red; mace from Grenada orange-yellow.

Blades of mace

ORIGINS & CHARACTERISTICS

The fruits of the nutmeg tree are not unlike apricots. The tree is believed to have originated in the Molucca Islands of the East Indies, but it is now cultivated in many countries such as Indonesia, Brazil, Sri Lanka and the West Indies. The Arabs spread the use of mace throughout the Arab world and subsequently all over Europe. During Tudor times in England it was used a lot and considered one of the finest, if not most expensive, spices available. When the Dutch East India Company controlled most of the world's spice trade during the seventeenth and eighteenth centuries, there was a story about how an official in the head office in Amsterdam sent a request to the governor of the Far Eastern colonies to grow fewer nutmegs and more mace because they got more revenue from mace—nutmeg being considered an inferior spice. He didn't realize that they came from the same tree.

Culinary Uses

Nutmeg and mace are used the most extensively by Europeans, both in sweet and savory meals. Unlike nutmeg, which is mainly used as a sweet spice, mace is a strong and aromatic savory spice best suited to baked fish, béchamel sauces, beef stews, casseroles and to season vegetables and potatoes. It should be added just before serving; a little can be grated over the top of any dish.

Ground mace

Storage

Mace in its whole form is known as blades of mace and loses its flavor quite quickly; however, it is fairly pungent and should be kept separate from other spices or it will taint them. It should be kept in a tightly lidded glass jar.

Medicinal Uses

Mace is used to treat stomach disorders such as diarrhea, dysentery and indigestion.

Myristica fragrans *produces both nutmeg and mace.*

NUTMEG

Myristica fragrans

The inner seed of the nutmeg tree, lying inside the filigree covering of mace, is the nutmeg. A nutmeg is quite large—about half an inch (1½ cm) long—and extremely hard. For this reason they are never used whole but is always grated. Once the seed has been separated from the mace, it is left to dry. It can then be grated in very small quantities in hot spicy drinks and used to flavor and sweeten desserts with its warm and highly aromatic taste.

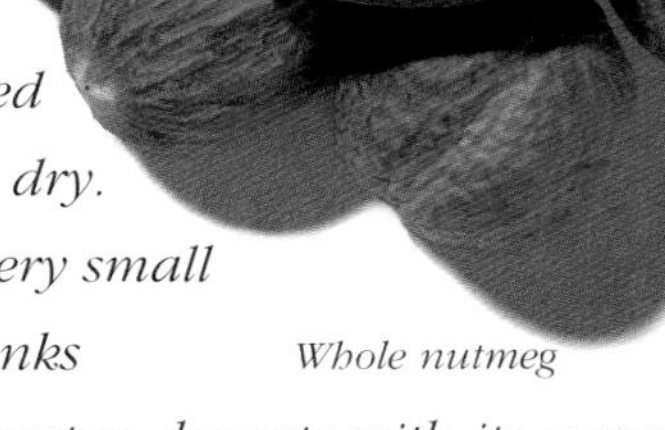

Whole nutmeg

Origins & Characteristics

Nutmeg trees grow in hot, tropical places and are extremely difficult to grow. The nutmeg has always been cheaper to produce than mace because it requires little processing before it can be sold, whereas mace has to be dried carefully to prevent decay. The oil of small or damaged nutmeg seeds is extracted and used in the cosmetic industry.

Ground nutmeg

CULINARY USES

You can grate nutmeg over puddings, custards and ice cream, as well as use it to flavor hot spicy drinks such as mulled wine. It is a flavorful addition to stewed fruit such as apples and pears and is used in baking spicy cakes and biscuits.

MEDICINAL USES

In India nutmeg was used as a cure for headaches, insomnia and urinary incontinence. In small doses nutmeg is carminative and is used in treating flatulence and vomiting and for improving overall digestion.

STORAGE

Nutmeg is its own best storage container. Whole spices will keep three or four years. Small quantities can be grated from the whole nutmeg when needed. They should be stored in lidded glass jars.

OTHER USES

Nutmeg is used in the cosmetic industry in soaps, shampoos and perfumes.

CAUTION

Nutmeg contains myristicin, which is a hallucinatory compound and should be regarded as a potential poison. As little as two whole nutmegs could be enough to cause death.

RECIPE

Baked Banana Custard with Nutmeg

You will need:

- 6 ripe bananas
- ⅓ cup light brown sugar (75 g demerara sugar)
- ⅛ oz (5 g) nutmeg, grated
- 1 tbsp (15 ml) lime juice
- 2 cups (500 ml) egg custard
- 2 oz (50 g) bread crumbs

Mash the bananas and mix with the sugar, nutmeg and lime juice. Place in buttered dish. Cover with bread crumbs and add a layer of egg custard. Sprinkle with a little nutmeg and bake at 350°F (176°C) for 35 minutes or until golden brown on top.

MYRTLE

Myrtus communis

Myrtle has long been considered a plant of love—it is named after Myrrha, who was a favorite priestess of Venus. Venus transformed Myrrha into the evergreen shrub to protect her from the unwelcome attentions of a suitor. When Paris gave Venus the golden apple for beauty, she was wearing a wreath of myrtle. Myrtle was also planted around her temple. Today it is still woven into bridal wreaths. An Arabic story tells of how Adam gave Eve a sprig of myrtle to declare his love—and she gave him an apple.

Origins & Characteristics

Myrtle is an evergreen shrub that grows quite tall—up to 16 feet (5 m)—with glossy leaves that are quite aromatic. The flowers are cream-colored and give way to blue-black berries. In the wild, myrtle grows in dry, hilly conditions in North Africa, southern Europe and the Middle East. The fruits are known as mursins. The flowers can be dried for potpourri, and the leaves and fruit can be used either fresh or dried as an aromatic spicy flavoring for game and roasted meats.

Myrtle (Myrtus communis)

The flowers of myrtle can be dried for potpourri.

Culinary Uses

The branches and leaves, burned on a grill, give meat a delicate, spicy flavor. You can use the fresh leaves to stuff game birds and the dried leaves to flavor stews and casseroles. The fruit, dried and ground, can be added to any savory dishes. The flavor is quite sweet but spicy—not unlike juniper berries.

Medicinal Uses

Myrtle is a carminative and expectorant and is thought to be helpful in cases of chest infections. The oil is extracted and used to treat acne. In China the dried and powdered leaves were used as an astringent dusting powder for babies when they were wrapped in swaddling clothes. For a tea that may relieve psoriasis and sinusitis, infuse the myrtle leaf—you may need to add honey for taste. A cold compress of the leaves can be used for bruises and hemorrhoids.

NIGELLA

Nigella sativa

Nigella is known by many other names including nutmeg flower, black cumin, Roman coriander and fennel flower and is a popular spice in Turkey and Tunisia as well as Greece, Egypt and India. The seeds of this pretty, annual herbaceous plant are black and can be dried and ground to provide a fruity-tasting spice. It is related to Nigella damascena, *love-in-a-mist, with which it is often confused. The two plants are very similar, but only* Nigella sativa *should really be used as a spice. The seeds of love-in-a-mist are distilled for an essential oil used in perfumes and lipsticks. They both smell faintly like strawberries. The flowers of* Nigella sativa *are small and white with a blue tinge.*

Nigella seed

Origins & Characteristics

Nigella grows wild throughout the whole of Asia and the Middle East, where it has traditionally been used in the same way in which we use black pepper today. In India, where the seeds are called *kalonji,* they are used as a pickling spice. In the Bible they are referred to as "fitches," from the Hebrew word *ketzah,* meaning "vetch." There are 14 varieties of nigella—the most common being love-in-a-mist—and they are mostly grown for their use in dried flower arrangements.

Culinary Uses

You can use the seeds to flavor curries, meat dishes, chutneys, pickles, sauces and cooked vegetables. The Bengalis use them as a flavoring for fish dishes. The seeds can be ground in a pepper mill and used in the same way you would use black pepper. The seeds can be added to breads and pastries to give a little pungency. Because the seeds do have an irritant effect, they should be used sparingly.

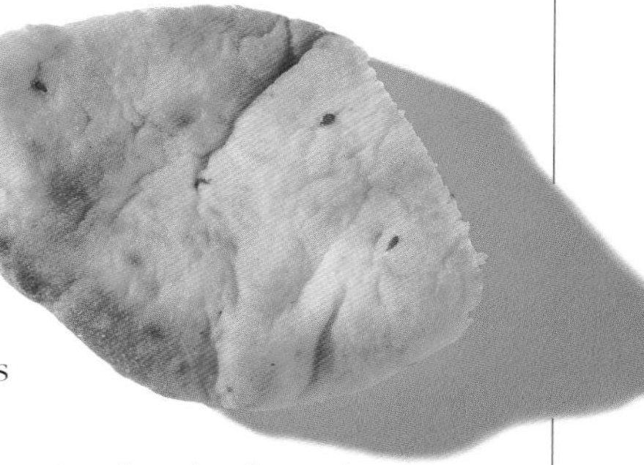

Nan bread is flavored with nigella.

Medicinal Uses

Traditionally nigella was given to nursing mothers to increase milk production and to help the uterus recover. The seeds are said to benefit digestion and reduce inflammation or irritation in the stomach lining.

Other Uses

Love-in-a-mist is easy to grow and makes a good flower for dried arrangements (it may take over because it is very invasive). *Nigella sativa* needs more sun and well-drained soil to take well. Sow seeds in the autumn or spring and do not try to transplant. Do not try to grow both as they will cross-pollinate.

The flowers of nigella (Nigella sativa)

POPPY

Papaver somniferum

The tiny blue-black seeds of the lilac-colored opium poppy, as it is commonly called, were used as a spice by the Sumerians as long ago as 4000 B.C. Nowadays it is cultivated in many countries both for its use as a culinary spice and for its medicinal qualities—it is used to make morphine and codeine.

Poppy seed

ORIGINS & CHARACTERISTICS

Opium poppies grow wild in the Middle East; they were first taken to China a thousand years ago. They have been used for their pain-relieving properties in ancient Greece, Egypt and Italy, as well as India and the Middle Eastern countries. Opium is obtained from the flesh of the unripe seed heads—the seeds themselves do not contain any of the drug. The plant grows around 4 feet (1¼ m) tall compared with the bright red corn, or field, poppy of Europe. The opium poppy also has a variety with white flowers.

Poppies (Papaver somniferum)

Infusion of poppy seeds

Culinary Uses

In Middle Eastern cooking the seeds are used to flavor sweet dishes and to make cakes, puddings and strudel fillings. In India, which produces an opium poppy with yellow seeds, the seeds are called khas khas and are used to flavor meat dishes. In most European countries the seeds are sprinkled onto newly baked bread to impart a nutty flavor. There is a Jewish three-cornered pastry called hamantaschen, which has a filling completely made of poppy seeds. You can try making cakes of poppy seeds with honey—they were given to the athletes of ancient Greece for extra energy before they took part in the Olympics.

Medicinal Uses

Opium poppy seeds are used for treating cystitis and pyelitis; make a diffusion and add honey to taste.

> **Caution**
>
> In some countries there may be a legal restriction on growing opium poppies; all parts of the plant, except the seeds, are poisonous. The seeds should not be given to anyone suffering from hay fever or any other allergic condition.

Recipe

Noodles with Poppy Seed

You will need:

- 8 oz (200 g) noodles
- ⅓ oz (10 g) unsalted butter
- 2 tsp (10 ml) poppy seeds
- salt and black pepper

Cook the noodles and add unsalted butter, poppy seeds, salt and pepper to taste. Stir well and eat. This works well as a side dish with a rich meat stew like goulash.

QUASSIA

Picraena excelsa

This spice is also known as Jamaican quassia, or bitter ash. It is similar and closely related to Japanese quassia (Picraena ailanthoides) *and Surinam quassia* (Quassia amara). *They are all deciduous trees from tropical America, India or Malaysia. The word "quassia" describes the bitter compound extracted from the wood and bark; at one time brewers used it instead of hops to flavor beer.*

Quassia chips

ORIGINS & CHARACTERISTICS

The quassia tree grows very tall—over 80 feet (25 m)—and looks a little like the ash tree. It has small, pale-yellow flowers. The wood is used in the form of chips, which are used to flavor tonic wines and beers. If you fill wooden cups made from this tree with water and leave them to stand overnight, you will have a bitter drink that is said to be good for stimulating the flow of gastric juices in the stomach and sharpening the appetite.

Culinary Uses

Quassia chips have an intensely bitter taste but no smell. When added to water or alcohol, they produce a yellow color. Quassia is used in the production of bitters, which were traditionally used in the spring to increase the secretions of digestive juices and stimulate sluggish stomachs, thus restoring the appetite—especially important after a winter of heavily salted and stodgy food.

Quassia amara *tree*

Medicinal Uses

Only small doses of quassia should be taken for general revitalization. Quassia is also used to treat rheumatism and fevers, stomach disorders and dyspepsia. A tea made from the wood chips is said to be a cure for alcoholism, and an infusion used as a shampoo is said to clear up dandruff. It can also be taken internally as a tea to kill roundworms.

Recipe

Quassia Tea

You will need:

- 1 oz (30 g) quassia chips
- 2⅔ cups (600 ml) cold water

Steep the chips in water for two hours. Strain and drink. This is said to be equally suitable as a cure for dyspepsia or, poured on the hair, as a cure for lice.

ALLSPICE

Pimento officinalis

Allspice is also known as Jamaican pepper and pimento. None of its names is really helpful—it is not a spice combination, and it is not a pepper. Moreover, "pimento" is a word that was used during the Middle Ages to describe any spice. "Allspice" is the name given to this aromatic spice by John Ray (1627–1705), an English botanist who thought it tasted like a combination of cinnamon, nutmeg and cloves. It is said to have first been brought back to Europe from its native Jamaica by Christopher Columbus. It was also used by the Aztecs to flavor chocolate. Allspice is cultivated in Jamaica on plantations known as pimento walks.

Allspice berries

Ground allspice

Origins & Characteristics

Allspice is the dried fruit of a tree that is native to Central and South America. The flowers are small and white, and the fruits are gathered unripe and dried in the hot sun until they turn a reddish brown. The tree can grow to an enormous height—over 50 feet (15 m).

Culinary Uses

Allspice should be bought whole and ground as needed. You can use it in much the same way you would use any of the three flavors it resembles—in hot spicy drinks and mulled wine; as a pickling spice; for puddings and custards. It can also be used for meat and fish dishes to which it gives an unusual and spicy flavor. It's especially good with lamb—some say it tastes of juniper berries. The leaves are used to make bay rum, and the flowers can be infused for a tea. You can add it as a powder to curry dishes and use it to flavor shellfish. If you can buy the whole berries, you can grind your own—or try adding a couple to your pepper mill to add a little zest to your black pepper.

Medicinal Uses

The oil is distilled and used for flatulent indigestion. It improves the overall digestion and is said to have a tonic effect on the nervous system.

Cosmetic Uses

You can grate a little into your bath water as an antiseptic and anesthetic—as well as for its beautiful aroma.

ANISEED (ANISE)

Pimpinella anisum

The oval-shaped, aromatic seeds of Pimpinella anisum *are one of the world's oldest known spices. The ancient Romans were the first to really discover and use the pungent and spicy aniseed to flavor their cakes, which they ate after heavy meals to settle their stomachs. Anise, as it is also called, is the flavor in the popular Greek drink ouzo.*

Dutch aniseed

Aniseed is used to flavor ouzo.

Origins & Characteristics

Aniseed grows wild throughout the Middle East, but it can also be cultivated in any moderately warm climate. It grows about 1½ feet (45 cm) tall, with broadish leaves and small cream-colored flowers that give way to tiny, light-brown hairy seeds. It was first cultivated by the ancient Egyptians and then spread throughout the Arab, Roman and Greek worlds. It has been grown commercially for a very long time but is now being slowly replaced by *Illicium verum*—star anise (see page 80) because it is cheaper to grow.

Culinary Uses

The fresh leaves can be used to flavor curries and spicy meat dishes, while the seeds can be chewed to sweeten the breath afterward. The taste is similar to fennel—sweet and spicy—although the leaves have a more delicate flavor. It is used to flavor candy that young children love. And it is also used to flavor various liqueurs such as ouzo, pastis and arak.

The flowers of anise
(Pimpinella anisum)

Medicinal Uses

Aniseed has warming and stimulating properties and it is these properties that make it useful for treating circulation problems and digestive disorders. It is also soothing for the lungs as an expectorant and is used to both flavor and activate cough medicines. More mysteriously, it is said to avert the evil eye. The oil is used in the production of toothpaste, and aniseed tea is used for settling the digestion and improving overall digestion.

Recipe

Aniseed Cakes

You will need:

- 3 medium eggs
- ½ cup light brown sugar (100 g demerara sugar)
- 1½ cups (150 g) whole wheat flour
- 2 tsp (10 ml) aniseed powder
- 1 tsp (5 ml) baking powder

Beat the eggs, add the sugar and beat for three more minutes. Mix the dry ingredients together and fold into the beaten eggs and sugar. Drop a spoonful of the mixture into each depression of a cupcake tray and let stand for 12 hours. Bake at 325°F (163°C) for 12 minutes or until the cakes brown nicely. Eat while they are still hot—spread with a little honey for total indulgence.

CUBEB

Piper cubeba

Cubeb is an unusual and very hot spice grown in Sumatra, Penang and New Guinea. It is also known as Java pepper, tailed pepper and tailed cubebs. It is the unripe fruit of a climbing pepper plant that grows like a vine. The dried unripe berries are used, and they look the same as the dried berries of black pepper—both come from the same family and are closely related. Cubeb berries come with little tails attached and, once dried, have a wrinkled, leathery appearance. Compared with pepper, cubeb is a lot more fiery and aromatic. It is used a lot in Indonesian cooking. If the berries are split open, some will have a small seed inside them, while others will be hollow.

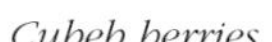

Cubeb berries

Origins & Characteristics

Cubeb likes rich clay soil with high humidity and lots of shade. It grows well in subtropical forests. The fruits are picked unripe and dried for use in powders, tinctures and liquid extracts or distilled for their oleoresin and oil, which are used by manufacturers to flavor sauces, relishes, bitters and even tobacco. The oil is also used in the production of perfumes and toiletries.

Culinary Uses

Cubeb is used widely in Indonesian food as a hot and spicy pepper addition to rice dishes, curries and fish. It has a taste similar to allspice and can be used to replace this spice when necessary. Be careful—it can be quite bitter if too much is used.

Medicinal Uses

Because of its warming properties, cubeb is said to relieve coughs and bronchitis, sinusitis and throat infection. Traditionally in Indonesia it was used as an antiseptic against gonorrhea, but there is no evidence of its effectiveness. When the oil is added to tobacco, it is said to relieve hay fever, asthma and pharyngitis. An infusion is made by steeping 1 tsp (5 ml) of powdered cubeb in 1 cup (250 ml) of hot water—a mouthful can be taken three times a day to relieve upset stomachs, indigestion and urinary infections.

Recipe

Hot Indonesian Rice

You will need:

- 2 onions, finely chopped
- cubeb
- coriander
- cardamom
- turmeric
- 3 cups (250 g) cooked rice, cold
- 3 bananas, as unripe as possible
- 4 eggs

Brown the onions and add the spices—you need to experiment to adjust the quantities to suit your own taste; you could start with ¼ tsp (1¼ ml) of each and adjust accordingly. Add the rice to the onions and spices. Slice the bananas lengthwise and fry. Cook the eggs quite dry—omelet style—and then slice. Serve the rice on a plate with the bananas and sliced eggs around it.

PEPPER

Piper nigrum

Black pepper is not related to sweet peppers. We get peppercorns from the climbing vine Piper nigrum, *which grows in Southeast Asia. The berries are picked unripe and green and left to dry in the sun. Berries that are left to ripen turn red—these are picked and soaked to get rid of the outer dark husk; the inner peppercorn is then dried to become white pepper. The unripe berries pickled in brine are called green pepper, and ripe ones are called pink pepper. Pepper has always been a valuable, expensive spice—we get the term "peppercorn rent" from the way pepper was used to pay taxes and rent during the eighteenth century—and in Roman times it was the most expensive of all spices.*

Black peppercorns

A forest of Piper nigrum

ORIGINS & CHARACTERISTICS
Originally a native of the Malabar coast, pepper is now grown in tropical regions throughout the world; mainly in India, the East Indies and Asia. Black pepper has a strong, pungent flavor, while white pepper has a milder flavor but is sharper, hotter and less aromatic. Peppercorns can be bought whole or ground, but ground pepper does lose its flavor more quickly.

Clockwise from top: ground black pepper, black and red pepper, tropical mixed peppercorns, coarse ground black pepper, ground white pepper

Culinary Uses

Pepper contains a volatile oil that actually helps in the digestion of meat and high-protein foods by stimulating the digestive juices. There are few savory dishes that do not benefit from a little black pepper being added to them after they have been tasted. White pepper is generally used in pale-colored dishes in which the use of black pepper would spoil the appearance. Sauces can be made from the whole peppercorn; they are also used in pickling spices and marinades.

Medicinal Uses

Pepper is said to be very good for stimulating the digestion, warming the bronchial passageways and relieving congestion.

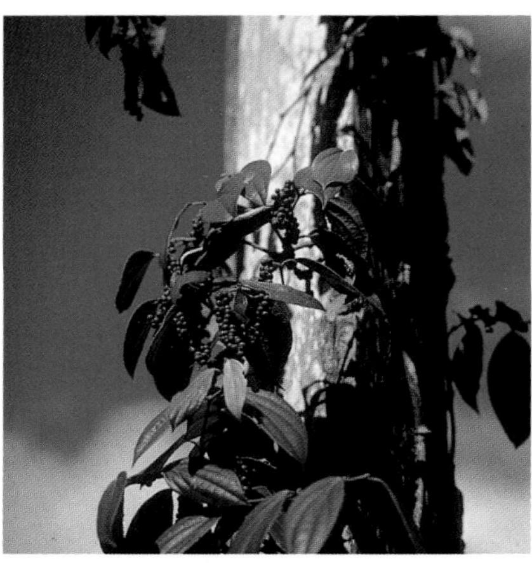

Piper nigrum *is a perennial vine.*

SUMAC

Rhus coriaria

There are two distinct types of sumac that can be used as spices—the Middle Eastern variety Rhus coriaria, *known as Sicilian sumac, and the North American sumac* Rhus aromatica. *Altogether there are more than 250 species of sumac. Some are quite poisonous, so care needs to be taken to make sure the right ones are used. The Chinese sumac* Rhus chinensis *is used widely in herbal medicine for treating coughs and mouth ulcers but has no culinary use. Sumac is not very well known in the West but can be procured from some Middle Eastern shops in its ground form.*

Ground sumac

Origins & Characteristics

Sumac is valued for its high tannin content and its astringent properties. It is related to poison ivy and grows wild as a tall shrub in thickets. The roots are harvested and dried, and the outer bark is stripped off. The fruits are collected when ripe, left to dry and then powdered for use.

Sumac is often used to decorate hummus.

Culinary Uses

In Lebanon the dried fruits are used in the same way in which we use lemon juice in cooking—as a souring agent. The seeds are crushed and then steeped in water to extract the juice. You can also buy sumac powder, which you add to savory dishes to give them a sharpish bite. In Turkey powdered sumac is commonly added to hummus, both to enhance the flavor and to act as a decoration. The North American native peoples used to make a cordial drink from the fresh red berries.

Medicinal Uses

Sumac is taken internally for treating severe diarrhea, and the root bark is used to treat dysentery. The fruits are used for treating urinary infections. The root bark is also used externally for treating hemorrhoids. A tea made from the bark or leaves is said to be good as a gargle for sore throats. The North American native peoples made a poultice from the fresh red berries to treat the irritation of poison ivy.

Other Uses

The tree's bark and leaves can be used as a dye.

> **Caution**
>
> Make sure you don't confuse the sumacs—some species are poisonous. Do not use the ornamental sumac.

Sumac (Rhus coriaria) *is a deciduous shrub.*

SESAME

Sesamum indicum

Sesame is a valuable and important addition to any cook's spice cupboard. It is also one of the earliest spices known to have been used both for its seeds and the oil contained in them. It is recorded in use in Egypt around 5,000 years ago, and there is evidence that it was being cultivated commercially in India as far back as 1600 B.C. Sesame was once believed to have magical powers. Ali Baba's famous phrase, "open sesame," probably springs from the seedpods' tendency to burst open suddenly.

Sesame seed

Origins & Characteristics

Sesame is a native of India, Indonesia, Africa and China; it grows well in sandy soil and needs a hot climate. It is a tall annual with white, trumpet-shaped flowers that turn into seed capsules about 1 in (2½ cm) long. They burst open when ripe and have a sweet, nutty flavor when lightly roasted. Some cultivated varieties do not burst, which makes them easier to harvest.

The Greek sweetmeat halvah is made from ground sesame seed.

Culinary Uses

The ground sesame seed is used as a paste in tahini, which is used in Greek cuisine and is made into halvah, a sweetmeat eaten with strong coffee in the Middle East. Sesame seeds are sprinkled onto bread and cakes. Toasted sesame seeds can be added to vegetables and cheese sauces and used instead of bread crumbs on fish pies. Sesame oil is used widely in cooking. Sesame seeds are also an important alternative to nuts for anyone with a nut allergy. They are used commercially in the production of margarine and cooking oils and even in soaps and lubricants.

Medicinal Uses

There are few conditions that have not been treated at some time with sesame seeds. This spice can help with hair loss, dysentery, dizziness, headaches, osteoporosis and boils. Because the seeds are very high in calories, they are good for convalescent people. They also make a mild and gentle laxative.

Sesame (Sesamum indicum)

Cosmetic Uses

The oil from sesame is used by Mediterranean women for dry skin conditions because it softens and penetrates well. It is also a good suntan oil because it absorbs most of the ultraviolet rays and is resistant to water, so it will not wash off if you go swimming.

WHITE MUSTARD

Sinapsis alba

The seeds of the white mustard are larger and much milder than those of the black mustard and are a pale brown or yellow. They are used in American mustard and mixed with black mustard to make English mustard. They are not used in French mustard. The herbalist Culpeper recommended that white mustard be applied to the soles of the feet in a poultice for "fevers and rheumatic and sciatic pains—to act upon the nerves whenever a strong stimulating medicine is wanted and not excite heat," while Pliny once observed that mustard "has so pungent a flavor that it burns like fire." Pliny also noted 40 remedies that were made using mustard.

Yellow mustard seed

White mustard (Sinapsis alba)

ORIGINS & CHARACTERISTICS White mustard is thought to have originated in the Mediterranean but will grow well in any temperate, dry climate in heavy, sandy soil. It is an annual, growing about 3 feet (1 m) tall, with yellow flowers that turn into seed pods about 1 inch (3 cm) long. The seeds are harvested, dried and ground.

CULINARY USES

White mustard has a pleasant, nutty flavor and is not as hot as black mustard, so it can be used more freely in cooking. The seeds can be used for pickling and can be sprouted with cress to make "mustard and cress"—because the mustard seeds grow more quickly they should be sown three days later. A mustard made with white mustard seeds is quite mild and is traditionally used to accompany American hot dogs and barbecued meat. Use a little grape juice with your mustard powder if you want to reduce its fieriness—use cold water if you want it full strength.

MEDICINAL USES

In Chinese medicine white mustard is used to treat bronchial congestion, colds, coughs and rheumatic joint pains.

CAUTION

Mustard contains substances that can irritate mucous membranes and is also a skin irritant, so home medicinal use should be avoided.

RECIPE

Herb Mustard

You will need:

- 2 oz (60 g) white mustard seed (use powdered if you can't get the seed).
- ¼ tsp (1¼ ml) herb pepper
- 2 oz (60 g) Mignonette pepper
- ⅓ oz (7 g) each of thyme and marjoram
- ¼ tsp (1¼ ml) lemon peel
- 1 pinch dried rosemary
- ¼ tsp (1¼ ml) orange peel
- 1 tsp (5 ml) honey
- 1 tsp (5 ml) wine or herb vinegar
- pinch of turmeric

Grind the mustard as necessary and add all other ingredients. Mix to a paste and use with cold meats—do not store; consume immediately.

TAMARIND

Tamarindus indica

Tamarind is known as the date of India, because it has been cultivated in India for centuries. It is widely used in Asian cooking. It is also used in Africa, Iraq and the countries bordering the Persian Gulf in southwestern Asia, in chutneys, curries and relishes. In Tudor times it was appreciated in England as a refreshing summer cordial, tamarind water, having probably been introduced to Europe by the Crusaders.

Tamarind pods

Origins & Characteristics

Tamarind grows as a large, dark pod on the tamarind tree, which is a native of tropical eastern Asia. The fruits can be eaten fresh or dried to make a souring agent and used as one would lemon juice. The taste is both sweet and sour, aromatic and spicy. The tamarind tree grows to a height of some 100 feet (30 m) and can reach more than 30 feet (10 m) in girth. It is now cultivated in the West Indies and has become an important spice ingredient in Mexican cooking.

Tamarind seed

CULINARY USES

Tamarind can be purchased as a fibrous, black, sticky pulp known as tamarind paste, which is the husk without the seeds. You extract the flavor by soaking it in hot water to which a little sugar has been added, and then squeezing it. It is a useful flavor to add to curries, meat or fish, and it has a stronger taste than either lemon or lime juice. It is also available in a dried and ground form.

Taramind block

The flower and fruit of tamarind (Tamarindus indica)

MEDICINAL USES

Tamarind makes an excellent laxative—its action is quite gentle. It is also used to treat fevers, asthma, jaundice and dysentery. Women who experience morning sickness in early pregnancy can eat the fruit to relieve the nausea. It is also said to increase appetite and aid digestion.

RECIPE

Tamarind Water

You will need:

- 2½ oz (50–70 g) tamarind paste
- 8 cups (2 l) water
- 3 tbsp (45 ml) sugar
- ½ sliced lemon

Soak the tamarind paste in the water overnight. Strain and add the sugar and lemon. Bring to a boil and simmer for five minutes. Let cool and strain again. This refreshing cordial makes a pleasant cold summer drink. You can add a little fruit or a sprig of mint to serve.

FENUGREEK

Trigonella foenum-graecum

Fenugreek is also known as bird's foot and greek clover and is grown throughout the world for its medicinal and culinary uses. The seeds have a mild curry flavor and a bitter aftertaste. It is probably best known in the West for its use in the Middle Eastern sweetmeat halva. Because of its ability to restore nitrogen to the soil, fenugreek is used in the East today as cattle fodder. It is also unusual in being a good source of protein.

Fenugreek seed

ORIGINS & CHARACTERISTICS

Fenugreek was probably first grown and recognized as a useful spice in Assyria some time around the seventh century B.C. It spread to India and China and is now used worldwide. In Egypt it is sold as a dried plant called *hilba* as a remedy for painful menstruation. The leaves are picked in summer and used fresh or dried in infusions. The seeds are collected and dried to be powdered or used whole. The Egyptians used it as an ingredient in their embalming fluids. In Yemen it is ground to a paste and added to vegetable dishes.

Ground fenugreek

Culinary Uses

In India the dried leaves of fenugreek, called *methi*, are a valuable addition to curries. The seeds can be left to sprout and used as a salad vegetable. The ground seeds are used in chutneys and relishes—mango chutney often has the whole seeds in it. The seeds can be lightly roasted to reduce the bitter aftertaste. In Ethiopia it is used as a condiment and in baking bread. You can use the seeds in fried foods, stews and pastries.

Dried fenugreek leaves

Fenugreek
(Trigonella foenum-graecum)

Cosmetic Uses

For an infusion that can be used for washing the face and hair, infuse the seeds by using 2 tsp (10 ml) of seeds steeped in 1 cup (250 ml) of cold water for six hours. Then boil for one minute and let cool. This infusion is said to improve skin condition and hair quality. You can always mix the seeds with oil for a stimulating massage oil.

Medicinal Uses

Traditionally fenugreek has been given to men suffering from impotence and to women to bring on childbirth. The seeds can be infused to treat gastric inflammation, colic, insufficient lactation, poor appetite and digestive disorders. In Chinese herbal medicine they are used to treat kidney disorders and edema.

> **Caution**
>
> The seeds should not be given to pregnant women because the saponins that the seeds contain are also used in oral contraceptives and could bring on miscarriage by stimulating the uterus.

VANILLA

Vanilla planifolia

The Spanish brought vanilla to the Old World from South America, and it became one of the world's most important flavorings. It is said that Thomas Jefferson introduced it to North America upon his return from France because he missed its taste in ice cream. Now it's one of the most popular flavors.

Vanilla pods

Origins & Characteristics

The Aztecs used vanilla to flavor chocolate. Vanilla is the pod of the climbing orchid, which originated on the east coast of South America. The flowers are small and green and are fertilized by hummingbirds. When it is grown outside South America, as in Indonesia, which now produces around 80 percent of the world's vanilla, it has to be pollinated by hand—there are no hummingbirds in Asia. The beans (also called pods) are picked unripe and treated with steam to ferment them. The vanilla crystals, known as frost, grow on the outside of the bean, which, when dried, is long, thin and quite dark. Synthetic vanilla is now widely available, but it does not have the taste of true vanilla.

Store vanilla pods in sugar in an airtight container.

Culinary Uses

The Aztecs were right—vanilla flavors chocolate superbly. But you can also use it to flavor custards, ice creams, cakes, rice and other puddings, mousses and soufflés. (Use the whole beans in preparing creams to extract the vanilla flavor from the crystals.) The beans should then be removed, carefully dried and stored and reused. Ideally they should be stored in sugar in an airtight container. The flavor will then leak into the sugar, which can also be used as vanilla-flavored sugar. Essence of vanilla is made by crushing the beans and soaking them in alcohol (the kind you choose depends on the flavor you require).

Vanilla (Vanilla planifolia) *has waxy, fragrant flowers.*

Medicinal Uses

Vanilla has few medicinal uses apart from aiding digestion and improving appetite.

Other Uses

A concentrated form of vanilla is used in perfumery.

Recipe

Iced Vanilla Coffee

You will need:

- 2 cups (500 ml) strong coffee
- 1½ cups (375 ml) cold milk
- ¼ cup (63 ml) sugar
- 2 vanilla beans (pods)
- 3 tbsp heavy cream

Mix all the ingredients together and leave in the refrigerator overnight. Remove the beans, add ice and serve.

SZECHUAN PEPPER

Zanthoxylum piperitum

Szechuan pepper is also known as Japanese pepper, anise pepper, fagara, Chinese pepper, and rather charmingly, flower pepper, which comes from its Cantonese name fahjiu. *A warming stimulant, Szechuan pepper can be used as a condiment in much the same way as black pepper, but it is hotter and more aromatic, and so should be used in smaller quantities. In ancient times it was used as a flavoring in foods and wines that were offered to the gods.*

Dried berries

Origins & Characteristics

Szechuan pepper grows in the Szechuan region of China. It grows as a large tree but is now mainly cultivated as a shrub. The leaves are picked fresh and used in cooking, and the bark is stripped and dried for infusions and decoctions. The fruits are picked in summer just before they fully ripen and are dried to make the peppercorns. These can be used in a pepper mill or can be purchased already ground. It is very hot, so beware.

Culinary Uses

Chinese cuisine was often considered bland in the West until the discovery of Szechuan cooking, with its fiery pepper sauces and hot curries—all thanks to Szechuan pepper. The leaves can be used to flavor soups and savory dishes—especially meat. They can be boiled with sugar and soy sauce and even covered in batter and fried.

Medicinal Uses

Szechuan pepper is a stimulant that works on the spleen and stomach. It also has properties that may lower blood pressure. It is diuretic and antibacterial and is used in Chinese herbal medicine as a local anesthetic. It is very warming and, thus, good for relieving the symptoms of colds and flu.

The leaves and fruit of Zanthoxylum piperitum

Recipe

Szechuan-Battered Shrimp

You will need:

- 4 tbsp (60 ml) self-rising flour
- ½ tsp (2½ ml) Szechuan pepper
- pinch of salt
- 1 piece gingerroot
- 1 egg
- 5 tbsp (75 ml) water
- light oil for frying
- 3¾ cups (500 g) shrimp

Sift flour, pepper and salt and add finely chopped ginger. Add egg and water and beat to a batter. Heat the oil, dip each shrimp in

batter and deep fry for two or three minutes until golden brown. Serve hot, garnished with scallions and a twist of lemon. Alternatively, boil the shrimp and serve garnished with the pepper, salt, ginger, scallions and a twist of lemon.

GINGER

Zingiber officinale

Undoubtedly one of the most well-known and popular spices, ginger was used widely throughout Europe in medieval times to flavor meat dishes until it fell out of favor in the eighteenth century when the spice wars pushed the price up too high. It was first mentioned in Chinese herbal medicine 2,000 years ago and remains a useful and aromatic spice for use in both culinary and medicinal roles. The young rhizomes of the plant are used for fresh ginger, while dried ginger tends to come from older, more pungent rhizomes.

Fresh rhizome

Dried root ginger

ORIGINS & CHARACTERISTICS
Ginger is a perennial native to tropical Asia and is now cultivated in other tropical areas, especially Jamaica. It is the thick, fibrous root of *Zingiber officinale,* which grows around 3 feet (1 m) tall, with long spikes of flowers that are white or yellow with purple streaks.

Ground ginger

Culinary Uses

Fresh ginger is an important part of Chinese cuisine, but it can also be used to add flavor to savory dishes, especially meat. It can be used to flavor sweet dishes and is probably best known in the West as the flavoring in ginger ale. Preserved and crystallized forms are available commercially. Stem ginger is made from the young shoots. Fresh ginger should be peeled before it is cut into thin strips and added to cooking. Dried ginger is the unpeeled root that has been dried—it should be peeled before grating. Ground ginger can be bought commercially, but it loses its flavor quickly; it is best to buy dried and grind it or to buy it fresh if possible.

Chinese ground ginger

Medicinal Uses

Recent research has shown ginger to be excellent for settling the stomach, and it is now used as a travel sickness remedy. It is also a valuable source of vitamins A and B and is helpful to women suffering from morning sickness during early pregnancy. The fresh root, if chewed, is said to alleviate sore throats as will ginger tea, which is also good for easing colic and flatulence and stimulating the appetite in invalids.

Recipe

Ginger Tea

You will need:

- ½ tsp (2½ ml) powdered root ginger
- 1 tsp (5 ml) honey
- 1 cup (250 ml) boiling water

Mix the powdered root with honey in the boiling water; let cool before drinking. A little dash of brandy can be added to treat colds and flu.

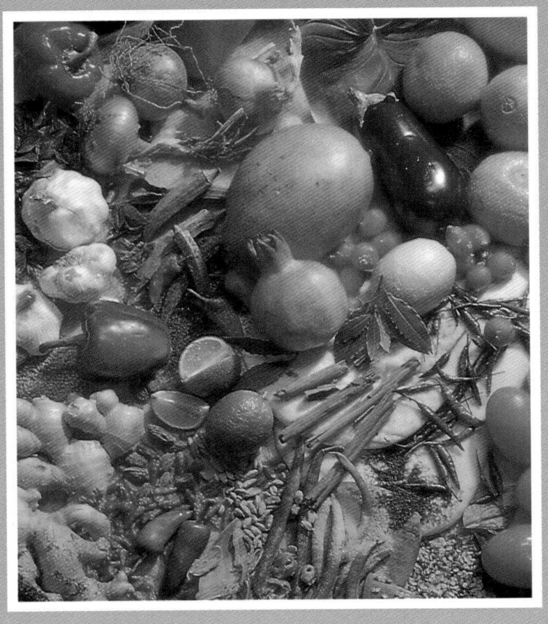

COOKING WITH SPICES

Every country uses spices in its cooking in one form or another. And in each country people from different regions will cook the same recipe in different ways, use different spices and quantities—and probably in every village in every region, there will be changes and additions to even the most basic of recipes. Here we will give you some ideas for basic spice recipes, but there are no rules—no exact quantities can be given for all tastes and preferences. Remember, where appropriate, to bottle and refrigerate as soon as possible.

No real cook would ever be without bouquet garni.

SPICY BUTTERS

An easy way to use spices in cooking is to make spicy butters. These are very easy to make and are useful for spreading on fish or meat before grilling or after as an accompaniment. Or try spreading them on sandwiches to spice them up, and adding a pat of spicy butter to vegetables—it makes all the difference! You cream the butter, preferably unsalted, and add the spices. You can add a little black pepper and salt to taste if you think it needs it. Form the butter into a roll and chill in the refrigerator. Each of the following recipes is for 9 oz (250 g) of butter.

Paprika Butter: Use 3 tsp (15 ml) of paprika. Good for cooking chicken and grilled lamb.

Mustard Butter: You will need 8 tsp (40 ml) of French or German mustard. Use with grilled meats and fish.

Juniper Butter: Crush 20 juniper berries before adding to the creamed butter. Use with grilled meats.

Horseradish Butter: Use 4 oz (100 g) of finely grated horseradish root. Use with grilled fish and meats.

Cumin Butter: Use 3 tsp (15 ml) of ground cumin seed. Use with vegetable dishes and cheese sauces.

You might like to experiment and make your own from the array of spices available. Some of the spices you could try include cayenne pepper, chilies, sweet peppers, cilantro or coriander, mustard seed, poppy seed and sesame seed.

SPICY OILS

Adding spices to oil imparts extra flavor to your cooking.

Oils, like vinegar, will take up the flavor of spices well as long as they have time to mature. You can add spices to virgin olive oil to impart the flavor to your cooking as you use the oil. Use 25 fl oz (750 ml) of olive oil and add six fresh chilies—green or red—10 juniper berries, 10 sprigs of lemongrass, two sprigs of rosemary, two crushed garlic cloves and 10 black peppercorns. Store for one month before using. You can make up several bottles at a time and experiment by adding other spices—you could make a milder oil by substituting sliced sweet peppers for the chilies; or use cilantro, dill, caraway and fennel seeds instead of peppercorns; or you could use bay leaves instead of rosemary and lemongrass. Be sure to store your oils in the refrigerator.

SPICY DRINKS

How cold winter would be without hot, spicy mulled wines to help us through it; somehow the heat seems to really penetrate and do us some good. But we do not have to limit ourselves to mulled wine—there are spicy punches, mulled ales, possets, spiced ciders, toddies, flips and wassails. In fact, any alcoholic drink can be served hot with some spices added to it.

Mulled Wine: Use a full red wine and add to it 3 tbsp (45 ml) of brown sugar, four cloves stuck into a small orange, 1 tsp (5 ml) allspice, 1 tsp (5 ml) grated nutmeg and three sticks of cinnamon. Heat gently—do not boil as this removes the alcohol—for about 10 minutes. Strain and serve with a slice of orange. Traditionally a well-beaten egg was added to the mull just before serving. You could try heating the mixture with a red-hot poker for that genuine touch.

Lambswool: Mix the flesh of four baked apples with (preheated) 4 cups (1 l) of strong dark beer, 2 cups (½ l) of white wine, one cinnamon stick, 1 tsp (5 ml) of nutmeg and 1 tsp (5 ml) of ginger powder. Remove the cinnamon and strain. You will need to squash the mixture through. Heat again and add a little sugar to taste.

Milk Posset: Heat 2 cups (½ l) of milk and add one glass of white wine. Stir in a pinch of ground ginger and a pinch of ground nutmeg, a little sugar and a squeeze of fresh lemon juice. Serve hot.

SALAD DRESSINGS

Spices can be added to your range of salad dressings to add that little extra bite. Spicy salad dressings make a change from the traditional French dressing and can really transform a humble salad into something special. Here are a couple of recipes to try. Both can be quickly prepared and then kept in the refrigerator for further use.

Spicy Chinese Salad Dressing

You will need:

- 1 garlic clove, crushed
- ½ red chili
- 1 tbsp (15 ml) sesame oil
- 1 tbsp (15 ml) sunflower oil
- 1 tbsp (15 ml) cider vinegar
- 1 tsp (5 ml) soy sauce
- 1 tsp (5 ml) sherry
- 1 tsp (5 ml) sesame salt

Make sure that you have removed the membrane and seeds from the chili. Mix all the ingredients together and store in a glass jar in the refrigerator. This salad dressing goes well with bean sprouts, stir-fried vegetables and tofu.

Spicy Cider Dressing

You will need:

- 6 tbsp (90 ml) cider
- juice of 1 lemon
- 2 tbsp (30 ml) sunflower oil
- 2 tbsp (30 ml) apple juice
- ½ tsp (2½ ml) ground allspice
- ½ tsp (2½ ml) nutmeg, grated

Mix all the ingredients together and store in a glass jar in the refrigerator. You may need to alter the quantities of spices to suit your taste. This dressing is sharp and gives salads a tangy lift without using too much oil.

PICKLING VINEGARS

Good cooks also need a pickling vinegar that can be used for a whole range of chutneys and relishes. There are two main types of pickling vinegar—sweet and malt. The sweet is for pickling fruit and the malt for pickling vegetables.

Pickling vinegar can be used for a whole range of chutneys and relishes.

Sweet Pickling Vinegar

You will need:

- 1 tbsp (15 ml) coriander seeds
- 1 tbsp (15 ml) whole cloves
- 5 blades of mace
- 1 tbsp (15 ml) whole allspice
- 2 cinnamon sticks
- 4½ cups (900 g) white sugar
- 5 cups (1¼ l) white wine vinegar

Put the spices in a muslin bag. Mix the sugar and vinegar. Put the spice bag into the vinegar and leave to steep for six weeks in a sealed glass jar. Strain and use.

Malt Pickling Vinegar

You will need:

- 1 tsp (5 ml) whole cloves
- 2¼ tsp (6 g) white peppercorns
- 2¼ tsp (6 g) mace blades
- 1 cinnamon stick
- 2¼ tsp (6 g) fresh gingerroot
- 2¼ tsp (6 g) whole allspice
- 5 cups (1¼ l) malt vinegar

Put all the spices in a muslin bag and steep in the vinegar for five to six weeks in a cool place in a tightly sealed glass jar. Shake the jar occasionally. Remove the spices and strain. Use as required.

A traditional bouquet garni

Bouquet Garni

No real cook would ever be without a bouquet garni—that little bag of herbs and spices to flavor a casserole or stew for winter warmth. They are traditionally made in muslin bags, but you might like to try using the outer leaf of a leek—it will not break up during cooking.

You will need:

- 1 bay leaf
- sprig of thyme
- 1 clove
- 6 peppercorns

Place the ingredients in the bag—or leek leaf—and tie with string. Hang inside the pot while cooking, but tie it to the handle so that it can be retrieved prior to serving.

SPICY CHUTNEYS AND RELISHES

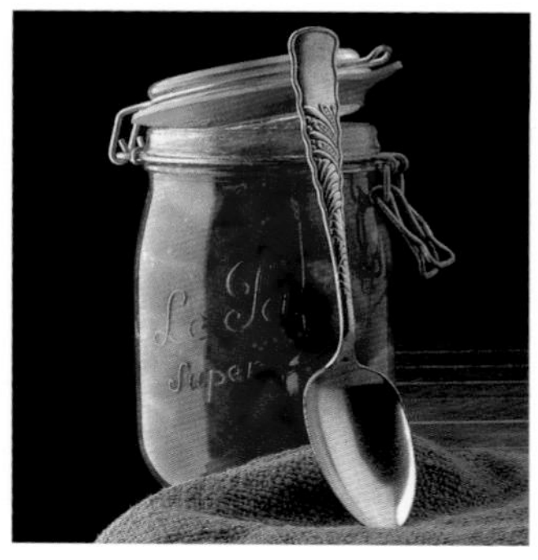

Chutneys are relishes of fruit and vegetables. They make a good accompaniment to cold meats, fish, meat pies and curries. They can range from relatively mild to very hot. The word "chutney" comes from the Hindu word *chatni*, which means "strong sweet relish"—and that's exactly what it is.

Sweet Pepper Chutney

You will need:

- 6½ lb (3 kg) large ripe tomatoes
- 1 lb (500 g) onions
- 3 garlic cloves, crushed
- 3 red sweet peppers
- 3 green sweet peppers
- 1 tsp (5 ml) ground mace
- 1 tsp (5 ml) ground black pepper
- 1 tsp (5 ml) paprika
- grated rind and juice of 2 lemons
- grated rind and juice of 1 orange
- 1 tsp (5 ml) ground ginger
- pinch of cayenne pepper
- 2 oz (50 g) salt
- 2 cups (450 ml) white wine vinegar
- 1 cup (250 g) brown sugar

Seed tomatoes after scalding and peeling them—you only want the flesh, not the seeds. Chop the onions and garlic and add to the tomato flesh in a saucepan. Prepare peppers by removing the seeds and membranes. Slice and add to the pan. Add all the other ingredients and heat gently until all the sugar has dissolved. Stir. Bring to a boil and simmer for two hours, stirring occasionally. When the chutney is thick and rich, you can store it in glass jars. Store in a cool place for two months before using—this is a mild chutney that will go well with cold meats and fish.

Spicy Lemon and Lime Relish

You will need:

- 2 cups (500 ml) olive oil
- 5 lemons
- 5 limes
- 2 tbsp (30 ml) black peppercorns
- 1 chopped dried red chili
- 1 tbsp (15 ml) cumin seeds
- 3 tbsp (45 ml) salt
- 4 garlic cloves, crushed
- 1 tbsp (15 ml) white mustard seeds
- 3 bay leaves
- 1 small piece of fresh ginger, grated

In a saucepan, heat the oil thoroughly and let cool. Slice the lemons and limes into quarters. Grind the peppercorns, chili and cumin seeds together and sprinkle over the lemons and limes. Add the rest of the ingredients and stir thoroughly. Let settle for one hour and then pour into a glass jar. Pour over the cooled oil and leave, sealed, in a warm place for one week, shaking every day. Then store in a dark cupboard for one month. The rinds will then have softened and taken on the spices and oil. Serve with hot curries and plain rice.

This relish should keep for up to six months—if you have not eaten it all by then—and goes extremely well with curries.

CURRIES

Most people think of India and China when they hear of curries, and although they do make up a large part of both Indian and Chinese cuisine, there are many other countries that have curry recipes as well such as Mexico, Thailand and the Caribbean countries.

Match your spices to the curry, so use cardamom, cinnamon, cloves and ginger if you want a fresh sweet flavor; turmeric and fenugreek for a slightly more robust sour taste; and cumin and coriander seeds for a fuller, more solid flavor. Only use 1 to 2 tbsp of ground spice blends in a curry for four people—this keeps the taste distinctive and delicate but not overpowering. Fry the spices when you begin cooking because this will develop their flavors, but be careful not to burn them because they will be bitter if you do. For Malaysian curries you should add lemongrass for that distinctive flavor. Thai curries are always part of a selection of dishes in a main meal, and the hotness is usually offset by a sweeter or blander dish; they often include lemongrass, galangal and kaffir lime leaves.

Curry powder (page 269) and garam masala (page 325), are both dry spice blends you can store for up to four months. You might like to make your own curry paste. You can use this immediately to cook any of the tikka curry dishes—these are hot curries using yogurt that were traditionally cooked in a *tandoor* (clay oven).

Garam masala

Curry Paste

You will need:

- 1½ tsp (7½ ml) cumin seeds
- 1 tsp (5 ml) garam masala
- 1 tsp (5 ml) garlic powder
- ½ tsp (7½ ml) paprika
- 1 tsp (5 ml) turmeric
- pinch of salt
- 2 tbsp (30 ml) wine vinegar
- 1½ tsp (7½ ml) coriander seeds
- 1½ tsp (7½ ml) chili powder
- 1 tsp (5 ml) dried mint
- 1 tbsp (15 ml) water
- 2 tbsp (30 ml) olive oil
- squirt of lemon juice

Grind the seeds in your coffee grinder (which you should keep specifically for this purpose if you do not want your coffee to taste too spicy afterward) and add to the other dry ingredients. Stir well, add the water, lemon juice and vinegar and mix into a thin paste. Heat the oil slowly in a heavy frying pan and stir in the paste. Cook gently until all the water has been absorbed (about 10 minutes). You can then use this paste as is, or you can store it in an airtight glass jar—you might like to pour a tiny amount of oil on top of the mixture to keep it really fresh. Once you have this paste it can be used to make a tikka masala—*masala* means "hot," by the way, so you have been warned.

Chicken Tikka Masala

You will need:

- 4 chicken breasts
- 4 tbsp (60 ml) plain yogurt
- 6 tbsp (90 ml) tikka paste
- 2 tbsp (30 ml) olive oil
- 1 clove garlic, crushed
- 1 onion, chopped
- small piece of fresh ginger, grated
- 1 red chili, chopped
- 1 tbsp (15 ml) almonds, ground
- 1 tbsp (15 ml) tomato purée
- 1 cup (250 ml) water
- 3 tbsp (45 ml) melted butter
- ½ cup (125 ml) heavy cream
- dash of lemon juice

To serve:

- 1 tsp (5 ml) cumin seeds
- 4 sprigs of fresh coriander
- 10 fl oz plain yogurt

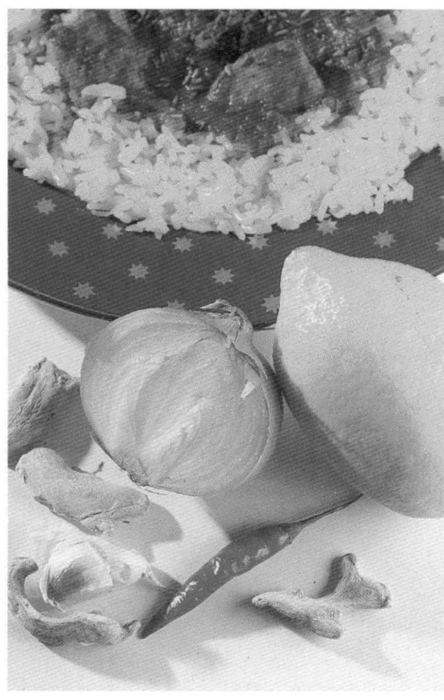

Skin and cut the chicken into cubes and put in a bowl with the yogurt and half of the tikka paste. Stir well and let marinate for half an hour. Heat the oil in a heavy pan and fry the garlic, onion, ginger and chili for four minutes and then add the other half of the tikka paste and fry for three minutes. Add the almonds, tomato purée and water and simmer for 15 minutes. Brush the chicken with the melted butter and grill for 15 minutes, turning until cooked through. You can now put the cooked tikka mixture through a blender if you want a smoother masala—or leave more coarsely prepared if you prefer. Add the cream and lemon juice to the pan with the tikka sauce and add the chicken. Simmer for five minutes. This should be served hot with nan bread and a garnish of toasted cumin seeds, fresh coriander seeds and plain yogurt.

And you probably want to know by now how to cook a spicy rice to accompany some of these curries.

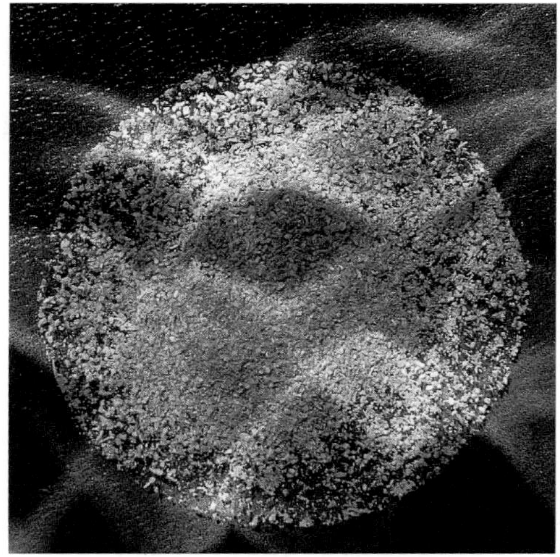

Coriander for spicy rice

Spicy Rice

You will need:

- 2 onions, finely chopped
- ½ cup (125 ml) vegetable oil
- 1 tsp (5 ml) turmeric
- ½ tsp (2½ ml) cumin
- ½ tsp (2½ ml) coriander seeds
- ½ tsp (2½ ml) cardamom
- ¼ tsp (1 ml) cloves, finely ground
- 1¼ cups (250 g) rice
- pinch of salt
- 2 cups (500 ml) hot water

Brown the onions in the hot oil in a heavy pan, add the spices and fry for two minutes. Add in the rice, washed and drained, and the salt, and brown for two minutes. Add the water so that it just covers the rice (about 1 inch [2½ cm]) and cover and simmer for 15 minutes—or until all the water has been absorbed. Fluff with a fork and serve hot. This is a basic recipe, and you can add any other spices that you want—a little cayenne pepper will give the rice a little bite—or you could swap the turmeric for paprika if you want your rice red rather than yellow. For a plain rice you can leave out the spices and just color it with turmeric or paprika. In India rice is usually fried before boiling, while in China the rice is usually boiled then fried with the meat and vegetables. To make a pilau rice you can add almonds and raisins—lightly sauté them before adding them to the cooked rice.

SWEET AND SPICY TREATS

After you've eaten all that spicy food, what could be better than something a little spicy-sweet to cleanse the palate and sweeten the breath? Spices are not only good for savory dishes but also for candy, puddings and desserts. You may like to try the following recipes.

Cardamom Ice Cream

You will need:

- 16 whole green cardamom pods
- 1 cup (250 ml) whole milk
- 1½ cup (350 ml) heavy cream
- 4 egg yolks
- ⅓ cup (75 g) confectioner's sugar

Bruise 10 of the cardamom pods and heat with the milk and half the cream to almost the boiling point for two minutes. Let cool for 10 minutes. Remove the seeds from the remaining cardamom pods and crush. Whisk the egg yolks with the sugar. Strain the milk mixture and add to the eggs and sugar. Whisk thoroughly and heat until it begins to thicken. Remove from the heat and allow to cool. Whip the other half of the cream and add the crushed cardamom seeds. Fold into the cooled milk and egg mixture. Freeze for two hours. Remove from the freezer and whisk. Return to the freezer overnight or for at least 12 hours.

Spicy Winter Compote

- 1 cup + 2 tbsp (175 g) each of dried peaches, pears, apricots and raisins
- ¾ cup (125 g) confectioner's sugar
- 2⅔ cups (600 ml) water
- ⅔ cup (175 ml) red wine
- 6 allspice berries
- 2 cinnamon sticks
- 6 cloves
- 1 vanilla bean
- 8 peppercorns
- ⅔ cup (175 ml) port

Soak the dried fruit in hot water for 10 minutes. Add the fresh pears, peeled, cored and quartered. Add the sugar and cook over a low heat for five minutes. Add everything else except the port and simmer gently for four minutes. Remove from the heat, add the port and let steep for 10 minutes. Serve warm—it is very good with the cardamom ice cream.

Cardamom Honey Dressing

You will need:

- ½ pint (300 ml) clear honey
- 2 tbsp (30 ml) lemon juice
- a few drops of orange-flower water
- ½ tsp (2½ ml) cracked cardamom seed

Beat honey in a mixer until light in color. Gradually add in the lemon juice and orange-flower water. Stir in cardamom seed. Keep in an airtight jar. This is a delicious dressing for fruit salads.

Vanilla growing up palm

SPICE COMBINATIONS

By tradition there are various spice combinations that have become known and loved throughout the world. India has produced many spice mixtures for its vast cuisine, possibly the most well known being garam masala, while Europe's famous combination is quatre-épices. There are spice mixtures that are used for specific purposes, such as pickling and pudding spice. However, the following recipes for some of these combinations are the subject of fierce debate and argument. You have been warned. For example, where we might suggest that garam masala is made with only 4 tsp of black cumin seeds, some authorities would argue vociferously that you simply cannot make a good garam masala without using at least five. Or we might suggest that a good curry powder would have, among its other ingredients, 1 tsp of black pepper to 2 tsp of cinnamon, but others will disagree and say that you absolutely, and without exception, must have exactly 2¼ tsp. Combining spices is that sort of area—it allows everyone to find their own particular favorite and become an instant expert. We hope you too will follow this path and become a spice combination connoisseur.

Try to buy seeds and spices that are as fresh as possible. Heat the seeds in the oven for a few minutes or in a heavy frying pan until you can detect the strong aroma. Then you should grind the seeds—a coffee grinder will work for this, but you may find that your coffee tastes a little strange for a while. Or you could have a grinder dedicated specifically for grinding spices. Once ground, the seeds should be put through a coarse strainer to remove any stalks, husks or foreign matter such as small stones. Keep the spices separately in airtight glass jars in a cool dark place and only mix combinations together in quantities that you can use in a week or two at the most; spice combinations will lose their potency quite quickly after that.

All of the following recipes are ones we have tried and like—you may, however, wish to experiment and find your own combinations. All of the recipes are given in teaspoons (ml in parentheses); the quantities refer to flat teaspoonfuls.

It is probably impossible to buy a curry powder in India—people there always mix their own—and you may well be unhappy with the commercially prepared ones—so why not make your own?

Hot Curry Powder

- 2 tsp (10 ml) chili powder
- 1 tsp (5 ml) cloves
- 2 tsp (10 ml) cardamom pods
- 2 tsp (10 ml) ground cinnamon
- 2½ tsp (12½ ml) ground cumin
- ½ tsp (2½ ml) ground fenugreek
- 1 tsp (5 ml) ground nutmeg
- 2 tsp (10 ml) ground black pepper
- 1 tsp (5 ml) mustard seed
- 1 tsp (5 ml) black poppy seed
- 1 tsp (5 ml) curry leaf

Mild Curry Powder

- 1 tsp (5 ml) chili powder
- 1 tsp (5 ml) ground black pepper
- 1 tsp (5 ml) ground cumin
- 4 tsp (20 ml) coriander seeds
- 1½ tsp (5 ml) ground turmeric
- 1 tsp (5 ml) cardamom pods
- 1 tsp (5 ml) ground fenugreek

Mild curry powder. Clockwise from top left: ground fenugreek, ground black pepper, ground turmeric, chili powder, coriander seed, cardamom pods, ground cumin

Garam masala is often mistaken for curry powder, but it is not the same. It might be as hot and as spicy, but it was a different flavor altogether. You can make a dry masala or a wet paste masala. Here are recipes for both.

Garam masala. Clockwise from top left: ground cinnamon, cloves, ground mace, cardamom pods, ground cumin, ground black pepper, bay leaves

Dry Garam Masala

- 3 tsp (15 ml) ground black pepper
- 2 tsp (10 ml) ground cinnamon
- 2½ tsp (12½ ml) ground cumin
- 2½ tsp (12½ ml) cloves
- 1½ tsp (7½ ml) ground mace
- 1½ tsp (7½ ml) cardamom pods
- 2 tsp (10 ml) bay leaves

Wet Paste Garam Masala

- 6 tsp (30 ml) coriander seeds
- 3 tsp (15 ml) ground black cumin
- 3 tsp (15 ml) cardamom pods
- 1 tsp (5 ml) bay leaves
- 4 tsp (20 ml) ground black pepper
- 1 tsp (5 ml) ground nutmeg
- 3 tsp (15 ml) ground cinnamon

Add the juice from two lemons (or limes) and make into a paste.

Chinese Five-Spice

Chinese five-spice is used extensively in Chinese cuisine. We have suggested equal quantities for the blend as a starting point—you can then experiment as you will. Be warned, though, that this combination is quite hot.

- 1 tsp (5 ml) fennel seed
- 1 tsp (5 ml) aniseed
- 1 tsp (5 ml) star anise
- 1 tsp (5 ml) ground cassia
- 1 tsp (5 ml) cloves

There is a Japanese equivalent, known as seven-flavor spice, which includes pepper leaf, sesame seed, poppy seed, hemp seed, rapeseed and dried tangerine peel. It may be best if you buy this one commercially prepared because getting some of the ingredients may be difficult—if not illegal—in some countries.

Chinese five-spice. Clockwise from top: cloves, ground cassia, star anise, aniseed, fennel seed

French Quatre-Épices (Four-Spice)

This recipe is a traditional French spice mixture that is used with cold meats and as a general spice blend for seasoning—it is quite hot.

- 6 tsp (30 ml) ground white pepper
- 1 tsp (5 ml) whole cloves
- 1 tsp (5 ml) ground ginger
- 1 tsp (5 ml) ground nutmeg

French quatre-épices. Clockwise from top left: ground ginger, cloves, ground white pepper, ground nutmeg

OTHER COMBINATIONS

You might like to try your hand at alino criolo, which is a Venezuelan combination of annatto seed, fresh oregano, ground cumin, paprika, garlic salt and black pepper. Fresh garlic is added just before using this in cooking stews and casseroles.

Or how about sambal, which is a spicy relish much loved in India and China? You need fresh chilies, a little sugar, salt, oil, some lemon juice, onion, lemongrass and dried shrimp. They are all blended together to make a hot, spicy picklelike relish to accompany any Indian or Chinese dish.

Others include: Cajun mix, used with Mexican fried beans, which consists of paprika, chili, cumin, mustard and oregano; pumpkin pie mix, which consists of cinnamon, allspice, nutmeg and ginger; and zahtar, used to flavor meatballs and hamburgers—sumac, roasted sesame seeds and thyme.

THE SWEET PEPPERS

Some people have never tried sweet peppers (*capsicum annuum*) because they think they are just fat versions of chilies. Nothing could be further from the truth. Sweet peppers are juicy and tasty without any of the fire that chilies have. Although all chilies are capsicums, not all capsicums are chilies. Sweet peppers are mild and sweet. They can be sliced and eaten raw, added to salads, stir-fried, added to casseroles and stews or stuffed. They can be grilled on their own as vegetables. They are also known as "pimentos" or "bell fruit."

Technically the green sweet peppers are unripe fruit, but they taste very similar to the red and yellow varieties, although they may be a little more bitter. You can blanch them for a minute or two before cooking to remove the bitter flavor. You can also get cream-colored peppers. Before cooking them, you should slit them open and remove the seeds and membrane. These can be quite hot and bitter. If you buy them canned, the seeds should have been removed already, although there should be no need to buy them as such anymore—fresh sweet peppers are now available yearround in most countries.

Sweet peppers should be sliced lengthwise rather than across their flesh as the flavor and juice tend to stay in better.

When buying sweet peppers always look for smooth, firm skins and a good color. There shouldn't be any softness or discoloration. If they have gone soft in any places, they have already started to go bad and should not be bought. Peppers will keep in the refrigerator for three or four days or in a cool pantry for two or three days.

To freeze them, remove the seeds and membranes and slice them lengthwise. Blanch them for two minutes. Cool them under cold running water for two minutes and then drain and freeze them. You can keep them for 12 months in a freezer. When you want to use them, you can add the frozen slices directly to any recipe. If you prefer pepper halves, blanch them for three minutes and defrost for an hour before using.

Sweet peppers are the main ingredient in ratatouille (a French vegetable stew). They make a good accompaniment to grilled meat or baked potatoes.

Ratatouille

You will need:

- 2 eggplants
- salt
- 5 tomatoes
- 1 large green sweet pepper
- 1 large red or orange sweet pepper
- 6 medium zucchini
- 3 tbsp (15 ml) olive oil
- 2 medium onions
- 2 garlic cloves
- ½ tsp (2½ ml) coriander seeds
- salt and pepper to taste

Slice the eggplants, sprinkle them with a little salt and let drain. Chop the tomatoes after skinning them. Crush the garlic cloves. Slice open the sweet peppers and remove the seeds and membranes. Slice the zucchini. Peel and coarsely chop the onions.

Heat the oil and gently cook the onions, garlic and peppers for about 10 minutes. Add the eggplant and the remainder of the ingredients. Cover and simmer for about 45 minutes, stirring occasionally to prevent the ratatouille from sticking. You can try experimenting by adding a little Tabasco sauce if you like your ratatouille a little hotter. Garnish your ratatouille with a little finely chopped parsley if you want to add some color.

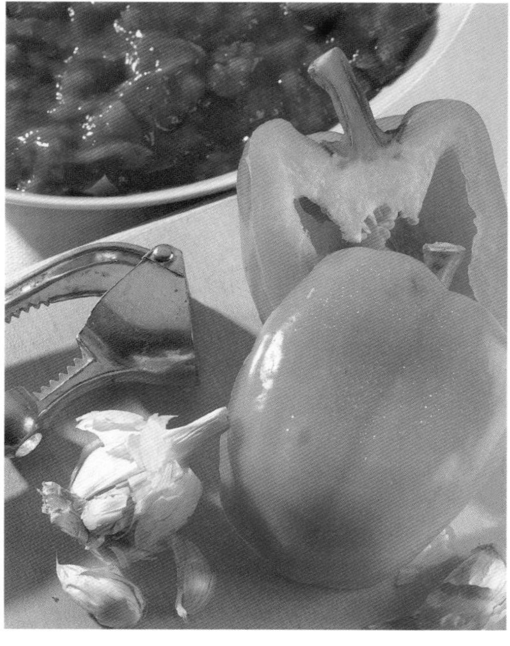

Grilled Sweet Peppers

You will need:

- selection of sweet peppers

You can use any color of peppers, but remember that the green ones may be a little more bitter than the red or yellow ones. Slice your peppers into two halves and remove the seeds and membranes. Lightly toast on the grill on both sides until the flesh just begins to bubble and brown. You can serve grilled sweet peppers just as they are—hot and succulent. The same technique can be used for adding sweet peppers to kebabs—just cut them into slightly smaller pieces. They slide onto skewers well and should be cooked until the flesh bubbles.

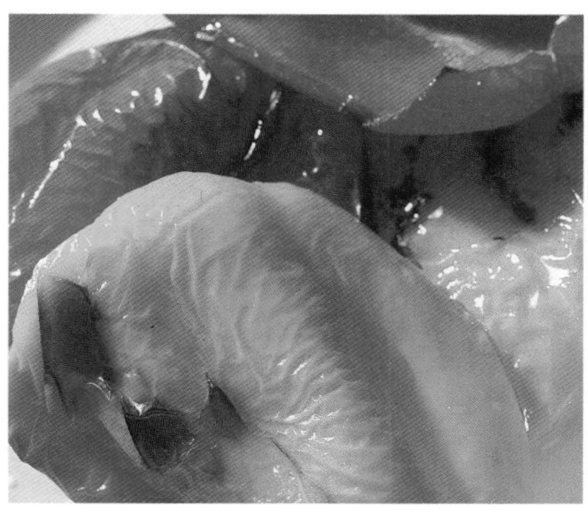

Basque Piperade

You will need:

- 1 large red and 1 large green pepper
- 6 tomatoes
- 2 onions
- 1 garlic clove
- 4 tbsp (50 g) butter
- 6 eggs
- 3 tbsp (45 ml) milk
- 10 slices of bacon

This is a recipe from the Basque region of Spain.

Prepare the vegetables and garlic in the same way as for ratatouille and cook them all in the butter for eight minutes. Beat the eggs and milk as you would for an omelet. Pour over the vegetables and reduce heat to a simmer. Fry the bacon separately. When the eggs are just set but still creamy on the top, lay the cooked bacon over them and serve hot.

THE CHILIES

No one really knows who grew and used the first chilies—but we do know it was around 9,000 years ago in the Amazon region of South America. Today there are more than 150 varieties of chilies, and they are grown worldwide but principally in Mexico, California, Texas, New Mexico, Arizona, Thailand, India, Africa and Asia.

It was the original inhabitants of Mexico who first discovered chilies and used them in their cooking. Once the Spanish and Portuguese explorers tasted them, their use spread to Europe and beyond. It was not too long before they had made it as far as China. Today chilies are known for their fiery pungency and for enhancing Mexican and Asian cuisine.

Chilies are members of the *capsicum* family (Latin for "box"—a box of seeds). Chilies are the fruit of the *Capsicum frutescens* plant, which will grow in any warm, humid climate, and they are easy to grow at home in pots. They make interesting and useful houseplants. They will cross-pollinate easily, so keep them separate if you want to stick to a particular variety. By tradition the smaller chilies have always been regarded as the hottest, but that may not always be true. Chilies range from mildly hot to the extremely hot, and great care must be exercised when handling them. Ideally you should wear thin surgical rubber gloves and wash your hands afterward. Never rub your eyes or face when handling chilies in any form—the oil they contain is an irritant and will burn. If you do get any on your skin, wash off with very large amounts of cold milk or soap and water. If you get any in your eyes, flush with lots of cool water. If you eat chilies and find them too hot, drink cold milk to reduce the fieriness. Keep chilies away from children.

Chilies come in all shapes, sizes and colors—from long thin ones to short plump ones; from red to green, purple, orange, yellow, cream and black. They can be bought fresh or canned, dried, pickled in brine or powdered. Dried chilies can be hotter than fresh ones, but canned ones are usually milder. If the seeds are used, the chilies will be hotter and more bitter.

Preparing Chilies

Fresh chilies should be sliced in half, and their seeds should be removed. You can then lightly grill them, and the skin will peel off easily. They are then ready to use. Some people like to grill them before removing the seeds because there is less risk of the volatile oil getting on their skin. To remove the skin of a chili, drop the chili into a plastic bag and peel it safely in that. Washing chilies will remove the oil—and the pungency. Dried chilies should be lightly roasted and then soaked in hot water for about 10 minutes to rehydrate them. You may need to remove their seeds.

Preparing chilies: once grilled, the skin should peel off easily.

Remember that the heat of the chilies is in the membrane rather than the seeds, so make sure you remove all of the membrane before use—chilies are hot enough without adding to their fieriness. When buying fresh chilies, look for firm, shiny specimens with good color. They should be dry and heavy. Any that are limp, dull or discolored should be rejected. When you get them home, rinse and dry them and store them in the crisper of your refrigerator. They should keep for two or three weeks. If you do not keep them in the refrigerator, they will deteriorate fairly quickly. They will also spoil if you keep them in a plastic bag because of the moisture build-up. Chilies are hot, but they also have a flavor. Experienced chili eaters will often claim they can experience quite delicate flavors and tastes in chilies that people less used to will not be able to discern. When you first start eating chilies, you will find they all just taste hot, but within a short period of time, you become tolerant to their heat and can both eat hotter varieties and experience their actual flavors. What one person describes as mild or hot may be completely different for another—only you can decide your own preferences. Do not be bullied into eating chilies that are hotter than you really like.

Chili Varieties

Chilies each have a unique flavor and heat level. On the following pages you will find some, but by no means all, of the most popular chilies—each has been graded from one to five for hotness—with five being the hottest.

Fresh Chilies

Anaheim: This is also known as the Californian chili or the New Mexican chili. It is about 6 in (15 cm) long and either bright green or, fully ripened, red. It looks a little like a sweet pepper (see page 226). When it is dried and powdered, it is sold as "Colorado chili powder." Quite mild—about a one.

Habanero: This is a distinct five+. It comes in any color from red to green to purple and is about 2 inches (5 cm) long. When it is ripe and red, it is said to have a fruity, tropical flavor, but the heat may not let you taste much. This is probably one of the hottest chilies available. It is grown in Central America and the Caribbean.

Anaheim chilies

Jalapeno: This is one of the most commonly used chilies and is grown in Mexico and across the North American Southwest. Dried and smoked, it is known as a chipotle. When fresh, it is a juicy, plump chili about 2 or 3 inches (6–8 cm) long and can be red or, when unripe, green. The red ones are much more flavorsome. A middling heat—a two or three.

Malaguetta: This is a very hot (and tiny) chili from Brazil. Its heat rating is about a five. It is thin and comes in green (unripe) and red (ripe).

Poblano: This one is quite mild—about a two. It is green or red, 4 to 6 inches (10–15 cm) long with quite thick flesh. When it is dried, it is known as an ancho. It comes from Mexico and California.

Scotch Bonnet: Here is another of the very, very hot ones (five+) and is grown in Jamaica and the Caribbean. It is only about 1 inch (2½ cm) long, but it packs a punch. It is usually described as having a smoky, fruity flavor, but the heat may stop you from tasting anything.

Scotch bonnet chilies

Serrano: This is a very thin chili, red or green in color and 2 inches (5 cm) long with quite a clean, sweet taste. It is fairly hot—about a four—but flavorful as well. The red ones are definitely sweeter than the green.

Bird's Eye: This is a tiny chili, but what it lacks in size it makes up for in strength! Very hot—five.

Dried Chilies

Chilies are dried because they last longer this way and are easier to transport. Here is a selection.

Ancho: This is the dried poblano chili. It has a sweet, fruity flavor and is quite mild—about a two. It is usually reddish brown with wrinkled skin.

Cayenne: This one is grown and dried in Louisiana and Mexico and is quite hot—about four or five. It is used to make the famous cayenne pepper. It is also what comes to mind when one thinks of chilies—about 2 to 4 inches (5–10 cm) long, bright red and tapering to a point.

Guajillo: A mild dried chili from central Mexico, it is widely available, 4 to 6 inches (10–15 cm) long with a rough, burgundy-colored skin and a slight bitter flavor. The skin is a bit tough and should be removed before using the chili.

Mulato: This is another popular mild dried chili, also from central Mexico, 4 to 5½ inches (10–14 cm) long with a dark brown skin. It has a smoky flavor reminiscent of licorice and rates a one or two for heat.

New Mexican: These come in many colors—from pale olive to bright scarlet. They are quite mild, a one or two, with a full chili flavor not masked by excessive fieriness.

Pasilla: This is a moderately mild chili, about a three, from central Mexico. It is about 6 inches (15 cm) long with an almost black skin, shiny and wrinkled. Some pasillas can be very hot, so choose carefully. You can also get powdered pasilla.

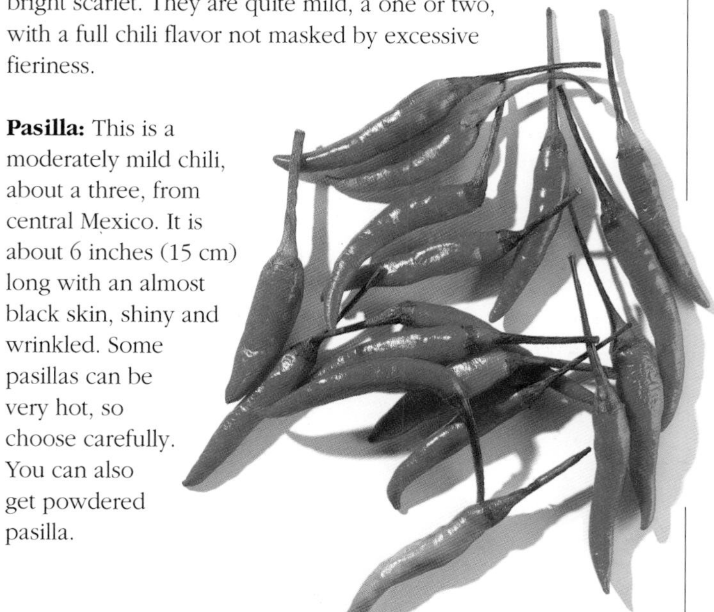

Bird's eye chilies

Using Chilies

Most people will have heard of chile con carne, but there are many other uses for chilies—where would India be without chilies for its curries? The Szechuan region of China produces some very hot chilies for use in Chinese cooking, but it is probably Mexican and Caribbean cuisine that most people associate with chilies—and rightly so. No true Mexican would go very long without eating mole poblano, which is the traditional dish of Mexico—and how about guacamole made with chilies and avocados? In tropical regions, chilies, with their fiery taste, are used to flavor bland tasting staple foods, and in India they are used in rice, as well as a staple ingredient in many curry powders. Chilies are now even used to flavor vodka. As stated before, always remember to exercise caution when using chilies, hold well away from your face when cutting them and don't rub your eyes. If possible, wear a pair of household rubber gloves. Fresh chilies help in digesting starches and are rich in vitamin C. But remember—a little goes a long way.

Mole Poblano

You will need:

- 4 large chicken pieces
- 1 onion, chopped
- 1 tbsp olive oil
- 1 each of pasilla, ancho and mulato chilies (or any 3 dried chilies if you cannot get these), chopped
- 2 cloves garlic, crushed
- 6 tomatoes, chopped
- 2 tbsp (10 ml) sesame seeds
- 2 tbsp (30 ml) whole almonds
- 2 tbsp (30 ml) peanuts
- ½ tsp (2½ ml) coriander seeds
- 1 square dark chocolate

Cook the chicken with the onions and olive oil in a large, heavy pan until the chicken is browned. Remove the chicken and let dry. Add the chilies, garlic and tomatoes to the oil and cooked onions and cook thoroughly for about 10 minutes. Grind all the nuts and seeds, add to the cooking chilies and cook for an additional five minutes. Take a little of the cooked juices, dissolve the chocolate in it and pour into the pan. Put the chicken back in and bring to a boil. Then simmer until the chicken is cooked through. You can add a little water if necessary. Serve hot with a fresh salad.

CUTTING THE MUSTARD

Mustard, being incredibly easy to grow and thriving in temperate climates, is not surprisingly one of the most common and widely used of all the spices. The Romans were probably first to recognize its importance in cooking, and they spread it to all the parts of their empire. As their empire collapsed and they retreated to Rome, they left behind many legacies—one being the use of mustard.

The name comes from two Latin words—*mustum* and *ardere. Mustum* means the "must"—the fresh grape juice from newly fermented wine, and *ardere* means simply "to burn"—and that is how mustard was made, with grape juice and at a burning hot temperature. But mustard should always be made with cold liquid—grape juice, vinegar, water; if it is made with hot liquid, the pungency and heat is eliminated. If that is what you prefer, that is fine, but to preserve the fiery nature of mustard, cold liquid must be used.

There are two basic types of mustard—brown and white. The brown mustard seeds are more aromatic and tasty, while the white ones are larger and hotter. Mustards the world over are combinations of these two types of seeds.

English mustard is made from a combination of both white and brown seeds (roughly 20 percent white and 80 percent brown) mixed with flour and turmeric. It is often sold as a dry, bright yellow powder. Cold water is added to this to make a traditional

English mustard is often sold as a dry, bright yellow powder.

hot English mustard. It should always be allowed to stand for 10 minutes to let the flavor develop.

French mustards are of two types: Dijon and Bordeaux. Dijon is made from brown seeds that are husked and ground and mixed with verjuice (unripe grape juice). Dijon mustard is used to flavor mayonnaise and sauces.

Bordeaux mustard is made with whole seeds and mixed with vinegar, sugar and tarragon. It is used as an accompaniment to cold meats.

French Dijon mustard

German mustards are very similar to Bordeaux mustards, but they are usually flavored with spices, herbs and caramel, which tend to make them darker and tastier. They are good with cold meats and sausages.

American mustard is made from powdered white seeds and flour, vinegar and coloring. It is excellent with hot dogs and hamburgers.

Mustard Combinations

English Whole-Grain: This is a pungent, hot mustard made from whole white seeds with white wine, black pepper and allspice.

English whole-grain mustard

Green Peppercorn Mustard: It is made with Dijon mustard with crushed green peppercorns added to it and is popular in Burgundy, where it is eaten with grilled meat. It is quite hot and spicy.

White Wine Mustard: This is another Dijon mustard made with white wine. Quite hot, it is used for flavoring sauces.

Tarragon Mustard: This Bordeaux-type mustard is flavored with tarragon. It is quite mild and is excellent with other spicy foods.

Düsseldorf Mustard: As its name implies, it is very popular in Düsseldorf. Although a type of German mustard, it is without the spices and caramel, but it is not nearly as mild as German mustard and is best eaten with spicy food.

Moutarde de Meaux: This is a Dijon mustard made with whole brown seeds—nicely hot and best eaten with foods that are not so spicy.

Coarse Grain Mustard: This is a type of Moutarde de Meaux which has white wine added to it. It is quite hot.

Florida Mustard: This is a Bordeaux mustard made with wine from the Champagne region rather than vinegar.

Once you have tried all of the commercially available mustards, you can try experimenting with your own. Try mixing white and brown seeds, husked or whole, adding herbs and spices, using vinegar or wine—even adding a little honey, caramel or garlic.

Mustard can be used in a vast variety of ways in cooking, adding extra zest to pickles, relishes and salad dressings. It would be a shame not to build on this still further by exploring all the different mustards you can make and adding even more flavor. Mustard makes a wonderful addition to all cheese dishes, really bringing out the flavor of the cheese. Cheese on toast will never taste the same again! And mustard mayonnaise spices up ordinary salad dishes.

Mustard Mayonnaise

You will need:

- 1 egg yolk
- ½ tbsp (2½ ml) mustard of your choice
- ½ tsp (2½ ml) Worcestershire sauce
- 1 tsp (5 ml) white wine
- salt and pepper to taste
- 3 drops Tabasco sauce
- 1 cup (250 ml) fine cooking oil such as sunflower or olive oil
- the juice of ½ lemon

Blend together everything except the lemon juice in a little of the oil. Add the rest of the oil—blending slowly. Then add lemon juice while still blending. This mayonnaise is excellent for salads.

SPICE VINEGARS

It is hard to believe that the vinegar we use to make vinaigrette dressing and to pickle and preserve spices and herbs is actually an acid—and so corrosive that you should only use stainless steel, earthenware, glass or enameled pots when using it in cooking.

Vinegar is made from the fermentation of wine, cider or malted barley and flavored with herbs or spices.

The best wine vinegar is made by slowly fermenting wine until it turns acetic. It should then stand for a month before use. You can get red wine vinegar and white wine vinegar. Both are fairly strong, so you should use wine of the same color to dilute them. Most people use white wine vinegar in vinaigrette dressing and mayonnaise because red wine vinegar will turn everything pink—red wine vinegar is, however, the most flavorful.

Malt vinegar is made from malted barley and is brown in color. This color is added by mixing the vinegar with caramel. Malt

From left to right: cider vinegar, red wine vinegar, malt vinegar, sherry vinegar.

vinegar used to be judged by its color—the darker the brown, the stronger the vinegar, but nowadays it is often colored artificially. Malt vinegar is best used for pickling.

Cider vinegar is, as its name suggests, made from fermented cider. It has a distinctive taste and is halfway between wine vinegar and malt vinegar in strength. Cider vinegar is best used for chutneys and fruity relishes.

You can also get sherry vinegar—made from sherry and used by French chefs to make poulet au vinaigre—as well as distilled vinegar and spirit vinegar. Distilled vinegar is colorless and used for pickling white onions. Spirit vinegar is very strong and flavored with lemon juice—it is slightly alcoholic.

To make the following spice vinegars, you can use any of the vinegars mentioned here, but a good white wine vinegar may be best, although a distilled vinegar will give you a purer flavor of the spices.

Basic Spice Vinegar

You will need:

- spice seeds—approximately 2–3 tbsp (30–45 ml) spice to 4 cups (1 l) vinegar

Lightly bruise any spice seeds in a mortar. Put the crushed seeds into the vinegar and shake well. Put the spice vinegar in a warm, dark place for two weeks and give it an occasional shake. At the end of this time, taste the vinegar. If you want a stronger tasting spice vinegar, strain off the mixture and discard the seeds. Use the vinegar with a fresh batch of spices and ferment again. Taste again at the end of two weeks. You can do this as many times as you want until you reach the required strength. Once will be enough with most spice vinegars. When you have the desired strength, strain off the seeds and store your new vinegar in a corked bottle. These vinegars can be used to make mayonnaise and vinaigrette sauces or poured over salads. They can also be used as pickling vinegars.

TYPES OF SPICE VINEGARS

Mustard Vinegar: Use 3 tbsp (45 ml) of crushed mustard seeds to 2 cups (750 ml) of vinegar (all recipes employ the same amount

of vinegar). You can use white or brown or try a combination of both.

Chili Vinegar: Use six hot red chilies and one whole garlic clove. Leave for two weeks and make sure you strain thoroughly. You can try experimenting with different types and different strength chilies.

Coriander Vinegar: Use 3 tbsp (45 ml) of crushed coriander seeds.

Ginger Vinegar: Use one whole root peeled and finely chopped.

Spicy Vinegar: Use 1 tbsp (15 ml) of crushed black peppercorns, 1 tsp (5 ml) of crushed celery seed, 1 tsp (5 ml) of peeled and chopped fresh gingerroot, one dried chili, one cinnamon stick, 1 tsp (5 ml) of allspice. Simmer all of the spices together in the vinegar. Let cool and store for two weeks. Strain and bottle.

Very Spicy Vinegar: You need two garlic cloves, six fresh hot red chilies, 2 tsp (10 ml) of black peppercorns, 2 tsp (10 ml) of juniper berries, four sprigs of lemongrass, four sprigs of rosemary. Put all of the ingredients into the vinegar and store for two weeks.

Quick Chili Vinegar: Add 2 tsp (10 ml) of hot chili sauce to the vinegar and use it immediately. Alter the amount of chili sauce to increase or decrease the fieriness.

Worcestershire Sauce: Although not strictly a vinegar, this can be used in the same way. You need six garlic cloves, 1 tsp (5 ml) of black pepper, ¼ tsp (1¼ ml) of chili powder, 1½ cups (350 ml) of vinegar, 5 tbsp (75 ml) of soy sauce. Blend all of the ingredients together in a blender. This is now ready to use, but store it in an airtight bottle and shake well before use each time.

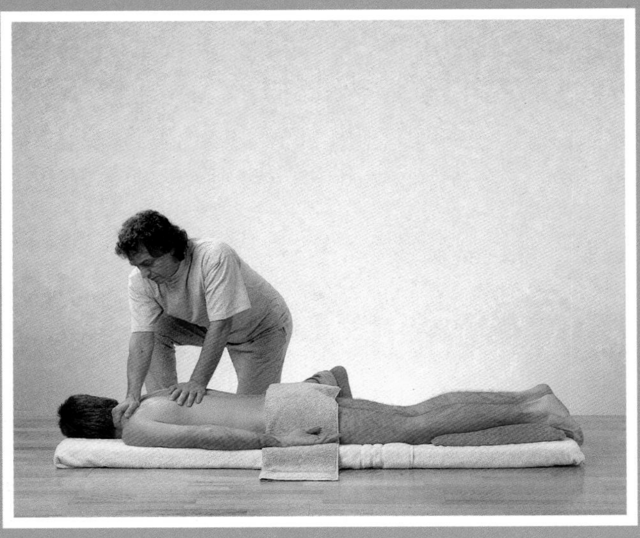

SPICES FOR BEAUTY, RELAXATION AND HEALTH

CAUTIONARY NOTE:

At all times it is recommended that you consult a health-care professional before embarking on a program of self-treatment. Spices are effective and safe when used in the correct circumstances. This book has been written to educate, and every effort has been made to make the book as accurate and as informative as possible, but the advice contained within is no replacement for professional guidance.

SPICES FOR BEAUTY AND RELAXATION

Traditionally in the West herbs have had a place in beauty treatments, while spices have been overlooked or considered too hot or pungent to have much use. However, some spices do have beneficial cosmetic uses, and we have included the following for your consideration. Bear in mind that certain skin types are more sensitive than others, so test each of the following potions and recipes before you use them.

In the Orient spices have been associated with beauty, perfume and color for thousands of years. The pungent aroma of spices was used to hide the smells of unwashed bodies and to purify and cleanse the air. Spices have also played a very important part in the manufacture of incense and are coloring agents in dyes for fabrics, carpets and silks.

In the hot climate of Eastern countries, spices were important for adding to oils to soothe and protect the skin from the harsh

Try making your own spicy blends of massage oils.

sun and to add to unguents to keep hair healthy and clean. Spices have been used both as cosmetics and as charms against evil and witchcraft since the earliest times. While nowadays it is easy to go out and buy whatever beauty products we need, nothing quite compares to making our own—an experience that enables us to partake again of a natural world in which the resources of nature are at our disposal.

It may be easier to buy synthetically produced perfumes, face creams, incense and massage oils, but it is not as satisfying as producing your own special and unique blends. Using spices in our beauty treatments creates an air of decadence, wealth, luxury and indulgence that may well be missing in commercial products. Perhaps we are not inclined to go as far as Emperor Heliogabalus, who bathed in hot baths of saffron and not only acquired a delicate aroma but also a healthy-looking golden glow, but we may well want to spice up our bathroom cabinet or add a certain something to the aroma in our homes. Spices are evocative and pungent—they bring the enigmatic Orient, or the sun of the Caribbean, or a hint of the mysterious lost civilizations of South America into our homes. They give us color and grandeur, fragrance and heat.

Using spice in incense goes back centuries.

Incense

Most people have at one time or another used incense to add a spicy aroma to their homes and maybe wondered where and how this tradition started. Perhaps the earliest cave dwellers discovered that a handful of certain leaves sprinkled on the dying embers of a cooking fire would produce a sweet smell that would mask the smells of leftover food, or maybe they used the spices in their cooking and when some fell into the heat of the fire, they liked the pleasant aroma. We will never know, but we do know that the ancient Egyptians and Babylonians used incense as part of their religious rites and that incense was used in China since the earliest times as a magic potion—a charm against restless ghosts. Whether you want some incense to settle your own ghosts, to add ritual and mystery to your home or merely to add aroma, there is nothing better than making your own. The following recipes produce incense that will soothe and relax you—and from a relaxed person comes inner beauty.

Traditionally there have been two ways to burn incense—loose and sprinkled onto glowing charcoal or blended with charcoal and gum and shaped into sticks or cones. The gummed incense needs a good draft to burn, which is why in churches the incense burner is swung backward and forward to produce a moving current of air to help the charcoal to glow.

Loose Incense

You will need:

- 1 oz (25 g) gum benzoin (from a pharmacist)
- 1 oz (25 g) powdered sandalwood
- ¾ oz (20 g) ground cassia bark
- ¾ oz (20 g) ground cardamom seeds
- ½ oz (15 g) ground cloves

Blend the ingredients together—you will find that the gum acts as a fixative. The cassia can be replaced with cinnamon; this is a basic recipe, so experiment.

Shaped Incense

You will need:

- ¼ oz (10 g) powdered sandalwood
- ¼ oz (10 g) ground cassia
- 3½ oz (100 g) gum arabic
- 1 oz (25 g) powdered gum benzoin
- 7 oz (200 g) charcoal

You need to crush the charcoal finely and add it to the dry ingredients. Mix the gum arabic with water to form a stiff paste, then stir in the rest of the ingredients. Form the incense into any shape you want and let dry for a day or two. Again you can use this basic recipe and add any other ingredients you like.

Remember that when burning incense, the fumes may be toxic, so make sure you have adequate ventilation.

PERFUME

Slice five vanilla beans and immerse in pure alcohol. Leave for six weeks but shake daily. At the end of this, strain the alcohol off, and you will have a pleasantly refreshing perfume.

Potpourri

A spicy potpourri will add a heavy, pungent scent to any room and give you an invigorating aroma. To make a dry potpourri, you can blend and grind any spices that you want—you can experiment and add spices as you try them in your cooking. A basic mixture would use rose petals as a base, or you could try crushed bay leaves. Then add to this base finely ground allspice, cassia, cinnamon, aniseed, nutmeg, vanilla bean, coriander seeds, cloves, ginger, cardamom and mace.

Here are two other combinations you might like to try:

A light, refreshing, spring-time potpourri mixture

You will need:

- 2 oz (50 g) caraway
- 2 oz (50 g) cardamom
- 2 oz (50 g) cinnamon
- 2 oz (50 g) fennel
- 2 marigold flowers
- 6 drops neroli essential oil
- 6 drops lemon grass essential oil

A rich potpourri mixture with an aroma of Christmas

You will need:

- 1 oz (25 g) cinnamon sticks
- 2 oz (50 g) cloves
- 2 oz (50 g) star anise
- 2 oz (50 g) juniper berries
- 2 oz (50 g) black pepper
- 2 oz (50 g) myrtle leaves
- 1 oz (25 g) rosemary
- 6 drops essential oil of frankincense
- 2 drops essential oil of cinnamon
- 6 drops essential oil of orange
- 2 drops essential oil of ginger

BEAUTY TREATMENTS

Hand Cream

You will need:

- 2 oz (60 g) vanilla beans
- 9 oz (250 g) pure lard
- 4 oz (120 g) gum benzoin
- 4 oz (120 g) spermaceti (from a pharmacist)
- 2 large cups (500 ml) almond oil

Put the vanilla beans and lard in a bowl with the gum benzoin, spermaceti and almond oil. Heat in a double boiler. Let cool and use as an all-over body lotion for massages. Aniseed makes a refreshing nerve tonic if a few drops of aniseed oil are added to the bath water—this is good for nervous headaches and tiredness. It is also good as a massage oil; add two drops of aniseed oil to two drops of nutmeg and rose and add this all to 1 tbsp of almond oil.

Other suitable essential oils of spices include: dill (for digestive problems and colic in children); fennel (for digestive problems); ginger (for nervous disorders); juniper (to help detoxify and cleanse); black pepper (to increase circulation); and lemongrass (for refreshment).

For a massage to aid digestion and colic, add 3 drops of essential oil of dill and 3 drops of essential oil of fennel to almond oil. For a refreshing and stimulating massage, add 1 drop essential oil of pepper and 3 drops of essential oil of lemongrass to 3⅓ tbsp (50 ml) of almond oil. Essential oils of spices are generally warming and stimulating and, if used too strongly, can be irritating to the skin. When using on someone with sensitive skin or with children, use half the recommended amount of essential oil.

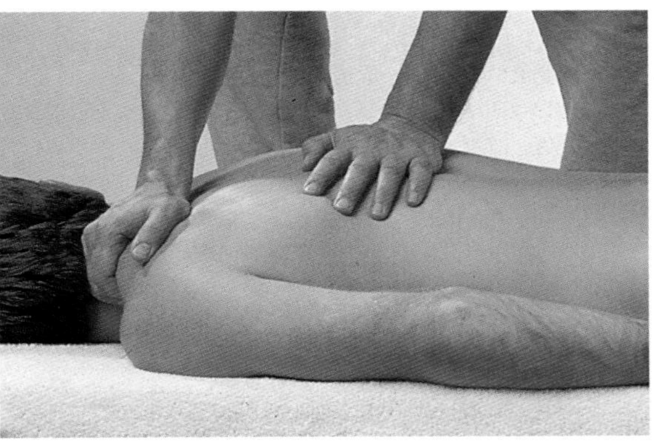

Cleansing Lotion and Aftershave

Nutmeg: For a soothing and firming lotion for breasts, infuse ½ oz (15 g) of nutmeg in 4 cups (1 l) of boiling water. Strain and soak the cloths in the liquid and leave on the breasts until the cloths cool. Repeat by warming the liquid.

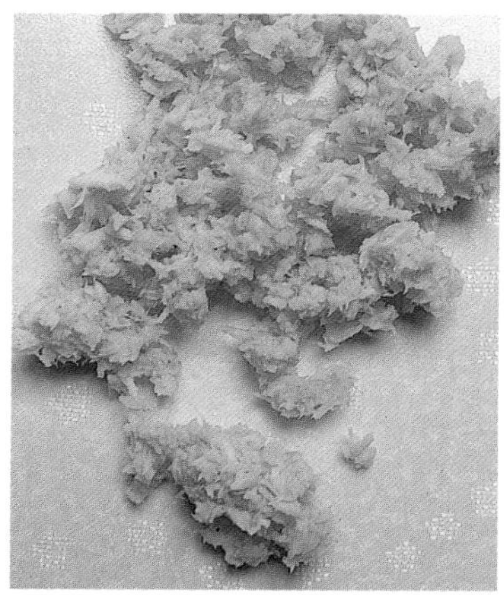

Horseradish has a use in skin care.

Horseradish: This spice makes a good cleansing lotion to get rid of pimples and blackheads. Slice the root and add to milk—9 oz (250 g) of root to 1 cup (250 ml) of milk—simmer over a low heat for one hour, then strain. Use the lotion on the face and forehead. Keep this bottled and in the refrigerator.

Coriander: This spice can be used to make a pleasant aftershave. Use 2 oz (60 g) of coriander seeds with 1 tsp (5 ml) of honey and 2 cups (½ l) of hot water. Let simmer for 20 minutes and cool. Add 1 tbsp (15 ml) of witch hazel and strain into a bottle. Keep the aftershave in the refrigerator, and it will be especially refreshing.

Eye Lotion

Fennel: For an eye lotion, simmer 2 oz (50 g) of crushed seeds in 2 cups (500 ml) of water for 30 minutes. Strain and let cool. Use this in an eye lotion using an eyebath to relieve inflammation.

Hair Preparations

Clove: This makes an excellent preparation with a pleasant scent for hair. Heat 1 lb (½ kg) of benzoate lard with 1 cup (250 ml) of almond oil and 2 tbsp (30 ml) of palm oil. Strain and add, while still warm, 2 tbsp (30 ml) of eau de cologne and 1 tsp (5 ml) of oil of cloves.

Saffron used as a final rinse tints hair a rich goldon color.

Star Anise: This is used in another good preparation for hair. Crush and boil 120 g of seeds in a cup of water and add the resulting oil to olive oil—1 tsp (5 ml) of oil of star anise to 10 tsp (150 ml) of olive oil. This helps the growth of new hair.

Saffron: For tinting fair hair a rich golden color, soak one dash of saffron in 2 cups (½ l) of boiling water. Let cool. The saffron water can be used as a wash after shampooing. Do not rinse—leave the hair wet and allow to dry naturally.

Rouge and Lipsticks

Safflower: A gentle rouge can be made from safflower. Soak a handful of safflower flowers in 2 cups (½ l) of boiling water. When cool, you will have a red liquid to which you add three parts rice powder and one part kaolin until you have a smooth paste. A little applied as a rouge or lipstick adds color to a pale face.

Beauty Soaps

Soap was first made and used in Rome nearly 3,000 years ago, and you can make your own spicy soaps quite simply.

Basic Soap

You will need:

- 9 oz (250 g) tallow
- 5 fl oz (150 ml) soft water
- 2 tbsp (30 ml) caustic soda
- dash of turmeric
- 1 tsp (5 g) ground caraway
- 1 tsp (5 g) ground sandalwood powder
- 1 ground clove
- 3 tsp (15 g) ground nutmeg
- 1 tbsp (15 ml) honey
- 1 tbsp (15 ml) olive oil

Melt the tallow in a pan. Pour the water into a separate pan and add the caustic soda. The caustic and water will react, causing heat, and you will have to allow it to cool down. Let the tallow also cool down. When both are lukewarm, pour the melted tallow and oil into the caustic soda and stir all the while—ideally use a whisk.

Add the dry ingredients (finely ground) and the honey and keep stirring. As you whisk you will suddenly find that your liquid turns into a thick, creamy paste. This is your soap. Turn it out into molds and let it set for 24 hours. Turn it out from the mold—by this time it will be quite hard—and leave it in a warm, well-ventilated cupboard for about two weeks. Then your spicy soap will be ready to use. It lathers easily and leaves your skin enriched and beautiful—and smelling aromatic and spicy.

This is a basic soap recipe—you can try experimenting and adding your own choice of spices. The turmeric adds yellow color—you might like to try paprika for a red tint or a little finely chopped parsley for green.

Caution

Caustic soda in its dry form will burn if it is allowed to come into contact with skin—wash it off with cold water immediately.

SPICES FOR HEALTH

In the thirteenth century Pope Innocent III passed an edict that no ecclesiastic should practice medicine for profit or shed blood in any way. Up until then all medical practitioners in Europe were in the holy orders. This edict meant that surgery passed into the hands of lay people, mostly barbers, while church priests and monks devoted their time to the search for cures based on natural plants. In effect, it meant that there was a considerable division between herbalists and surgeons—the latter in the holy orders concerned themselves more with the theoretical aspects of medicine. This led to an enormous upsurge in interest in plants that had an effect on a patient's condition. As the Spanish and Portuguese explorers came back from the New World with new plants and spices, these were seized on as being miraculous—and, in certain cases, as having far greater powers than they actually did. However, spices do have a natural

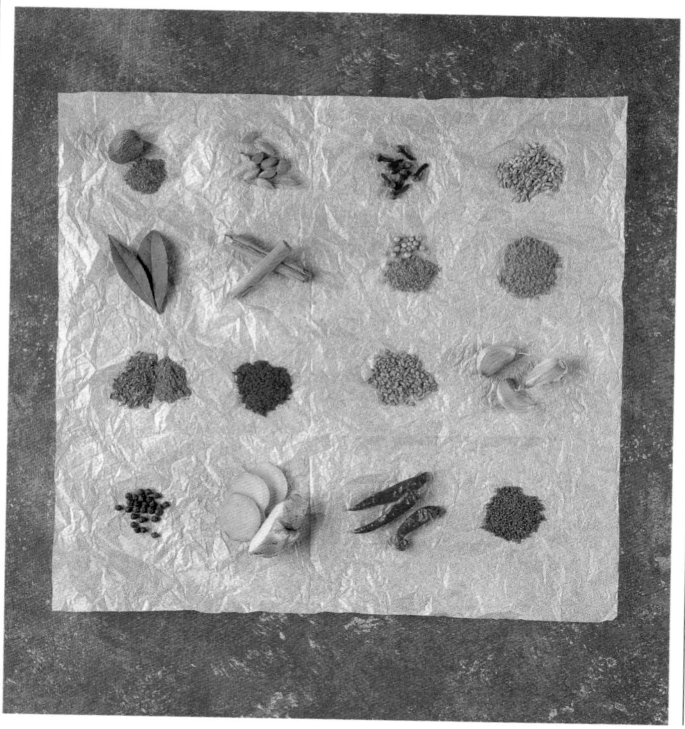

warming effect and are of some use against colds, coughs and flu symptoms. The following medicinal recipes should be taken only for the very mildest of conditions. Any illnesses that you would not normally treat at home should not be treated with spice remedies. Consult a qualified medical doctor if you are not sure.

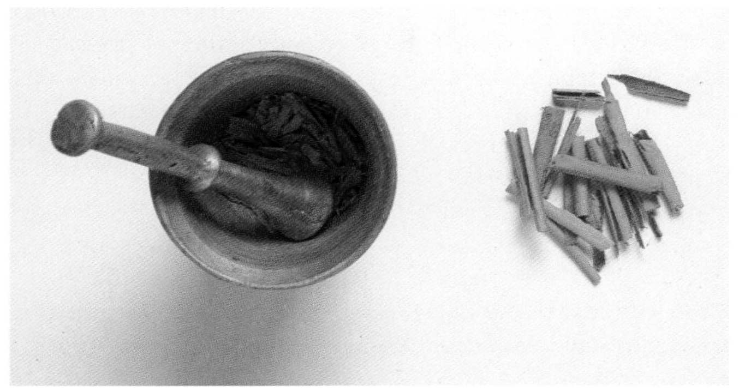

Colds and Coughs

Spices are warming—and what could be better to ward off the effects of cold winter conditions?

Cayenne Pepper Tea: Stir ½ tsp (2½ ml) of cayenne pepper into 5 fl oz (150 ml) of boiling water. Let cool and sip slowly. This is said to ward off a cold before it has had a chance to take hold, and it will certainly warm your whole system. You can substitute hot milk for the water if you prefer.

Ginger and Honey Tea: Stir ½ tsp (2½ ml) of dried ginger powder into hot milk and add 1 tsp (5 ml) of honey. This is a warming drink to reduce the symptoms of a cold.

Cardamom Tea: To reduce the effects of a winter flu fever, mix 1 tsp (5 ml) of basil with the seeds of one large cardamom pod and ½ tsp (2½ ml) of ground cinnamon in 2 cups (500 ml) of boiling water with 1 tsp (5 ml) of sugar. Infuse

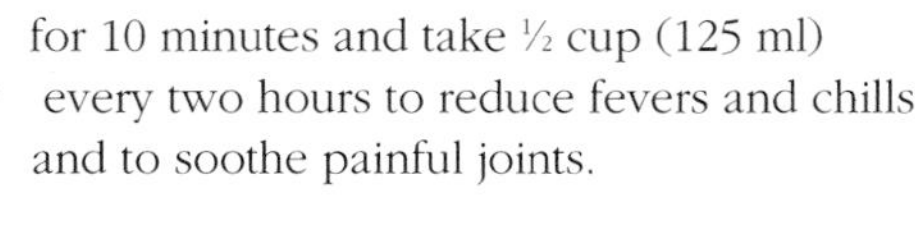

for 10 minutes and take ½ cup (125 ml) every two hours to reduce fevers and chills and to soothe painful joints.

Anise Tea: For soothing a cough and to loosen phlegm infuse 2 tsp (10 ml) of crushed aniseed in 1 cup (300 ml) of boiling water. Drink when cool.

Sedatives and Relaxants

When we cannot sleep or we feel the need for something to relax us when we are stressed, spice teas are natural, nonaddictive ways to help us.

Fennel, Dill and Anise Tea: To make a relaxing drink before bed to help you sleep, take crushed seeds of fennel, anise and dill—1 tsp (5 ml) of each—in 1 cup (250 ml) of hot water.

Tonic

Eating any of the sweet peppers increases vitamin C intake, and you can make teas from other spices to provide a tonic to help strengthen the whole system.

Ginseng Tea: Add 1 tsp (5 ml) of powdered ginseng in 2 cups (500 ml) of boiling water. Simmer for 15 minutes and sip slowly when cool.

Caraway Tea: Take 1 tsp (5 ml) of caraway seeds in 1 cup (250 ml) of hot water.

Caper Tea: Take 1 tsp (5 ml) of dried and ground capers in 1 cup (250 ml) of hot water.

Celery Tea: Take 1 tsp (5 ml) of ground celery seeds in 1 cup (250 ml) of hot water.

Fenugreek Tea: Take 1 tsp (5 ml) of ground fenugreek seeds in 1 cup (250 ml) of hot water.

Digestive Tonics

After the winter, when all people had to eat were salty, stodgy foods, they needed a good digestive tonic to cleanse the system and restore a sluggish stomach.

Fenugreek Tea (recipe above): Make a tea as a general tonic, and you will find it will also increase appetite.

Spicy Brandy Tonic: Steep 1 tsp (5 ml) each of crushed fennel, aniseed and caraway seeds in 2½ cups (600 ml) of brandy with ¼ cup (50 g) sugar. Let mature for four weeks—shake occasionally. Strain. Take ½ cup (125 ml) before meals.

Bitter Brandy Tonic: Take this as an aperitif before meals to settle the stomach; if taken half an hour before eating, it stimulates the appetite. To 4 cups (1 l) of brandy add 2 tsp (30 ml) of dried orange peel; 2 tsp (10 ml) of crushed cardamom seeds, ½ tsp (2½ ml) of ground cinnamon; ¼ tsp (1 ml) of ground cloves. Bottle this and store it for a month. Take 2 tbsp (30 ml) before meals.

Nutmeg Wine: Take this as an aperitif half an hour before meals. Add one whole grated nutmeg to 2 cups (500 ml) of red wine. Allow to steep overnight. Strain. Take 2 tbsp (30 ml) before meals.

Juniper Berry Wine: Soak 1 tbsp (15 ml) of juniper berries in 4 cups (1 l) of white wine. Sweeten with 1 tbsp (15 ml) of brown sugar. Let mature for one week and then strain and drink a glass or two as required.

Syrup of Juniper Berries: Take this after meals to settle the stomach. Simmer 4 lb (100 g) of juniper berries, fresh or dried, and the peel of one lemon in 4 cups (1 l) of water until they soften. Strain, add 2 tbsp (30 ml) of honey, bring to a boil and simmer until the syrup thickens. You can bottle and use immediately. To keep fresh, keep in the refrigerator. Take 1 tbsp (15 ml) after meals.

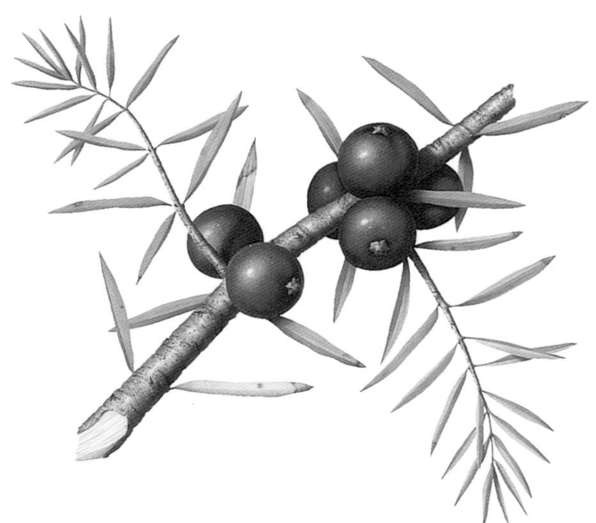

Ginger and Honey Mulled Wine: This is a good digestive tonic for those who suffer from winter chills or have poor appetites. Heat a little red wine, making sure the wine doesn't boil (or boil it for children if you want to get rid of the alcoholic content). Add some finely grated ginger according to taste and then leave to cool. Add honey—1 tsp to each glass.

Cinnamon Milk: This will act as a good digestive remedy. Take ½ tsp (2½ ml) of ground cinnamon in 1 cup (250 ml) of hot milk with a little honey added. This is good at night because it not only settles the stomach and cures indigestion, but it also induces sleep.

Cardamom Tea: Crush the seeds from one pod of cardamom and add to 1 cup (250 ml) of boiling water. Allow to cool and sip slowly. This relieves indigestion.

Digestive Teas: You can infuse the seeds of anise, cumin, coriander and caraway to make teas to settle upset stomachs. Any of these seeds can be infused in milk or can be chewed after meals. They also sweeten the breath.

Cardamom Coffee: In Arab countries this is called gahwa and is drunk hot and strong. It is considered so beneficial for settling digestion that you are not allowed to speak while the coffee-drinking ceremony is being carried out because it would only undo all the good work the coffee is doing. Crush green coffee beans and add crushed cardamom pods and seeds with a little ground clove (only a dash) to hot water and boil for two minutes. Strain and serve hot and black with sugar.

Laxatives

Either through poor eating habits or stress, we may sometimes experience constipation and laxatives may be necessary. Any long-term need for them should be referred to a qualified medical doctor.

Aniseed and Licorice Laxative: Soak 1 oz (25 g) of licorice root overnight with six dried figs or prunes—or both if you prefer. In the morning simmer with ½ tsp (2½ ml) of aniseed and 1 tsp (5 ml) of honey for 15 minutes. Remove the licorice and eat the fruit for breakfast.

Binding Agents

Again, any long-term need for binding agents to ease or cure diarrhea should be checked with a doctor.

Allspice Binding Agent: Add ½ tsp (2½ ml) of crushed allspice berries to 4 cups (1 l) of water and 1 tbsp (15 ml) of bilberries (soaked overnight). Bring to a boil and simmer gently for a few minutes. Allow to cool and add 1 tsp (5 ml) of lemon juice. Stir. Take a cup every few hours until the symptoms pass.

Rheumatism Remedies

Cinnamon: To relieve the pain of rheumatic joints, add a few drops of oil of cinnamon to olive oil and massage into the affected area to bring relief. Likewise, you can gently heat juniper berries in olive oil for an hour and allow to cool and use as a pain-relieving massage oil. Inflamed or swollen joints should not be massaged.

Juniper Berries: These can be used in a tea and taken internally to relieve the pain of rheumatic joints.

Toothache Remedy

Clove: To relieve toothache pain, simply clamp a whole clove to the painful tooth and leave for a while to relieve the pain—and then go straight to a dentist.

Spices for All-around Health

Star Anise: This is a diuretic and appetite stimulant and is also useful for relieving flatulence and nausea.

Licorice: This reduces inflammation and spasms, expels phlegm and soothes the bronchials.

Elecampane: The warming qualities of elecampane make it a good expectorant and a treatment for bronchitis, asthma and other pulmonary infections.

Dill: This is rich in sulfur, potassium and sodium.

Celery: A poultice of the leaves of celery can be used externally for fungal infections, and the seeds taken in small quantities internally are good for relieving gout, arthritis and inflammation of the urinary tract.

Horseradish: This is a diuretic. It increases perspiration, which can be good for some fevers. It can be made into a poultice to be used externally for wound infections, arthritis and pleurisy.

Java Galangal: This is a warming digestive and is useful as a remedy for diarrhea, gastric upsets that are sensitive to cold and incontinence.

Galangal: This can be taken internally for chronic gastritis, digestive upsets, gastric ulcerations and to relieve the pain of rheumatism.

Mustard: This can be used in the form of mustard plasters, bandages soaked in mustard, and applied as a poultice to relieve rheumatism, muscular pain and chilblains. They can be used to soak feet for relief from aches and strains and also to cure headaches and colds; use cold water to maximize the heating effect. People with sensitive skin should take care because it can cause blistering. In large doses it causes vomiting.

Safflower: This can be taken as a tea and is good for coronary-artery disease and menopausal and menstruation problems.

Capers: These are used to revitalize and increase digestion and appetite. They are good for gastrointestinal infections and diarrhea.

Chilies: These are revitalizing, help digestion and have a strong stimulant effect.

Cayenne: You can infuse cayenne to make a hot, fiery tea to stimulate the appetite and to relieve stomach and bowel pains and cramps.

Sweet Peppers: These contain large amounts of vitamin C. They also have revitalizing and antiseptic qualities and stimulate the digestive system.

Paprika: The warming qualities of paprika make it effective as a reliever of cold symptoms as well as a rich and valuable source of vitamin C.

Caraway: These seeds can be chewed for immediate relief of indigestion and colic as well as menstrual pains and cramps.

Grains of Paradise: The seeds are used internally in western Africa for a wide range of ailments including painful menstruation and excessive lactation.

Cassia: This is a major ingredient in cold remedies and is used for treating dyspepsia, flatulence and colic.

Cilantro: This is a useful remedy for minor digestive problems, and the coriander seeds can reduce the effects of some laxatives, which can produce painful stomach spasms.

Cumin: Minor digestive disorders may be helped if cumin is taken internally. It settles stomach upsets that cause migraines.

Turmeric: Taken internally, turmeric is good for digestive upsets and skin disorders.

Lemongrass: This can be taken internally by small children as a digestive aid. It can also be taken for mild fevers.

Cardamom: Taken internally, cardamom settles upset stomachs and counteracts the effects of dairy product allergies.

Cloves: Because they are a warming stimulant, cloves are useful for stimulating the digestive system. They can be taken internally for gastroenteritis and nausea, gastric upsets that are sensitive to cold, and impotence.

Asafetida: This cleans and restores the digestive tract and relieves stomach pains and colic.

Fennel: This relieves digestive disorders and reduces inflammation. It can be taken as a mouthwash and gargle for sore throats and ulcerated gums.

Juniper: This can be used for urinary tract infections—cystitis, urethritis and inflammation of the kidneys—as well as for gout and rheumatism.

Mace: This can be used to treat stomach disorders such as diarrhea, dysentery and indigestion.

Nutmeg: In small doses, nutmeg is a carminative, meaning it reduces flatulence and digestive discomfort. It is useful in treating flatulence and vomiting and for improving overall digestion.

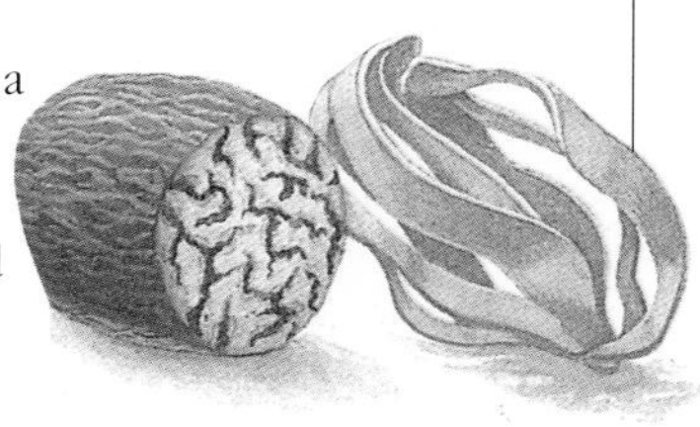

Myrtle: This reduces colic, flatulence and digestive discomfort, is an expectorant and is helpful in all types of chest infections.

Nigella: These seeds are said to benefit digestion and reduce inflammation or irritation in the gut lining.

Opium Poppy: This is useful for treating cystitis and pyelitis.

Quassia: This is used to treat rheumatism and fevers as well as stomach disorders and dyspepsia.

Allspice: The oil of allspice is distilled and used for flatulent indigestion. It improves overall digestion and has a tonic effect on the nervous system.

Aniseed: The warming and stimulating properties of aniseed make it useful for treating circulation problems and digestive disorders.

Fenugreek: These seeds can be infused to treat gastric inflammation, colic, insufficient lactation, poor appetite and digestive disorders.

Cubeb: Because of its warming properties, cubeb will relieve coughs and bronchitis, sinusitis and throat infections.

Pepper: This is very good for stimulating the digestion, warming the bronchial passageways and relieving the congestion of colds and flu.

Sumac: This is sometimes prescribed herbally for treating severe diarrhea, and the root bark is used to treat dysentery. The fruits are used for treating urinary infections.

Sesame: These seeds are used as a mild and gentle laxative.

White Mustard: This is used to treat bronchial congestion, colds, coughs and rheumatic joint pains.

Tamarind: This makes an excellent laxative—its action is fairly gentle. It is also used to treat fevers, asthma, jaundice and dysentery.

Vanilla: This has few medicinal uses apart from aiding digestion and improving appetite.

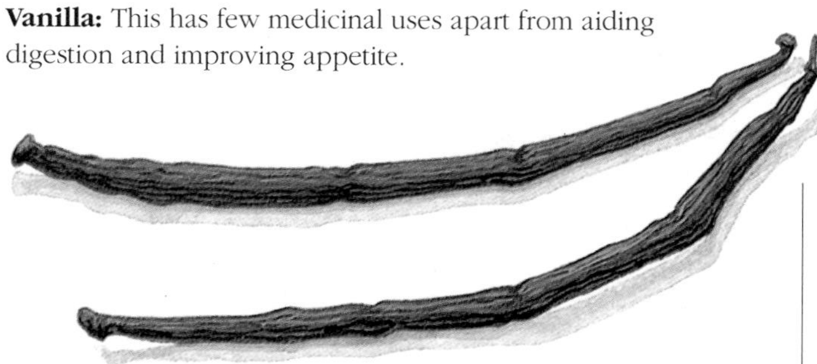

Ginger: Recent research has shown ginger to be excellent for settling the stomach, and it is now used as a travel sickness remedy.

Curry: The bark of the curry plant is used internally for digestive problems and the leaves are used as an infusion for constipation and colic.

Szechuan Pepper: This is a stimulant that works on the spleen and stomach. It also has properties that can lower blood pressure.

Saffron: You can infuse saffron to make an herbal tea that can be taken as a warming soothing drink to clear the head. It can also shake off drowsiness and bring on menstruation.

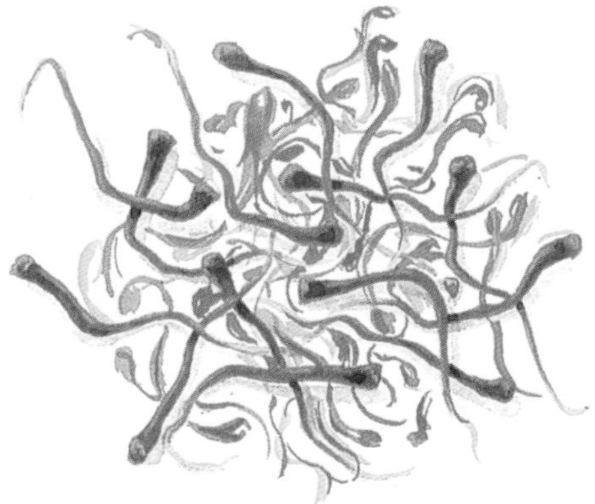

Cinnamon: This strong stimulant of the glandular system helps relieve stomach upsets. It is very warming, so it is good for relieving the symptoms of colds, flu and sore throats.

GLOSSARY

Addison's disease – disease caused by the underactivity of the adrenal glands

Adrenal glands – glands situated just above the kidneys

Adrenaline – hormone secreted by the adrenal gland that is released in response to physical and mental stress and initiates a variety of responses, including increasing the heart rate

Analgesic – relieves pain

Anemia – deficiency of hemoglobin in the blood

Antiallergy – reduces allergic reactions

Antibacterial – prevents the formation of bacteria

Antibiotic – prevents the growth of bacteria

Antidepressant – alleviates depression

Anti-inflammatory – reduces inflammation

Antimicrobial – destroys pathogenic microorganisms

Antiseptic – prevents the growth of bacteria

Antispasmodic – relieves muscle spasms or cramps

Aphrodisiac – increases sexual desire

Aromatherapy – therapeutic use of essential oils usually through massage

Bacteriostatic – prevents the growth of bacteria

Bitters – herbs that have a bitter taste that stimulate the appetite and aid digestion

Carminative – relieves flatulence and settles the digestive system

Cholagogic – stimulates the flow of bile into the intestine

Cicatrisant – promotes the healing of skin and formation of scar tissue

Colic – abdominal pain in the intestines

Cortisone-like action – reduces inflammation

Cystitis – inflammation of the bladder

Decongestant – helps eliminate nasal congestion

Diaphoretic – promotes sweating

Diuretic – stimulates the secretion of urine

Douche – application of liquid into the vagina

Dyspepsia – indigestion

Elixir – tincture with added sugar or syrup

Emmenagogue – stimulates menstruation

Essential oils – base materials in aromatherapy that are highly aromatic and volatile and are produced from plants by means of extraction, usually distillation

Expectorant – helps to expel mucus and relieves congestion in the digestive tract

Flatulence – large amounts of gas in the stomach and intestines

Flavonoid – substance responsible for the colors yellow and orange in herbs, fruit and vegetables

Histamine – substance released in response to allergic reactions

Holistic – approach that considers the patient's body, mind and spirit

Lactation – secretion of breast milk

Laxative – promotes the evacuation of the bowels

Mastitis – acute inflammation of the breasts

Mucilage – viscous liquid that forms a protective layer over the mucous membranes and skin

Nervine – a nerve tonic, it calms the nerves

Neuralgia – acute nerve pain

Osteoporosis – loss of bone tissue

Phlegm – mucus secreted by the respiratory tract

Pleurisy – inflammation of pleural membrane that surrounds the lungs

Rhizome – underground rootlike structure used as a food store by plants during the winter

Saponin – substance that forms a lather when mixed with water that is found in a variety of herbs and has a wide range of therapeutic properties

Sedative – relieves nervousness and induces sleep with a calming effect

Serotonin – hormone released from the pituitary gland in the brain

Sinusitis – inflammation of the sinuses

Tonic – herbs to strengthen and invigorate a specific organ, system or the whole body

Volatile – evaporates very easily when exposed to air

USEFUL ADDRESSES

Organizations

United Kingdom

Bioforce (UK)
Olympis B Park
Dundonald
Ayrshire, KA2 9BE

British Naturopathic Association
Frazer House
6 Netherhall Gardens
London, NW3 5RR

The British Herb Growers Association
c/o NFU
Agriculture House
London, SW1X 7NJ

Hadley Wood Healthcare Ltd. (UK)
67A Beech Hill
Hadley Wood
Barnet
Herts, EN4 0JW

Herbal Medicine Association (UK)
Field House
Lyle Hole Lane
Redhill
Avon, BS18 7TB

The Herb Society
134 Buckingham Palace Rd.
London, SW11 4RW

Herbal Suppliers

Enzymatic Therapy (UK)
P.O. Box 74
Potters Bar
Herts, EN6 5ZZ

National Institute of Herbal Medicine
9 Palace Gate
Exeter, Devon, EX1 1JA

Naturopathic & Herbal Schools and Universities

British College of Naturopathy & Osteopathy
Frazer House
6 Netherhall Gardens
London, NW3 5RR

Neals Yard Remedies (UK)
1A Rossiter Rd.
London, SW12 9RY

Power Health Products (UK)
10 Central Ave.
Airfield Estate
Pocklington
York, YO4 2NR

Swiss Health Products (UK)
Auchenkyle
Southwoods
Troon
Ayrshire, KA9 1RY

United States of America

American Association of Acupuncture and Oriental Medicine
1424 16th St., NW,
Suite 501
Washington, DC 20036

American Botanical Council
P.O. Box 201660
Austin, TX 78720
512-331-8868

American Herb Association
P.O. Box 1673
Nevada City, CA 95959

Bastyr University
144 N.E. 54th St.
Seattle, WA 98105
206-523-9585

Bioforce (USA)
P.O. Box 507
Kinderhook, NY 12106
518-758-6060

Enzymatic Therapy (USA)
825 Challenger Dr.
Green Bay, WI 54311
414-469-1313

National College of Naturopathic Medicine
11231 S.E. Market St.
Portland, OR 97216
503-255-7355

Canada

Enzymatic Therapy (Canada)
8500 Baxter Place
Burnaby, BC
V5A 4T8

Australia

National Herbalists Association of Australia
Box 65
Kingsgrove, NSW 2208

Short Correspondence (Non-Professional) Courses

United Kingdom

Nutrition with Herbal Medicine
The Edison Institute of Nutrition (UK)
P.O. Box 74
Potters Bar
Herts, EN6 5ZZ

United States of America

Nutrition with Herbal Medicine
The Edison Institute of Nutrition (USA)
2675 W. Highway 89A
Suite 1062
Sedona, AZ 86336

Canada

Nutrition with Herbal Medicine
The Edison Institute of Nutrition (Canada)
2 Bloor St. W. Suite 100
Toronto, Ont. M4W 3E2

ADDITIONAL READING

Day, Avanelle and Lillie Stuckey. *The Spice Cookbook*. David White Company, 1964.

Gunst, Kathy. *Condiments*. G. P. Putnam & Sons, 1984.

Herbst, Sharon Tyler. *The New Food Lover's Companion*. New York: Barron's Educational Series, 1995.

Pratt, James Norwood. *The Tea Lover's Treasury*. 101 Productions, 1982.

Rain, Patricia. *Vanilla Cookbook*. Celestial Arts, 1986.

Schapira, Joel, David and Karl. *The Book of Coffee and Tea*. St. Martin's Press, 1975.

Sobart, Tom. *Herbs, Spices and Flavorings*. The Overlook Press, 1982.

Stone, Sally and Martin. *The Mustard Cookbook*. Avon Books, 1981.

Townsend, Doris McFerran. *Herbs, Spices & Flavorings*. HPBooks, 1982.

Westland, Pamela. *The Book of Spices*. New York: Exeter Books, 1985.

ACKNOWLEDGMENTS

The Publishers would like to thank Kay Quigley, Darren Braithwaite, and Liz Day of Schwartz, McCormick UK Ltd, Haddenham, Buckinghamshire, England for advice and help in the supply of the vast majority of spices photographed for this book. We would also like to thank Joseph Flach of Peterborough, England, and Fox's Spices of Stratford upon Avon, Warwickshire, England, for advice and the supply of some of the more unusual spices (Fox's Spices are available by mail order on Tel: (00 44) 1789 266420, Fax: (00 44) 1789 267737.

The author would like to thank Roni Jay for her help with the research for this book and all the wonderful explorers, cooks, chefs, cookery writers and spice merchants who have gone before and fired my imagination about spices.

INDEX

Bold page numbers refer to directory entries